MULTINATIONAL INDUSTRIAL RELATIONS SERIES

No. 11

MULTINATIONAL ENTERPRISES AND THE OECD INDUSTRIAL RELATIONS GUIDELINES

by

Duncan C. Campbell
and
Richard L. Rowan

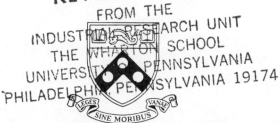

Industrial Research Unit
The Wharton School, Vance Hall/CS
University of Pennsylvania
Philadelphia, Pennsylvania 19104
U.S.A.

Copyright © 1983 by the Trustees of the University of Pennsylvania
Library of Congress Catalog Number 82-81083
MANUFACTURED IN THE UNITED STATES OF AMERICA
ISBN: 0-89546-039-4
ISSN: 0149-0818

Foreword

The Wharton School's Industrial Research Unit has engaged in an active research and publications program pertaining to many aspects of international labor and industrial relations. Several major studies have been published since 1972 including *Multinational Collective Bargaining Attempts: The Record, the Cases, and the Prospects; Multinational Union Organizations in the Manufacturing Industries;* and *Profit Sharing, Employee Stock Ownership, Savings, and Asset Formation Plans in the Western World.* In addition, monographs have been issued covering the political, economic, and labor conditions in various countries including Venezuela, Brazil, Mexico, the Philippines, and India. Research is now underway that will lead to the publication of studies on topics such as an international comparison of hours of work, international trade secretariats in the white-collar field, and additional country studies.

Codes of conduct for multinational enterprises became an important topic in the international labor field in the early 1970s. Intergovernmental bodies, such as the Organization for Economic Cooperation and Development (OECD), the International Labor Organization (ILO), and the United Nations (UN) have issued, or are planning to issue, guidelines for multinational enterprise behavior. The OECD was the first agency to come forth with a code including guidelines on employment and industrial relations.

The present monograph examines the response of multinational enterprises and unions to the employment and industrial relations guidelines as issued by the OECD. General oversight and implementation of the guidelines are conducted by the OECD Committee on International Investment and Multinational Enterprises (CIIME) which receives input from its constituent groups from business, the Business and Industry Advisory Committee (BIAC), and labor, the Trade Union Advisory Committee (TUAC). An effort is made in this monograph to assess the "cases" that have been brought before the CIIME by the unions alleging violations of the guidelines by multinational firms. Multinational enterprises appear to have voluntarily observed the guidelines as may be witnessed by the fact that there has been a paucity of "cases" since the code was issued in 1976.

The writing of this monograph was sponsored by the Exxon Education Foundation, the Monsanto Fund, the Rockwell International

Charitable Trust, and by thirty firms in the international business community and undertaken at the suggestion of members of the U.S. Business and Industry Advisory Committee of the OECD. As usual, the Industrial Research Unit staff can be commended for its outstanding work in connection with this monograph. Professor Herbert R. Northrup, Director of the Industrial Research Unit, provided a critique of the monograph during all stages of its drafting. It has been a great pleasure to work with an extremely capable research associate, Duncan C. Campbell, senior research specialist and management instructor, whose intelligence, mature judgment, and initiative have made it possible to complete the study against stringent deadlines. Mario Gobbo also assisted in early drafting of the study. Our editorial staff, including Patricia Dornbusch and Richard Freeman, performed their duties in a capable and cheerful manner. Our administrative and office staff, including Margaret E. Doyle, O.P. Suri, Cynthia Smith, and Sherrie Waitsman all provided services in a patient manner.

RICHARD L. ROWAN, *Co-Director*
Industrial Research Unit
Professor of Industry
The Wharton School
University of Pennsylvania

Philadelphia
August 1983

TABLE OF CONTENTS

LIST OF TABLES

LIST OF FIGURES

FIGURE

CHAPTER I

Introduction

On June 21, 1976, a declaration by the member governments of the Organization for Economic Cooperation and Development (OECD) was issued concerning international investment and multinational enterprises and containing "Guidelines for Multinational Enterprises." These voluntary guidelines cover the following areas: disclosure of information, competition, financing, taxation, employment and industrial relations, and science and technology (Appendix A contains the text of the declaration).

The origin of the guidelines can be traced to many factors; however, the major reasons for their establishment include the following: publicity given to alleged malpractices on the part of some multinational firms in the early 1970s, union pressure and support for the guidelines, and a movement by the International Labor Organization (ILO) to formulate a code of conduct for multinational enterprises. The ILO's "Tripartite Declaration of Principles Concerning Multinational Enterprises and Social Policy" appeared in November 1977 (see Appendix B). The OECD evidently desired to issue the first set of guidelines in order to establish a precedent for a voluntary code and to protect business interests as much as possible. At least, in being first, some thought that the OECD might avoid more stringent regulations that could be forthcoming from the ILO or the United Nations (UN).

The decision by the OECD to develop a code of conduct for multinational firms has provided areas of confrontation that were not present in the earlier life of the organization. Founded in 1948 as the Organization for European Economic Cooperation (OEEC), the body was established as a provision of the Marshall Plan to ensure that the war-ravaged countries would work together toward their economic recovery. By 1960, this objective had been attained and, in recognition of the growing interdependence among the industrialized countries of the West, the United States and Canada joined the original eighteen members of the OEEC to form the Organization for Economic Cooperation and Development (OECD) on December

1

14, 1960.[1] The goals of the newly formed body were thus altered to encourage the economic growth of the member nations, to aid the less-developed countries both within and outside of the membership, and to promote the global expansion of trade.[2] In 1964, Japan became a full member of the OECD, followed by Finland (1969), Australia (1971), and New Zealand (1973). Yugoslavia participates in the body as a partial member.

The OECD member countries account for 20 percent of the world's population, 60 percent of the world's industrial output, and 70 percent of its trade.[3] In the more than twenty years since its founding, the OECD has provided a mechanism through which governments have exchanged useful information, research studies have been professionally prepared, comparative data on international economic conditions have been developed in a reliable manner, and conferences have been held which stimulated new ideas and constructive solutions to problems in areas such as economic policy, energy utilization, development cooperation, trade and financial policies, social affairs, manpower, and education.

The OECD's structure is diagrammed in Figure I-1. As the figure shows, the organization's structure is dominated by the council, which consists of representatives of all the member countries. Beneath the council sits the executive committee, whose principal functions include the preparation of the council's work (i.e., the executive committee forwards draft decisions and recommendations to the council for approval), the coordination, upon the council's instruction, of the work of other bodies within the OECD, and the initiation of policy discussions on interrelated economic issues.

The bulk of the OECD's detailed research and discussion occurs in the committees, each of which is comprised of representatives of the member states and the principal roles of which are to prepare annual programs of work for approval by the council. The individual committees may also set up working groups to aid in the research and preparation of their work. The Committee on International Investment and Multinational Enterprises (CIIME), which is responsible for the supervision of work pertaining to the guidelines, is part of the Financial and Fiscal Affairs division of the OECD. A special working group within the CIIME, the Working Group on the Guide-

---

[1]The original eighteen members were Norway, Sweden, Iceland, Denmark, Germany, Turkey, Greece, Italy, Austria, Switzerland, the Netherlands, Belgium, Luxembourg, France, Spain, Portugal, Ireland, and the United Kingdom.

[2]Organisation for Economic Cooperation and Development, *OECD at a Glance* (Paris, 1977), p. 2.

[3]*Ibid.*, p. 5.

lines (or "Lévy group," after the name of its chairman) aids the CIIME in its supervisory functions.[4]

FIGURE I–1
Structure of the OECD

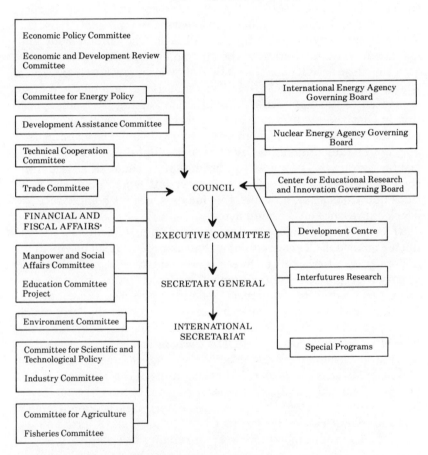

[a]Includes, among others, the Committee on International Investment and Multinational Enterprises.

Source: Organisation for Economic Cooperation and Development, *OECD at a Glance* (Paris, 1977), p. 3

[4]Mr. Philippe Lévy is from Switzerland.

Committee on International Investment and
Multinational Enterprises (CIIME)

Representatives on the CIIME are drawn from national government echelons and usually come from agencies whose work pertains to financial and investment matters. Business interests are represented before the CIIME by the Business and Industry Advisory Committee (BIAC), and labor's interests are represented by the Trade Union Advisory Committee (TUAC). The employment and industrial relations section of the guidelines appears to have generated the most activity for the CIIME; however, few representatives who have a specific background in industrial relations have been appointed to the committee. The difficulty arising from this situation is that the significance of technical and practical labor problems discussed before the committee by trade unionists and others may not be fully understood by those with almost exclusively financial backgrounds. Delegates to the committee can seek advice from their departments of labor and employment when industrial relations questions arise; however, this may not always compensate for a lack of presence on the committee.

BIAC. The bureau of the Business and Industry Advisory Committee of the OECD consists of a chairman, four vice chairmen, an honorary treasurer, and business representatives from each of the twenty-four participating nations. The latter representatives are usually appointed by employers' federations in member countries. In addition, there is a permanent secretariat staff in Paris which includes a secretary general, four department heads, and four members of an administrative staff. The Paris office, which is headed by Secretary General Yolande Michaud, handles arrangements for meetings at the OECD, coordinates meetings of the committees and groups of experts, and prepares staff papers. Committees on international investment and multinational enterprises, economic policy, and energy and raw materials have been formed; and approximately ten working groups of experts in areas ranging from capital markets to education are operational.

Unlike TUAC, the BIAC staff must handle the whole range of OECD activities including labor and industrial relations. As noted below, TUAC works selectively on industrial relations issues and its general secretary, Kari Tapiola, has a considerable trade union background. There is no specific counterpart to Tapiola in the Paris office of BIAC who is able to spend full time on labor-management matters.

TUAC. The Trade Union Advisory Committee to the OECD consists of national trade union centers such as the AFL-CIO in the United States, the Federation of German Trade Unions (Deutsche Gewerkschaftsbund—DGB) in West Germany, and the Trade Union Congress (TUC) in the United Kingdom (see Table I-1). A secretariat

TABLE I-1
Affiliation Fees Paid to TUAC in 1981
(in French Francs)

Acronym	Full Name	Country	Dues
DGB	Deutscher Gewerkschaftsbund	Germany	152,650.00
OGB	Österreichischer Gewerkschaftsbund	Austria	33,840.00
ACTU	Australian Council of Trade Unions	Australia	–
CSC	Confédération des Syndicats Chrétiens	Belgium	23,614.72
FGTB	Fédération Générale du Travail de Belgique	Belgium	19,350.00
CLC	Canadian Labour Conference	Canada	27,950.00
CSN	Confédération des Syndicats Nationaux	Canada	3,440.00
FTF	Faellesradet for Danske Tjenestemands og Funktionaerorganisationer	Denmark	5,697.50
LO-DK	Landsorganisationen i Danmark	Denmark	25,456.00
STV	Solidaridad de Trabajadores Vascos	Spain	2,365.00
UGT	Unión General de Trabajadores	Spain	5,354.76
AFL-CIO	American Federation of Labor and Congress of Industrial Organizations	United States	293,066.16
SAK	Suomen Ammattiliittojen Keskusjarjesto	Finland	19,780.00
TVK	Confederation of Salaried Employees in Finland	Finland	6,288.00
CFDT	Confédération Française Démocratique du Travail	France	21,694.00
CGC	Confédération Générale des Cadres	France	9,450.00
CGT-FO	Confédération Générale du Travail—Force Ouvrière	France	19,458.00
FEN	Fédération d' Education Nationale	France	10,554.00
TUC	Trades Union Congress	Great Britain	113,500.00
GSEE	Greek General Confederation of Labor	Greece	2,257.00
ICTU	Irish Congress of Trade Unions	Ireland	11,825.00
ASI	Icelandic Federation of Labour	Iceland	1,094.00
CISL	Confederazione Italiana Sindicati Lavoratori	Italy	53,708.84
UIL	Unione Italiana del Lavoro	Italy	6,000.00
DOMEI	Japanese Confederation of Labor	Japan	30,100.00
SOHYO	General Council of Trade Unions of Japan	Japan	64,464.72
CGT-LG	Confédération Générale du Travail de Luxembourg	Luxembourg	688.00

TABLE I–1 (continued)

Acronym	Full Name	Country	Dues
LCGB	Letzburger Christlicher Gewerkschaftsverband	Luxembourg	322.00
LO-N	Landsorganisasjonen i Norge	Norway	14,620.00
CNV	Christelijk National Vakverbond in Nederland	Netherlands	5,384.00
NKV	Nederlands Katholiek Vakvarbond	Netherlands	6,880.00
NVV	Nederlands Verbond van Vakverenigingen	Netherlands	15,867.00
UGT-P	União Geral dos Trabalhadores de Portugal	Portugal	–
LO-S	Landsorganisationen i Sverige	Sweden	39,914.00
TCO	Tjänstemännens Centralorganisation	Sweden	20,532.50
CNG	Christlich Nationaler Gewerkschaftsbund der Schweiz	Switzerland	2,279.00
SVEA	Schweizerischer Verband Evangelischer Arbeiter und Angestellter	Switzerland	301.00
USS	Union Syndicale Suisse	Switzerland	9,868.50
TÜRK-IS	Confederation of Turkish Trade Unions	Turkey	20,750.00
HISTADRUT	General Federation of Labour in Israel	Israel	–
			1,100,363.70

Sources: Financial data from TUAC; Abbreviations from A.P. Coldrick and Philip Jones, *The International Directory of the Trade Union Movement* (New York: Facts on File, Inc., 1979).

is maintained in Paris with a general secretary, Kari Tapiola, and several staff members, one of whom is responsible for the work done on multinational firms. Tapiola comes from the Finnish trade union movement, and prior to his position in Paris, he served as special labor assistant to Klaus Sahlgren, formerly director of the UN Centre on Transnational Corporations (CTC) in New York. The primary mission of TUAC is to prepare a trade union response to issues arising at the OECD level. Before the issuance of the guidelines in 1976, TUAC had a low profile at the OECD and concerned itself mainly with preparing a trade union position in regard to broader economic issues. This changed with the issuance of the guidelines as the OECD moved to establish a code of conduct for the practice of employment and industrial relations.

The introduction of the guidelines has forced the OECD into the posture of a quasi-regulatory agency. It is, moreover, the employment and industrial relations section of the guidelines that has altered the posture of the organization by introducing strong, third-party involvement in the forms of active trade union initiatives and discussions between multinational firms and governments. International Trade Secretariats (ITSs), such as the International Metalworkers' Federation (IMF) and the International Federation of Commercial, Clerical, Professional and Technical Employees (FIET), have figured prominently in this third-party involvement. In a practical sense, ITSs have played an intermediate role in collecting and submitting instances of alleged infractions of the guidelines. In a broader sense, however, they have constituted a major voice in favor of consultations with management at the parent company level, multinational bargaining, and the enforced international regulation of multinationals. The employment and industrial relations guidelines also have provided a forum in which multinational bargaining can be encouraged by international trade union officials in spite of the intention stated in the umbrella, or "chapeau," clause that precedes the guidelines, which refers the behavior of the multinational enterprise to the context of local law and practice.

CHALLENGES TO THE GUIDELINES

Needless to say, the trade unions in particular were anxious to seek interpretations of the guidelines once they had been issued. In late 1976 and early 1977, two separate events occurred in Europe that led to international trade union activity before the OECD and the ILO. Cases pertaining to the Badger (Belgium) NV Company,[5] and the Hertz Corporation in Copenhagen, Denmark,[6] created the first real challenges under the OECD guidelines.

Several months following the publication of the guidelines, on March 30, 1977, these two "cases" and ten others were submitted by TUAC to the CIIME "to illustrate the types of problems which in the experience of the trade unions, the implementation of the Guidelines involves." The guidelines, although voluntary, were obviously not intended to be ignored. Yet, that the implementation of the guidelines should involve "cases" of alleged infractions by individual enterprises alluded to a judicial or quasijudicial function that the CIIME clearly did not have.

An annex issued with the declaration of the guidelines on June 21, 1976, stated that it would be the function of the CIIME to "periodically or at the request of a member country hold an exchange of

[5]See Chapter IX, pp. 152-57.
[6]See Chapter XI, pp. 183-88.

views on matters related to the Guidelines and experience gained in their application." The CIIME, it was provided, would also periodically invite the views of both TUAC and BIAC, again on "matters related to the Guidelines." Although, on the proposal of a member government, the CIIME might decide to invite an individual enterprise to express its views if it so wishes, "the Committee shall not reach conclusions on the conduct of individual enterprises."[7]

At the early stage of the original "cases" submitted to it, the CIIME was reluctant to express interpretations of the guidelines on the basis of alleged infractions by individual companies. This reluctance was made manifest when, on the day following the presentation of TUAC's submission, the CIIME, in executive session, was requested by the Belgian government representative to issue an interpretation of the guidelines allegedly violated by Badger (Belgium) NV: "The U.S. delegates objected to such an action on the ground that they were not sitting as a judicial or semi-judicial body nor involved in a complaint procedure and that the case in question was already in the courts where it properly belonged."[8] A majority of other delegates agreed, and the request for an interpretation was refused.

The episode remains highly significant, for it illustrates the source of meanings embodied in the guidelines. Do or should these emanate from the interpretations of an international body on the basis of individual cases of supposed infractions? Or, rather, do the guidelines "recognize the primacy of local law and practice" and rely on these latter for meaning to be endowed them? The belief that the latter criteria should predominate is the basis of business support for the guidelines.

THE 1979 REVIEW OF THE GUIDELINES

When the guidelines were published in 1976, a review was scheduled to take place after three years, or by June 1979. Hearings were conducted by the CIIME during 1978, at which time both TUAC and BIAC presented their positions to the committee. A report reviewing the guidelines was issued by the CIIME in 1979.[9]

[7]USA-BIAC Committee on International Investment and Multinational Enterprises, *A Review of the OECD Guidelines for Multinational Enterprises: Employment and Industrial Relations* (New York, 1978), p. 32.

[8]*Ibid.*, p. 33.

[9]Organisation for Economic Cooperation and Development—Committee on International Investment and Multinational Enterprises, *The Review of the 1976 Declaration and Decisions on International Investment and Multinational Enterprises* (Paris, 1979).

BIAC reiterated its support for the guidelines; however, in regard to the review, its position can be described as one of insisting on no changes in the guidelines on the grounds, first, that there had not been enough experience in three years to evaluate the results of the guidelines; second, that because companies had agreed to abide voluntarily by the guidelines it would be a mistake to "rock the boat" early in the game by attempting to revise the language in the guidelines; and third, that a review, not a revision, of the guidelines was intended for 1979 when the document was first issued in 1976.

TUAC, on the other hand, sought the right to revise and to introduce changes in the language of the guidelines. Considerable effort was expended by TUAC to uphold the right of the trade unions to be recognized and to be able to bring specific charges against multinational companies. As the result of one much celebrated case, the language of one paragraph of the guidelines was changed.[10] As far as textual changes in the guidelines are concerned, this was the sole major amendment.

The CIIME's report did, then, constitute a review, not a revision, of the guidelines. The commentaries included in the report, however, contain language that may enhance TUAC's position in the CIIME's consideration. Three review paragraphs, in particular, appear to mark important gains for the unions. Paragraph 60 of the review report held that

> the thrust of these provisions of the Guidelines is towards having management adopt a positive approach towards the activities of trade unions and other bona fide organisations of employees of all categories and, in particular, an open attitude towards organisational activities within the framework of national rules and practices.[11]

This paragraph may be in conflict with national law and practice; for example, it would seem to go far beyond the United States National Labor Relations Act (NLRA), both in encouraging unionization generally and in approving the organization of supervisory, salaried, and managerial employees. Moreover, were the activities of ITSs to be understood as deserving of a "positive approach" by management? Or does the meaning of "other bona fide organisations of employees" exclude the ITSs which, themselves, are not organizations of employees, but of unions?

The questions, as raised, constitute an advance for unions, for they introduce a discussion of multinational collective bargaining.

---

[10]See Chapter XI, pp. 183–88.
[11]OECD—CIIME, *Review of the 1976 Declaration*, p. 33.

Review paragraphs numbers 61 and 62 are also relevant in this regard:

> 61. While not explicitly addressing the issue, the Guidelines imply that the management of [multinational enterprises] MNEs should adopt a co-operative attitude towards the participation of employees in international meetings for consultation and exchanges of views among themselves provided that the functioning of the operations of the enterprises and the normal procedures which govern relationships with representatives of the employees and their organisations are not thereby prejudiced.
>
> 62. The Committee has not considered the question of the conduct of collective bargaining at an international level, for which there are no real examples, although there has been some development of trade union efforts to co-ordinate approaches to multinational enterprises on a cross-country basis. The question has been raised, however, whether the Employment and Industrial Relations Guidelines could put obstacles in the way of recognition by the management of an MNE, in agreement with the national trade unions it has recognised and consistent with national laws and practices, of an International Trade Secretariat as a "bona fide organisation of employees" referred to in Paragraph One of the Guidelines. It is the Committee's view that no such obstacle exists or was intended in the Guidelines.[12]

These paragraphs lean toward the concept of multinational bargaining. Few employers deem it their obligation to support, encourage, or even cooperate with union or secretariat-sponsored multinational employee meetings, as is proclaimed proper by Paragraph 61. The attitude of most companies is that such meetings should be neither encouraged nor discouraged. To cooperate can mean to assist in setting the stage for multinational bargaining and the attendant risks which management clearly believes are involved. Because international union organizations regard consultation as a prelude to bargaining, such management fears may be realistic.

Paragraph 62 suggests an affirmative answer to the question of whether ITSs deserve a positive approach by management. Despite the fact that they are federations of organizations, not of employees, and have not hitherto been considered unions as such, ITSs have seen their status enhanced by the 1979 review. Most significantly, a combination of Paragraphs 60, 61, and 62 could well be interpreted to mean that a refusal by a multinational corporation to meet with an ITS or with an ITS and a committee of national unions to consult, or even to bargain, on a multinational basis is a breach of the OECD guidelines.

---

[12]*Ibid.*

BIAC reacted strongly to the above mentioned paragraphs and has stated the following:

> In connection with the references made in the Report to the Employment and Industrial Relations section of the Guidelines, BIAC reaffirmed that the introduction of this section firmly sets each of these guidelines within the framework of law, regulations and prevailing labor relations and employment practices, in each of the countries in which enterprises operate, and this introduction is overriding for all matters regarding employment and industrial relations. The Report states that the thrust of the provisions of the first two paragraphs of the Guidelines on Employment and Industrial Relations is towards having management adopt "a positive approach towards the activities of trade unions" and "an open attitude towards organizational activities." BIAC recalled that the Guidelines paragraphs to which the OECD's commentary referred, as well as the introduction to the Employment and Industrial Relations section, had been carefully and explicitly phrased. BIAC stated its intention to continue to rely on this phrasing.
>
> The participation by employees in international meetings for consultation and exchange of views among themselves was also treated in the Report. This subject, in the view of BIAC, should be handled by a reference to the language employed on this point in the ILO Tripartite Declaration which provides that representatives of workers should not be hindered from attending such meetings.
>
> BIAC restated another point it previously made relating to the International Trade Secretariats, which were mentioned in the Report: while these bodies may have a role to play within the overall trade union system, they cannot be regarded as organizations of employees in the context of the Guidelines.[13]

It appears that the BIAC position may have mitigated some of the effects of the language in Paragraphs 60, 61, and 62. TUAC, on the other hand, will continue to push for more effective and binding rules and regulations, as well as access to those it considers to be real decision makers in the ranks of management.

In June 1982, the CIIME met to consider the final draft of an interim report on activities that have taken place under the guidelines in the three years since the 1979 review. Significantly, TUAC, in presentations informing the CIIME of its views, further elaborated on an implementation structure for the guidelines. BIAC, meanwhile, continued to express its support for the guidelines, but cautioned that the continued issuance by the CIIME of clarifica-

---

[13]Business and Industry Advisory Committee, *A Report for Business on the OECD Guidelines for Multinational Enterprises*, (Paris, 1980), pp. 15–16. *See also,* Business and Industry Advisory Committee, *Report on the Promotional Activities of Member Organizations,* (Paris, 1981), for a statement on the positive action taken by employer groups to promote the guidelines.

tions on the guidelines for employment and industrial relations, which would further constrain the activities of multinational firms, ran the risk of eroding support for the guidelines. The next full-scale review of the guidelines is scheduled for 1984.

THE PRESENT STUDY

The perception that voluntary guidelines somehow constitute a way station on the road to more binding mechanisms at the international level has been evident in the way the ITSs and TUAC have used the guidelines during their six-year existence. There has been a concomitant tendency for the unions to equate the "voluntariness" of the guidelines with their "insignificance," on one hand. But on the other hand, the unions have used the guidelines as a skeletal structure upon which to base claims for, and enhance the credibility of, multinational bargaining. Such efforts have been lent prestige through their association with an intergovernmental agency.

The present study does not deny that there have been instances in which multinational enterprises, whether willfully or by neglect, have erred in their comportment within a host country. Nor does this study repudiate the usefulness of the guidelines in codifying what, at their inception, was viewed as "good practice for all."[14] Yet, the relatively small number of alleged infractions of the guidelines by multinationals that have been brought before the CIIME by TUAC provides testimony to the generally good comportment, and thus good reputation, of multinational firms. Chapter II provides an overview of the accomplishments of multinationals in the areas of employment and industrial relations.

Emphasis must be placed on the "alleged" status of infractions brought before the CIIME. The CIIME has no judicial function: it neither solicits examples of individual enterprises' conduct under the guidelines, nor performs any "fact finding" of its own. It does not reach conclusions on the conduct of individual companies. Rather, the nine paragraphs of the section in the guidelines on employment and industrial relations commend their adherence by enterprises "within the framework of law, regulations and prevailing labor relations and employment practices, in each of the countries in which they operate"—the "chapeau clause" of the guidelines on employment and industrial relations. The issues introduced by TUAC through its submissions to the CIIME have invariably arisen from the conduct of entities at the national level. It is at this

---

[14]Paragraph 9 of the General Policies Section, see Appendix A.

level—if the "chapeau clause" of the guidelines is to have any meaning—that both the source and solutions of industrial relations matters reside.

The local and national contexts of industrial relations law and practice are characterized by great variety across countries. So diverse is one national setting from another that a comprehensive survey of twenty-four OECD member countries would greatly expand the scope of the present study. Effort has been made, therefore, to focus attention, where appropriate, on the United States and the member countries of the European Community (EC).[15]

Chapters III through XII, therefore, relate the individual employment and industrial relations guidelines to the richness of law and practice at the national level in these countries. The aim in these chapters is to discuss the range of meaning embodied in the language of each guideline. For just as local law and practice vary among settings, so, too, must the specific meanings of general guidelines.

Within these chapters, several of the cases to have come before the CIIME are discussed in detail. The aim of these discussions is twofold: first, to balance the unions' allegations through reference to all available information, rather than to present just one side of the story; and second, to illustrate the meaning of the guidelines through examination of the local contexts in which these disputes occurred and, from such a perspective, to view the extent to which a company's comportment adhered to or deviated from the meaning of the guidelines. In the final chapter, several conclusions are drawn which provide an overview of the study.

---

[15]France, Germany, Belgium, the Netherlands, Luxembourg, United Kingdom, Ireland, Italy, and Denmark are frequently referred to in the course of this study, as are Spain, Sweden, Austria, and Switzerland, although the latter are not members of the EC.

CHAPTER II

Overview of
the Industrial Relations Performance of
Multinational Enterprises

A recent study, submitted by the International Institute for Labour Studies to the European Commission, the body whose role it is to initiate policy research and discussion within the European Community (EC), concludes: "National industrial relations norms condition labor-management relations, particularly as regards information disclosure, consultation and negotiation, in transnational enterprises to a greater degree than their transnational character."[1] The finding is significant, both because it highlights the disparity between perception and fact, and because it concurs with other research undertaken by such bodies as the International Labor Organization (ILO), the Organization for Economic Cooperation and Development (OECD), and the European Community (EC) itself. Their analyses, along with others, "demonstrated that multinationals adapted to the local industrial relations rules and to the local climate."[2]

The performance of multinational enterprises in the area of industrial relations thus appears to conform to the "chapeau clause" of the OECD Guidelines on Employment and Industrial Relations, the clause which compels multinationals to adhere to the guidelines "within the framework of law, regulations and prevailing labor relations and employment practices, in each of the countries in which

---

[1]International Institute for Labour Studies (Geneva), *Pilot-Study on Relations Between Management of Transnational Enterprises and Employee Representatives in E.C. Countries,* submitted to the Commission of the European Communities (1977), p. 62.

[2]Roger Blanpain, *The OECD Guidelines for Multinational Enterprises and Labour Relations, 1976–1979: Experience and Review,* English text rewritten by Michael Jones (Deventer, The Netherlands: Kluwer, 1979), p. 15.

they operate."³ Notwithstanding the available evidence, however, multinational enterprises (MNEs) continue to arouse the suspicion, voiced by trade union and other officials, that they constitute a challenge to local self-determination. The basis of this challenge is a certain perception of the power of a multinational enterprise to operate independently of local standards. It is useful, therefore, to balance this perception with what data exist regarding the scope, structure, and content of multinational industrial relations.

MULTINATIONALS AND EMPLOYMENT

Logically prior to a discussion of industrial relations is the subject of the impact of MNEs on employment. A recent ILO study on the employment effects of multinationals has made a considerable contribution toward this end.⁴ Several surveys undertaken in the 1970s underscore the significant employment gains attributable to MNEs. Indeed, 40 percent of employment in industry in nine of the wealthiest industrial nations is accounted for by multinationals.⁵ Data collected by the OECD, moreover, estimate total employment in manufacturing in the developed countries at 90,000,000, of which one-third is employment attributable to multinationals.⁶

Multinationals in specific industries account for much of this employment. The ILO study observes that "MNEs have been found to constitute . . . a particularly high proportion of undertakings in industries which make relatively intensive use of technology."⁷ Although the data did not allow the attribution of any causal links between MNE involvement in particular industries and the growth of these industries relative to others, it was found that "MNEs in the industrial countries are largely concentrated in growth industries and are less noticeable in industries where the greatest structural problems. . . are presently encountered."⁸ The ILO study found, moreover, that it is difficult to substantiate the claim that MNEs are responsible for the decline of employment in struggling industries.⁹

---

³USA-BIAC Committee on International Investment and Multinational Enterprises, *A Review of the OECD Guidelines for Multinational Enterprises: Employment and Industrial Relations* (New York, 1978), p. 17.
⁴International Labour Office, *Employment Effects of Multinational Enterprises in Industrialised Countries* (Geneva, 1981).
⁵*Ibid.*, p. 1.
⁶*Ibid.*
⁷*Ibid.*, p. 33.
⁸*Ibid.*, p. 73.
⁹*Ibid.*, p. 74.

As a case in point of the impact of MNEs on an industry in which employment has declined, the study cites the case of the Swedish welding equipment industry. Between the years 1965 and 1977, domestic employment in this industry dropped 35 percent. Research found "that there was a small increase in total home-country employment in the two sample MNEs in the industry, in contrast to the marked decline in domestic firms; [and] that there was an especially rapid increase in staff employment (in the two sample MNEs), whereas production employees had dropped slightly, but less than for (non-MNE) national firms."[10]

The Issue of Job Export

Related to the Swedish example above is the issue of "job export," or the extent to which foreign direct investment has resulted in a net loss of domestic jobs. The question has stirred considerable debate, much of it occurring at the beginning of the 1970s. The AFL-CIO's Industrial Union Department (IUD) concluded, for example, that 900,000 jobs had been lost in the United States between 1966 and 1971 as a result of the expansion of U.S. multinationals abroad.[11] The figure, based on data from the Bureau of Labor Statistics and the U.S. Department of Labor, represents the researchers' calculations of jobs generated by the increase in

---

[10]*Ibid.*, p. 61. Other factors clearly condition the employment effects of MNEs, as Hans Günter notes in his summary of ILO publications on the subject:

A general impression conveyed by these papers is the diverse strength and nature of MNE employment impact the world over . . . .Thus the employment impact of MNEs in a small industrialised country, like Belgium for instance, which has a heavy concentration of foreign MNEs in the manufacturing sector (No. 16), differs from that in a major industrialised country, like the Federal Republic of Germany, which has a much lower penetration rate of foreign MNEs, an important proportion of domestic MNEs and a highly developed labour market and income protection policy (No. 17). The situation is again different in a country such as the United Kingdom, where the foreign enterprise penetration has increased at a steady rate during the last 10–15 years in an environment of rising unemployment and rapid industrial change (No. 20). On the other hand, in a country like Nigeria (No. 25), as in other developing countries, much disguised unemployment exists, public efforts for employment creation (while mostly in the small-scale industries) have had a decisive influence also on the employment performance of MNEs. Still, it can be safely concluded that in all countries where multinationals have established subsidiaries, industrialised and developing, MNEs have acted as elements of dynamic change contributing not only to employment opportunities but also to the social concerns connected with change. Hans Günter, *ILO Research on Multinational Enterprises and Social Policy: An Overview*, Working Paper No. 15 (Geneva: International Labour Office, 1981), p. 18.

[11]Subcommittee on International Trade of the Committee of Finance of the U.S. Senate, "An American Trade Union View of International Trade and Investment, AFL-CIO," in *Multinational Corporations* (Washington, D.C., 1973), pp. 59–86.

exports versus those that would have been required to produce the
increase in imports to the United States from U.S.-owned subsidiaries abroad.

The AFL-CIO's study provoked controversy not only over its
finding of a net export of jobs attributable to MNEs, but over the
very reasons behind foreign direct investment. The extended parameters of the debate introduced a needed complexity into the discussion of the job-export issue. Thus, for example, the notion of "defensive expansion," or the need to establish foreign subsidiaries to
defend market shares initially acquired through exports, was raised
to counter the unions' charge that the search for "cheap labor" pro-
pelled domestic companies to establish subsidiaries abroad.[12] Subsequent analyses of the job-export issue have had "at least the merit
of identifying a number of issues to be considered in the context,"[13]
accounting to a greater degree for the complexity of the employment effects of multinationals.

An example of a more comprehensive view of the job-export question appears in the research of R.G. Hawkins.[14] Using data from the
U.S. Department of Commerce, Hawkins sought to gauge not only
the loss of jobs resulting from foreign direct investment, but also
gains in domestic employment directly and indirectly related to
such expansion, and the creation of jobs owing to the establishment
of foreign subsidiaries in the United States. A principal finding was
that "total U.S. jobs have not suffered at the expense of U.S. foreign affiliate operations. But some industries have lost output and
jobs while others have gained."[15] In its review of research undertaken on the issue, the ILO study also concludes that although no
evidence of massive job export exists, "this does not exclude . . . the
export of individual jobs or of certain categories of jobs through
production transfers or expansion abroad."[16]

It is significant that a review of the evidence does not support the
contention that the multinational enterprise's expansion results in a
net export of jobs: "As an overall conclusion, from the more specific
calculations reviewed, it can be noted . . . that the effects of MNE
expansion abroad on the total domestic employment volume in the
industrialised home countries in question have probably not been

---

[12]See, for example, B. Stobaugh, "How Investment Abroad Creates Jobs at
Home," *Harvard Business Review*, Vol. 50, No. 5 (Sept.–Oct. 1972), pp. 118–26.

[13]ILO, *Employment Effects of Multinational Enterprises*, p. 85.

[14]R. G. Hawkins, *Jobs, Skills and U.S. Multinationals*, a statement to the Subcom-
mittee of International Economic Policy, Committee on International Relations, U.S.
House of Representatives (Washington, 1976).

[15]*Ibid.*, p. 85.

[16]ILO, *Employment Effects of Multinational Enterprises*, p. 59.

very important, generally and proportionately, either in a positive or a negative sense."[17] A summary of the findings of studies of the job-export issue appears in Table II-1.

Precipitating from the job-export question has been that of what effect the expansion of multinationals may have on the structure of employment. Some evidence suggests that the effect may parallel the more general phenomenon of shrinking volume in production jobs in manufacturing and growth of white-collar employment.[18] Although analyses of this question are inconclusive, the issue itself has occasioned much debate, fueled in part by the fact that the jobs apparently eliminated may largely be traditional, union jobs.[19]

Job Security

It would seem that because of the worldwide economic downturn and high levels of unemployment, discussion of the effects of multinationals on employment has attracted renewed poignancy. Just as the job-export issue won considerable attention a decade ago, so the present economic climate has perhaps accentuated the "foreignness" of the foreign subsidiary, creating a perception equating such foreignness with employment instability. To cite a representative view: "Recently, there have been some highly publicized plant closures by MNEs in both Belgium and Scotland which have served to exacerbate oft-expressed union and government fears that employment in host-country MNE subsidiaries was inherently unstable."[20] Here again, there are limits to the available data; however, the evidence that exists appears to contradict these fears of employment instability.

The ILO study of the effects of multinationals on employment offers a synthesis of their performance in the area of job security. "Despite particular MNE features, most of the government replies received for the present study give the impression that as regards

---

[17]*Ibid.*, p. 86.

[18]*Ibid.*, p. 60.

[19]*Ibid.* The U.S. component study for the ILO's research notes:

To the extent that U.S. investment abroad eliminates jobs on a gross basis or, in the case of defensive investment, that the employees who lost their jobs would have lost them anyway, the skill, industry, and location mix of those eliminated jobs will differ from the characteristics of the jobs created through export stimulus and managerial staff accretions as a result of the foreign operations . . . .It becomes a problem of a structural mismatch between the jobs eliminated and the jobs created, even if the latter dominate. One of the obvious results is that the jobs that are eliminated will be almost exclusively production jobs and, if the MNC parent is unionized, predominently union jobs.

[20]*Ibid.*, p. 62.

TABLE II-1
Summary of Studies on
Multinational Enterprises' Effects
Upon Employment (U.S.)

Study	Type of Analysis or Source of Information	Main Conclusions	Net Effect on Employment
Business International	Sample survey of 86 companies	Between 1960 and 1970, exports by multinationals increased more rapidly than U.S. exports. In same period, employment in the United States grew more quickly in multinationals than in other sectors.	Positive
Emergency Committee on American Trade	Sample survey of 74 companies	Between 1960 and 1970, employment in multinationals grew by 3.3 percent, whereas employment in U.S. manufacturing grew at a rate of 1.4 percent per year. Foreign subsidiaries stimulate U.S. exports.	Mainly Positive
National Foreign Trade Council	Sample survey and case studies of more than 50 companies	Most foreign investments are made to extend or maintain foreign markets. In most cases U.S. domestic investment is not a valid alternative to foreign investment.	Positive
Ruttenberg, AFL-CIO Study	Analysis based on official data	Multinationals are largely responsible for deterioration in U.S. balance of payments and loss of U.S. jobs. Technology transfer harms U.S. employment and balance of payments.	Negative (loss of 500,000 jobs, 1966–1969)

Stobaugh and Associates	Combination of nine case studies and various data	Multinationals have positive effects on employment. Foreign investment is made to preserve existing markets or open new ones. Effect on trade balance is positive.	Positive (increase of 600,000 jobs)
U.S. Chamber of Commerce	Sample survey of 158 companies	Between 1960 and 1970, employment in multinationals grew more quickly than total U.S. employment. Multinationals made foreign investments to preserve markets or to overcome trade barriers.	Positive

Source: International Labour Office, *The Impact of Multinational Enterprises on Employment and Training* (Geneva, 1976), pp. 23–24.

employment security there is, on the whole, no significant difference in industrialized countries between multinational and other enterprises."[21] Clearly, the perception of "inherent" instability attaching to MNE employment suggests a sort of protectionism and implies a "preference" for closure of an MNE's foreign subsidiaries over its home-country operations. Such an implied preference is not borne out by the available evidence, evidence that "seems to support the hypothesis that . . . the propensity of MNEs to close down enterprises or to undertake mass dismissals has usually been no greater than that of national firms."[22]

In Belgium, where the presence of both multinationals and unemployment are particularly high, the issue is perhaps more acute. Roger Blanpain notes that some researchers have stated "without too much evidence to sustain their assertion, that job security is less guaranteed in new foreign firms than in former Belgian firms that have been taken over."[23] No evidence of such behavior has been found in a similar study on the United Kingdom; and in Belgium, moreover, other studies have tended to contradict such an assertion. Thus, in a climate of rising unemployment, "the fear of a massive withdrawal of foreign MNEs from Belgian territory has certainly not materialized."[24] Indeed, one study indicates that foreign subsidiaries in Belgium have in fact fared better than domestic firms, concluding that

> it would seem that the relatively favourable employment performance of foreign enterprises as compared with Belgian companies is connected with a relatively higher productivity and profitability of the foreign enterprises and the fact that their integration in a larger multinational group possibly gives them more leeway to absorb temporary difficulties. Thus, somewhat in contrast to other evaluations, in the Belgian case the international character of MNEs has been regarded as a positive factor for employment stability.[25]

---

[21]*Ibid.*, p. 61.

[22]*Ibid.*, p. 62.

[23]Roger Blanpain, "Multinationals' Impact on Host Country Industrial Relations," in *Multinationals, Unions, and Labor Relations in Industrialized Countries* R. F. Banks and J. Stieber, eds. (Ithaca, New York: New York State School of Industrial & Labor Relations, Cornell University, 1977), pp. 131–32.

[24]*Ibid.* See also Hans Günter, *ILO Research on Multinational Enterprises and Social Policy: An Overview* Working Paper No. 15 (Geneva: International Labour Office, 1981), p. 13:

Both with respect to the larger-term global employment trend in manufacturing and with regard to the effect of the recession, MNEs appear to have displayed in various countries a somewhat greater employment increase than the rest of manufacturing or resisted better recessionary employment decline (in particular in Belgium and the United Kingdom).

[25]ILO, *Employment Effects of Multinational Enterprises*, p. 63.

The extent to which empirical evidence contrasts with some perceptions of the multinational—here, for example, with regard to
employment stability—raises complex questions about the performance of MNEs in the area of industrial relations in general. Many
of these perceptions appear linked to a view of the MNE as an "independent agent of change."[26] Specifically, "the scope which MNEs
may have for transferring activities between countries has sharpened fears that such enterprises may enjoy considerable discretion-
ary power to act as independent agents in promoting the international allocation of resources and employment."[27] To a certain
extent, a discussion of the industrial relations performance of
MNEs is the attempt to dissociate "sharpened fears" from fact.

THE STRUCTURE OF MNE INDUSTRIAL RELATIONS: DECENTRALIZATION

Blanpain observes that "the local labor relations system may
compel the multinational corporation first to decentralize the handling of industrial relations and, second, to adjust to local conditions."[28] A good indication of this decentralization exists in that,
almost without exception, the local employee relations personnel are
host-country nationals. In fact, however, MNE industrial relations
executives have long argued that what "compels" decentralization
in industrial relations is simply good business practice, and that
"multinationals are well aware that there are significant differences
between countries in their industrial relations systems, that they
must respect these differences to avoid serious conflicts and difficulties, and that they must employ indigenous managers who have
local understanding and knowledge to be primarily responsible for
the conduct of most industrial relations issues."[29]
One study of collective bargaining in industrialized market economies has noted that the impact of multinationals on the local bargaining structure has been minimal in those instances in which the
foreign subsidiary has successfully integrated itself into the structure of existing practices.[30] Such integration moreover, has been
found to vary, depending upon the particular country, the degree of

---

[26]*Ibid.,* p. 64.

[27]*Ibid.*

[28]Blanpain, "Multinationals' Impact," p. 125.

[29]B. C. Roberts, "Comment," in *Multinationals, Unions, and Labor Relations,* pp. 50–51.

[30]M. Beckers, J. P. Frière, F. Saucier, and G. Torrisi, *La Belgique Face aux Inves-
tissements Etrangers* (Louvain: Université de Louvain, 1973), pp. 82–84.

compulsoriness of the local industrial relations system, and the national origin of the MNE. Becker's study of the impact of foreign investment in Belgium found that foreign subsidiaries generally conform to the local structure in "integrated" regions of that country, *i.e.*, regions characterized by a higher percentage of industry and established labor-management relations.[31] Similarly, an ILO study has concluded that in France and Belgium, "union recognition difficulties among foreign multinational subsidiary firms, or other firms of generally comparable size . . . in the industries under study in this report have been conspicuous by their absence."[32] Similar findings characterize the structure of bargaining in Sweden and Germany as well.

On the other hand, research undertaken by the ILO and other groups suggests that in the absence of a clearly defined existing structure, foreign subsidiaries of MNEs "have had a decentralizing effect where the policies followed . . . with respect to collective bargaining have been independent of those of the employers' associations in the industry in the host countries of their subsidiaries."[33] Although the data are incomplete, others have suggested that multinationals have played a significant role in the continuing shift of the locus of industrial relations toward the plant level.[34] Blanpain, however, concludes that it is yet too early to endow any findings in this area with certainty, and observes that "in the intermediate term . . . fundamental characteristics of industrial relations systems are likely to remain basically unchanged."[35]

As with the cases that have come before the OECD's Committee on International Investment and Multinational Enterprises (CIIME), a disproportionate amount of the research on the impact of MNEs on industrial relations appears to focus on the United Kingdom and Belgium, countries that have similar industrial relations systems. Both have "well-developed systems of 'voluntary' industrial relations, with a rather strong degree of unionization . . . no legally bind-

---

[31]*Ibid.*

[32]International Labour Office, *Multinationals in Western Europe: The Industrial Relations Experience* (Geneva, 1976), p. 6.

[33]Blanpain, "Multinationals' Impact," p. 131.

[34]International Labour Office, *Collective Bargaining in Industrialised Market Economies*, (Geneva, 1979), p. 129:

On the other hand, [MNEs] have had a decentralizing effect where the policies followed by multinational enterprises with respect to collective bargaining have been independent of those of the employers' associations in the industry in the host countries of their subsidiaries . . . .To this extent, multinational enterprises have in certain countries contributed to general movement towards a more decentralised bargaining structure.

[35]Blanpain, "Multinationals' Impact," p. 134.

ing collective agreements; collective bargaining at different levels (national, regional, and plant); and employer associations that play an important role in collective bargaining as well as in representing employers' interests with governmental authorities."[36] Significantly, in his summary review of research done on the subject in these countries, Blanpain observes that the "findings on the United Kingdom and Belgium by and large do not support the conclusion that the multinationals, up to now, have really had a great impact."[37]

The general finding noted earlier that multinationals have adapted to the local context of their operations also implies this process of decentralization. Indications of this decentralization are reflected in the great extent to which multinational subsidiaries have joined the appropriate employers' association and have recognized and bargained with the local trade unions.[38] Controversy over trade union recognition does exist, and tends toward localization, particularly in countries of "voluntarist" industrial relations, such as the United Kingdom. There, it is also true, the issue is more specifically recognition of trade unions by U.S.-owned subsidiaries. In their study of the issue, however, Steuer and Gennard have concluded that nonrecognition of trade unions is no more a problem among foreign than among domestic firms.[39] The authors further note that the issue of trade union recognition is apparently linked to the "size" as well as to the "foreignness" of a company: "When trouble over nonrecognition arises with a foreign-owned company it tends to get greater union and press publicity and has perhaps created the impression that domestic firms are less anti-union than the foreign company."[40] Here, as in the case of job security, the issue of foreignness itself may distort the perception of MNE performance. As an ILO study on the industrial relations practices of MNEs observes: "Even a handful of difficult cases may make them appear as though all or nearly all multinationals have been difficult on the matter of recognition."[41] Steuer and Gennard conclude that this has not been the case and, moreover, that the issue of size may add a further distortion to the discussion: "the foreign company often

---

[36]*Ibid.*, p. 124.
[37]*Ibid.*, p. 133.
[38]Günter, *ILO Research on Multinational Enterprises*, p. 5.
[39]J. Gennard and M. D. Steuer, "The Industrial Relations of Foreign Owned Subsidiaries in the United Kingdom," *British Journal of Industrial Relations*, Vol. IX, No. 2 (July 1971), p. 155. *See also*, International Labour Office, *Multinational Enterprises and Social Policy* (Geneva, 1973), pp. 92–93.
[40]*Ibid.*
[41]ILO, *Multinationals in Western Europe*, pp. 3–4.

starts big in this country, altering the recognition and the power relations between the employer and the unions, compared to domestic firms."[42]

The Locus of Decision Making and the Scope of Industrial Relations

Although evidence suggests that one possible impact of MNEs on the structure of industrial relations is a decentralizing influence, another salient issue that has emerged in recent years involves the claim that MNEs present a highly centralized structure whose ultimate decision-making authority is lodged in corporate headquarters. From the dual claims of information disclosure and worker participation in decision making, therefore, trade unions have argued that, owing to their transnational power, MNEs represent an unfair match in collective bargaining. A hypothetical example helps to illustrate the complexity of this issue.

It may be difficult to separate fact from contention in a union official's charge that local management, claiming pressure from corporate headquarters, threatens to transfer production facilities unless management gets its way in negotiations.[43] If no such pressure exists and the claim is being used merely as a tactic in negotiations, then this may arguably constitute an abuse of bargaining power. Such a contention might come close to the truth, however, as in the situation of an unprofitable subsidiary whose continued existence is underwritten by financing from the parent company. If, under such circumstances, the parent company makes known through local management its intention that unless certain conditions are met production will be transferred to a location outside the country, does the charge of abuse still hold? Clearly, the decision to close an unprofitable subsidiary cannot in itself be viewed as either unwise or unethical in the context of business economics.

A further distinction is useful. The former instance, the union official's charge, is an industrial relations matter. The latter set of circumstances, in the view of most managers, is a corporate matter

---

[42]Gennard and Steuer, "The Industrial Relations of Foreign Owned Subsidiaries," p. 155.

[43]Allegations of this nature have in fact been made. For example, summarizing views held by the European trade unionists interviewed for the ILO report on MNE industrial relations, the report concludes:

While unionists felt no pressing need for full-scale transnational collective bargaining devices . . . dissatisfaction with this or that bargaining (or related) practice of some multinational companies was expressed. The issues engendering such dissatisfaction and occasional friction include: . . . the fear that production might be moved or new investments curtailed, as a company bargaining tactic. (ILO, *Multinationals in Western Europe*, p. 67.)

with industrial relations repercussions. The former case, then, is over management's conduct in collective bargaining; the latter, over corporate investment decisions. The first instance involves the locus of decision making in the MNE, and the second case verges toward the issue of the scope of industrial relations.

Although not an implication that abuses such as the one hypothesized in the first case have never occurred, it appears that an MNE's ability to transfer physical and human capital independently of national law and practice is overstated. The ILO study on the employment effects of multinationals notes that "the available evidence is mixed as to the extent to which multinational enterprises do, or can in fact exercise discretion in decisions to transfer production abroad on the large scale."[44] As Gennard and Steuer observe: "British unions have suffered little from the effects of 'runaway' industry, *i.e.* the potential ability of the multinational to move its production from one country to another."[45] This view is shared by other researchers: "Although the power of corporate headquarters may be virtually absolute in the long run, it may be far less than unions often suggest in the short run."[46] Later pages of this study will confirm that the supposed "absolute power" of the multinational to transfer production is in fact considerably constrained by the foreign subsidiary's adherence to national law and practice.

With regard to the locus of decision making, several factors appear to influence the degree to which a corporate headquarters is involved in the industrial relations decisions of its subsidiaries. As Ben Roberts observes,

> there is evidence that technological, cultural, and ideological factors play an important role in determining the locus of decision making between headquarters and subsidiary managements. Companies with a high capital-to-labor ratio (such as chemical processing, oil production and refining, and manufacturing companies) tend to have a greater headquarters' influence than labor-intensive companies, especially in the early years of an expansion overseas. The degree of interdependence in the production process between countries is also of considerable importance. When subsidiaries in overseas countries are dependent on a single source of supply, corporate headquarters will inevitably be drawn into industrial relations decisions that may crucially affect various subsidiaries and the ultimate profitability of the corporation as a whole.[47]

---

[44]ILO, *Employment Effects of Multinational Enterprises*, p. 69.
[45]Gennard and Steuer, "The Industrial Relations of Foreign Owned Subsidiaries," p. 144.
[46]Roberts, "Comment," p. 50.
[47]*Ibid.*

An important distinction must be drawn, however, between the open lines of communication among subsidiaries and their parent company and the actual locus of decision making in the area of industrial relations. In a survey of thirty British multinationals, only three firms said that "their headquarters staff were frequently involved in the preparation for negotiations, collective bargaining, and the settlement of disputes."[48] David Blake analyzed the industrial relations practices of U.S. multinationals and found that the day-to-day conduct of industrial relations, including contract administration and grievance procedures, was characterized by the autonomy of the subsidiary.[49] Headquarters became involved only in the areas of industrial relations conflict, such as strike settlement.[50] Generally, the following view of one multinational executive appears to corroborate the available evidence: "It would be a brash corporate management that would substitute its judgment of an industrial relations situation for the judgment of the local management. If they do, they are asking for trouble."[51]

One area in which headquarters' involvement is particularly great, however, is in negotiations over, and changes in, the company's pension plan. The reason for a higher degree of parent-company involvement in this area is clearly attributable to the fact that pensions represent a long-term financial commitment.[52]

As the second hypothetical example indicated, the question of centralized decision making may be inextricably bound up with competing perceptions of the scope of industrial relations. One American employee relations executive provides the following definition:

> Broadly defined, industrial relations questions generally involve remuneration and conditions of employment, including employee benefit plans, recruitment and training of employees, recognition of trade unions or other employee representatives, establishment of collective bargaining and grievance procedures, and resolution of disputes that might arise concerning these matters. Management decisions about new or redeployed production facilities are not as such, industrial

[48]*Ibid.*, p. 51. See also, B. C. Roberts and J. May, "The Response of Multinational Enterprises to International Trade Union Pressures," *British Journal of Industrial Relations*, Vol. 12, No. 3 (November 1974), pp. 403–17.

[49]D. Blake, "Comment," in *Multinationals, Unions, and Labor Relations*, p. 85. See also, D. Blake, "Cross-National Cooperative Strategies: Union Response to the MNCs," *Multinational Corporations and Labour Unions*, selected papers from a symposium in Nijmegan, Netherlands, May 1973.

[50]*Ibid.*

[51]J. Belford, "Comment," in *Multinationals, Unions, and Labor Relations*," p. 135.

[52]ILO, *Multinationals in Western Europe*, p. 31.

relations questions. The effects or impact of those decisions on employees, however, are the concern of management industrial relations executives, and in most firms these effects are an appropriate subject for consultation and bargaining with recognized representatives of designated groups of employees.[53]

As this definition implies, the debate over the locus of decision making in multinational firms focuses mainly on the matter of investment decisions.

Trade unions, particularly in Western Europe, have been considerably active in bringing this issue to the forefront of public attention and have rallied the support of some governments and international bodies as well. Roberts has stated that

the extent to which unions have established a right to negotiate or to be consulted on these matters is contentious in all countries. In fact, it is precisely this situation that has led European unions to press their governments to compel both domestic- and foreign-owned corporations to provide advance information about their plans. The closure of plants and transfer of production facilities from one country to another is the primary factor in the belief of unions that multinational enterprises are fundamentally a different species from national enterprises and, therefore, must be regulated by an extension of national or international law, or by the internationalising of the bargaining process.[54]

Nonetheless, it appears that the unions' perception of MNEs as "different species" than national firms in the area of investment and transfer of production facilities is contradicted by the available evidence.

In the case of Belgium, it was noted that employment stability may in fact be greater for foreign-owned than for domestic firms. As Roberts further observes, "once a company has made an investment, it may be locked in. Companies have often taken immense losses before pulling out, finally deciding that the loss is killing them. . . . In these decisions multinationals behave much like national firms."[55] Here as elsewhere, moreover, their behavior is subject to national law and collective agreements. Examples of prolonged loss prior to final plant closure, ultimately requiring the sanction of the host country's courts and after the requisite consultation with the unions, are discussed below.[56]

Concern over job security, information disclosure, and participa-

[53]Robert Copp, "Locus of Industrial Relations Decision Making in Multinationals," in *Multinationals, Unions, and Labor Relations,"* p. 44.
[54]Roberts, "Comment," pp. 49–50.
[55]*Ibid.,* p. 50.
[56]See Chapter IX, p. 146.

tion in decision making—all to some degree facets of the same prism
of union interest—will doubtless continue to be areas of contention
in industrial relations, especially if the present recessionary climate
and high unemployment continue. It is significant, however, that to
the extent that MNEs have largely obeyed national law and practice, union interest in the locus of decision making and the scope of
industrial relations exists quite independently of the behavior of the
foreign subsidiary in its host country.

THE CONTENT OF INDUSTRIAL RELATIONS

There is general agreement that the wages, fringe benefits, and
working conditions in foreign subsidiaries of multinationals are at
the very least equivalent to those paid by national employers and
that multinationals are often among the better-paying employers.[57]
The ILO study on the employment effects of multinationals
remarks that "in all industrialized market economy countries for
which comparative data are available, the share of foreign MNE
subsidiaries in total industrial value added and the total wages bill
exceeds their share in industrial employment. Foreign MNEs are
thus often seen as paying higher wages and salaries."[58] Similarly,
another ILO study on wages and working conditions found, with
regard to the latter, that working conditions in MNE subsidiaries
either matched or compared favorably with those of national
employers of equivalent size.[59]

Higher fringe benefits, too, appear to be one of the advantages of
multinational firms. Thus, "there was general concensus, as a report
in a 1970 OECD trade union meeting concluded, that multinational
enterprises 'often provide better fringe benefits than domestic companies.' The report of the International Organisation of Employers
[IOE] on multinationals states that these companies 'are certainly
at the top' as regards fringe benefits, and 'especially as regards pensions.'"[60] The IOE report, the result of a survey of 400 multinationals, further notes that although pensions tend to be centrally ad-

[57]H. Gunter, *ILO Research on Multinational Enterprises*, notes that the ILO studies "tend to support the thesis that in industrialized host countries, when MNEs
deviate from prevailing patterns and levels of remuneration, this deviation is more
often than not in the direction of better rates . . . .Somewhat similar patterns seem to
exist with regard to the working conditions practices," p. 23. On the latter subject,
see also, ILO, *Multinational Enterprises and Social Policy* , pp. 63–82.
[58]ILO, *Employment Effects on Multinational Enterprises*, p. 57.
[59]International Labour Office, *Wages and Working Conditions in Multinational
Enterprises*, (Geneva, 1976), pp. 49–50.
[60]ILO, *Multinationals in Western Europe*, p. 31.

ministered, the authority for establishing wages, fringe benefits, and working conditions tends to reside with the host-country subsidiary.[61]

The relative achievements of multinationals in the area of wages, fringe benefits, and working conditions have, however, met with the contestation of some European unions, particularly in Belgium and the United Kingdom, which have expressed the fear that the rationale for these better conditions is to keep the unions out or otherwise to undermine the solidarity of the union movement. "The policy of high benefits, special training programmes, special company parties, internal house organs and the like create a special kind of attachment of workers to such enterprises. In turn this may lead to disinterest on the part of workers in the ordinary union organisations of the country."[62]

The data needed to resolve this argument are unavailable, but the argument itself has a curious status as an issue. Is a company, whether national or multinational, at fault in providing higher than average wages and benefits in the hopes that its employees choose not to join a union? This question is discussed in greater detail in Chapter III. Gennard notes, meanwhile, that evidence exists which indicates that in the United Kingdom domestic and foreign firms alike have provided higher fringe benefits as a means of keeping unions out.[63]

Other reasons are available that seek to explain the better wages and fringe benefits provided by multinationals. One of these suggests that the higher productivity of the foreign subsidiary allows for higher wages. It is noted, as well, that multinational foreign subsidiaries are often characterized by a higher degree of capital intensiveness, which may result in higher productivity and, in turn, higher wages.[64]

Another view ascribes the phenomenon to successful management: "Multinational companies are almost without exception organisations with substantial operations and long experience in their own countries. Part of their growth and success can be attributed to their handling of manpower and skills as well as technical processes."[65] Similarly, another writer observes that "the evidence then suggests, strongly, if in a general way, that superior labour rela-

---

[61]*Ibid.*

[62]*Ibid.*, p. 41.

[63]J. Gennard, *Multinational Corporations and British Labour: A Review of Attitudes and Responses*, British-North American Committee, (London: Alfred H. Cooper & Sons, Ltd., 1972), p. 35.

[64]ILO, *Wages and Working Conditions*, p. 49.

[65]ILO, *Multinationals in Western Europe*, p. 35.

tions . . . have been one source of the [MNE] subsidiaries' superior
performance."[66] Gennard and Steuer note that "it is often suggested
that the foreign-owned subsidiary is more productive and profitable
than its domestic counterpart, and that this superior performance is
at least partly due to better labour utilization."[67] To the authors,
such a situation could create friction in host-country industrial relations. In their research, however, the authors found, using strike
patterns as a proxy for industrial content or unrest, that the foreign
firms actually fared better in the comparison than domestic firms.[68]

The Issue of Innovation

One vein of the considerable body of writing on multinationals
implies that any and all changes in industrial relations practices
introduced by the subsidiary of a foreign corporation are bad *per se*
by virtue of their foreign origin. There have, however, been examples of good change as well as bad attributable to the multinational
firm. A balanced view of such changes would undoubtedly conclude
that "some industrial relations decisions of multinationals have
been unacceptable locally, whereas others have been regarded as
constructive innovations."[69] How numerous examples of either category may be is, of course, a matter of much debate and few facts. In
his study of foreign firms in the United Kingdom, Gennard concludes that industrial relations innovations are responsible for the
higher productivity of the foreign firm. Moreover, "there is evidence
that the productivity gap between foreign and domestic firms is narrowing and reflects, among other things, a spreading of the industrial relations innovations of the foreign subsidiaries into the
domestic sector."[70]

---

[66]*Ibid.*
[67]Gennard and Steuer, "The Industrial Relations of Foreign Owned Subsidiaries,"
p. 143.
[68]*Ibid.*, p. 149:
If we look at the nature of strikes in the foreign owned and the domestic firms, we
see that the foreigners tend to have fewer of the very short and the very long stop-
pages. Their strikes tend to be of medium length. That could suggest more skillful
industrial relations. We might argue that a very short strike is often one that could be
avoided altogether through better grievance procedure and so on, and that a very
long strike tends to involve a miscalculation on at least one side.
[69]Belford, "Comment," p. 135.
[70]John Gennard, "The Impact of Foreign Owned Subsidiaries on Host Country
Labor Relations: The Case of the United Kingdom," in *Bargaining without Boundaries: The Multinational Corporation and International Labor Relations* R. Flanagan
and A. Weber, eds. (Chicago: University of Chicago Press, 1974), p. 88. See also, ILO,
Wages and Working Conditions, p. 50:
The favourable reputation sometimes enjoyed by multinational enterprises for
superior conditions of work and leadership in terms of advanced personnel practices

Others have asserted, however, that "there are many examples of multinational corporations attempting to impose foreign solutions that conflict with local traditions and values."[71] The imposition of foreign values implies potential industrial relations conflict, and such conflict clearly can be neither in the interest of the foreign firm, already a highly "visible" entity, nor in that of the local labor force. The view of an executive of a Canadian multinational may be representative: "Where the multinational innovates by convincing its employees and employee representatives. . .it can successfully innovate, but there must be some form of employee participation or involvement."[72] It is presumably in this means that change has been incorporated into local surroundings, accounting for the finding that MNEs "have modified their basic policies to come to terms with requirements of national environments."[73]

---

results from the natural tendency of these firms to export at least some of their employment practices from the home country. As a result of this, in a number of instances, multinational firms have been viewed as the source of desirable innovations in such areas as wage payment systems, career development, a more democratic work environment and alternative forms of work organisation. At the same time, this same tendency to export home country practices has been at the root of a number of adaptation problems encountered by these firms. There are reports that such difficulties have arisen because multinationals have, for example, resisted demands for certain types of fringe benefits not found in the home country, not always placed the same emphasis on secure and stable employment as normally found in the countries where they operate, and tried to implement wage payment systems not in accordance with local values.

[71]Blanpain, "Multinationals' Impact," p. 122.
[72]Belford, "Comment," p. 135.
[73]Roberts, "Comment," p. 52.

CHAPTER III

Paragraph 1

Enterprises should:

> respect the right of their employees to be represented by trade unions and other bona fide organisations of employees, and engage in constructive negotiations, either individually or through employers' associations, with such employee organisations with a view to reaching agreements on employment conditions, which should include provisions for dealing with disputes arising over the interpretation of such agreements, and for ensuring mutually respected rights and responsibilities.

The two most fundamental rights embodied in the wording of Paragraph 1 are those of freedom of association and union recognition. All industrial nations, whether through law or traditional practice, have delineated these rights in the context of their own societies. In addition, however, international agreements exist that speak to these issues. Thus, for example, International Labor Organization (ILO) Conventions No. 87 (1948), on the freedom of association and the right to organize, and No. 98 (1949), on the right to bargain collectively, have been ratified by the majority of industrial nations. Of the member states of the OECD, only the United States and New Zealand have not ratified Convention No. 87, but in each of these countries freedom of association is no less protected by law. Similarly, five of the OECD countries, the United States, Switzerland, New Zealand, the Netherlands, and Canada, have not ratified Convention No. 98, although each grants the convention's provisions in its national legislation.[1]

---

[1]Compared with many other countries, labor legislation in the United States is relatively extensive, a fact obviating the need for ratification of international conventions. More importantly, however, the United States does not ratify ILO conventions, as they would conflict, at least indirectly, with existing U.S. law, as illustrated by this passage from "Ratification of Seven ILO Conventions: The Process and Impact on Domestic Labor Law," (Washington, D.C.: Labor Policy Association, Inc., 1980), p. i.

Ratification in and of itself would probably not cause a convention to supersede existing domestic law. To do so, Congress would have to enact implementing legisla-

National Diversity

One might imagine that with national law and international agreement so comprehensive on the rights expressed in Paragraph 1, there would be little room for controversy over the paragraph's provisions. In fact, however, the broad wording of the paragraph, no doubt an effort at inclusiveness, masks the considerable diversity that exists at the national level. The following comparison of several countries yields the general conclusion that in some, the recognition of unions may be automatic whereas in others it may be the end result of a more lengthy (and more contested) process.

A nation's industrial relations system is the result of the historical accretion of custom and law and is never completely replicated in another nation. Even within such variety, however, the United States' system stands apart, particularly with regard to union recognition. In no other country are the steps toward union recognition so legally prescribed, nor the democratic principles of "majority rule" so ensconced in law. Therefore, union recognition in the United States is never automatic:

> In the well-unionized, mass-production industries of the United States, when a large unionized company opens a new plant, the union (or unions) must undertake a special organizational campaign to win its rights to bargain in that particular plant. In Europe, on the other hand, when a new plant is opened by either an old or a new employer in an industry where an associationwide agreement is already in effect, the employer is under pressure from both the employer association and the union to recognize the union and to accept the terms of the agreement.[2]

A simple majority among members of an appropriate bargaining unit in an election administered by the National Labor Relations Board (NLRB) is the criterion in the United States upon which union recognition—and the *exclusive representation* of that union—

---

tion. Ratification, nevertheless, could have serious indirect effects as the conventions could be used to support administrative or judicial action altering the interpretation and application of existing labor laws. For example:

Under present law, the National Labor Relations Act requires employers to bargain collectively with only certain types of employees. A convention regarding freedom of association and protection of the right to organize, however, could be read to require an employer to recognize a union which includes as members supervisors, plant guards and other excluded groups. Also, an employer could be forced to recognize unions other than the one selected by the majority as its exclusive bargaining representative. Further, the convention would conflict with domestic laws protecting union members from corrupt union officials, permitting those officials to exercise greater control over rank and file members.

[2]Everett Kassalow, *Trade Unions and Industrial Relations: An International Comparison* (New York: Random House, 1969), pp. 138–39.

is based. In many European countries, union recognition is neither the outcome of a polling of employee preference nor a right conferred only upon a majority. In addition, several unions often represent the same category of employees within the same plant. Indeed, in some European countries, there is no purely legal impediment to an employee being a member of more than one union.[3]

In some European countries the government also may play a major role in industrial relations and collective bargaining by legislating the coverage of a labor-management agreement, even for companies that are not organized or where union members are a minority. Broadly speaking, "if an agreement is judged to cover 50 percent of the workers in a given industry or occupation, the state can extend the terms of the agreement to cover the entire trade or occupation . . . .Laws to extend the terms of collective agreements operate in France, Belgium, the Netherlands, Germany, Austria, Switzerland and Luxembourg."[4] Australia and New Zealand have traditionally injected the state into the employer-union bargaining process by having government conciliation and arbitration tribunals make an award determining wages and other major terms of employment on an industry basis. Although there is currently considerable talk of collective bargaining as an alternative to compulsory arbitration in Australia, there has not yet been any real move away from the state-dominated industrial relations system.

In the Scandinavian countries, the strength of the trade unions and the traditional cooperation of employers' associations obviate the need for the legal extension of collective agreements. In Sweden, for example, such strength "makes it difficult for any substantial enterprise, especially a multinational one to 'hold out', and with association membership goes union recognition."[5]

The prevalence of industrywide bargaining in many European countries thus tends to render the issue of union recognition less significant there than in the United States. There have for some time been indications suggesting that the locus of industrial relations in European countries is increasingly becoming the plant or company level. With this shift, recourse to the legislated extension of collective agreements appears to be declining.[6] The influx of

[3]M. Despax and J. Rojot, "France," in *International Encyclopaedia for Labour and Industrial Relations,* Vol. III, Roger Blanpain, ed. (The Netherlands: Kluwer, 1979), p. 123.
[4]Kassalow, *Trade Unions and Industrial Relations,* p. 139.
[5]International Labour Office, *Multinationals in Western Europe: The Industrial Relations Experience* (Geneva, 1976), p. 7.
[6]Kassalow, *Trade Unions and Industrial Relations,* p. 140.

multinationals may have played a role in encouraging this transition. More tangibly, however, considerable improvements in wages and working conditions since the 1960s may have sponsored this shift: "Resort to extension of collective agreements has become less common, even in the countries where legislation permits it. This is the result of several developments: the principal one, perhaps, is that many individual companies now frequently give workers more than industry- or association-wide agreements require."[7] If the shift in the locus of industrial relations proves to be a major trend, one offshoot of this trend would conceivably be to accentuate the issue of union recognition and the form of collective agreements, even where these have been relative non-issues.

WHERE UNION RECOGNITION IS AN ISSUE

A brief analysis of the OECD Guidelines on Employment and Industrial Relations isolates several loci of contention within the wording of Paragraph 1. The first clause, 'respect the right of their employees to be represented by trade unions,' might seem clear enough but it does raise a number of questions: How many employees of a firm must indicate a desire for a union before an employer is required to respect this right? What is the procedure for indicating such a desire?"[8] Important questions all, and particularly so, it seems, in the context of both United States and British industrial relations, where the matter of union recognition is significant. It is perhaps no mere coincidence that two of the cases brought before the Committee on International Investment and Multinational Enterprises (CIIME) of the OECD involve British subsidiaries of U.S.–owned multinationals.

In the 1960s, one observer noted that

> the right of employees to form and join unions is not a protected right in the United Kingdom . . . .The method by which unions in the United Kingdom secure recognition from employers as employee representatives differs fundamentally from the U.S. practice. In Britain the recognition of a union as the bargaining agent of employees is usually the product of contractual arrangements . . . reinforced if necessary by imposition of economic pressure.[9]

---

[7]*Ibid.*

[8]USA-BIAC Committee on International Investment and Multinational Enterprise, *A Review of the OECD Guidelines for Multinational Enterprises: Employment and Industrial Relations* (New York, 1978), p. 18.

[9]Seyfarth, Shaw, Fairweather and Geraldson, *Labor Relations and the Law in the United Kingdom and the United States* (Ann Arbor: Univ. of Michigan, Bureau of Business Research, Graduate School of Business Administration), p. 23.

Despite the differences, a similarity that unites the United Kingdom and the United States is the ability, whether legal or practical, to withhold union recognition. A discussion of the charges brought by the unions against two American multinationals, Black & Decker and Citibank, is useful to an understanding of union recognition in the United Kingdom.

BLACK & DECKER'S SPENNYMOOR PLANT

Two British unions, the General and Municipal Workers' Union (GMWU) and the Amalgamated Union of Engineering Workers (AUEW) undertook organizing campaigns that culminated, in early 1977, in Black & Decker's refusal to grant recognition. The unions' claim was taken up by the International Metalworkers' Federation (IMF) which, through the Trade Union Advisory Committee (TUAC), submitted the case on March 30, 1977, to the CIIME.

The GMWU's efforts to gain recognition at Black & Decker appear to have been part of a regional recruitment campaign begun in 1975.[10] The union claimed to have recruited 290 new members at the Spennymoor site, 265 of whom were general process workers, and 25 of whom were office staff. The union further asserted that this membership extended

> throughout all areas of the factory, with the exception of the warehouse. The union demands recognition to be granted on a general basis covering all subjects suitable for joint regulation, and that recognition should be granted by the company to duly elected shop stewards of the union at plant level and to Regional and National officers when their assistance is requested by the factory shop stewards.[11]

The company, while promising to give full consideration "to all matters raised by elected shop stewards on behalf of their members,"[12] refused to grant "recognition and negotiating rights to regional and national officers of the (GMWU)."[13] In support of its decision, the company asserted that in a ballot that it had taken of its employees, the majority had responded that they did not wish to be represented by a union.

The GMWU took issue with the announced result of the ballot and claimed further that the company's procedure in having con-

---

[10]"Complaints on the Policy of Multinational Companies calling for application of the OECD Guidelines for Multinational Enterprises," Report on specific cases and recent developments submitted by the International Metalworkers' Federation through the Trade Union Advisory Committee (TUAC), March 11, 1977, p. 2.

[11]*Ibid.*

[12]*Ibid.*

[13]*Ibid.*

ducted a secret ballot without the assistance of the shop stewards was at fault.[14] The union applied for the assistance of the Advisory, Conciliation and Arbitration Services (ACAS) under Section 11 of the Employment Protection Act (EP Act) of 1975. Sections 11 through 16 of the EP Act endowed the ACAS with statutory authority to conduct an inquiry and make recommendations on requests for recognition submitted to it by an independent union (although not by an individual or an employer). "Once a recognition issue has been referred to ACAS under (Section) 11 of the EP Act it has only two routes. Either the union withdraws the reference (because agreement has been reached or its support is very low) or the results of the inquiry and any recommendation eventually appear as a published report."[15]

The endowment of statutory powers to the ACAS in the matter of union recognition came about under the policies of the Labour government in power from 1974 to 1979. With the election victory of the Conservative Party in 1979, however, Prime Minister Margaret Thatcher sought to undo many of the pieces of labor legislation enacted during the Labour government's tenure. The Employment Bill of 1980 removed Sections 11 through 16 of the EP Act of 1975, thus dismantling the ACAS's statutory powers in union-recognition cases. The removal of these sections had become predictable, for the ACAS had demonstrated a pronounced prounion bias in its inquiries into union-recognition disputes. The ACAS's chairman, moreover, had publicly stated that the agency wished to be relieved of its controversial duties in union-recognition matters.[16]

In the late 1970s, however, under Section 14 of the EP Act, the ACAS was empowered to conduct an inquiry to obtain the opinions of the workers "to whom the issue relates by any means it thinks fit." In the majority of instances, the favored approach by the ACAS was to poll worker preference by means of a questionnaire. But how first to determine "to whom the issue relates?"

In the absence of any discrete definition of what constituted a bargaining unit, the ACAS in practice appeared merely to accept the group proposed by the petitioning union. As one observer concluded, "if a union attracts substantial support in only part of what it would regard as its 'potential territory', ACAS will not intervene

---

[14]*Ibid.*
[15]"Results of ACAS recommendations," *Incomes Data Service,* Brief No. 105 (March 1977), p. 2.
[16]*Employment Gazette,* Vol. 87, No. 6 (January 1979), p. 540.

to say that the bargaining group should also include employees among whom the union has little support."[17]

The issue is obviously a substantive one, for it appears that disagreement over whose opinions should be polled delayed the ACAS from administering a ballot, and indeed was a major area of contention between employer and union: "The company says (the ballot) should be company wide, but the unions want it based on those workers they would wish to represent. The company claims that when it conducted an independent ballot of the whole work force two years ago 80 percent said they did not wish to be represented by unions."[18] Was the employer's defense foreign to the context of British law and practice?

The British Context

Definition of the bargaining unit, often an area of contention, may ultimately find legal resolution in the United States. In the United Kingdom, on the contrary, ambiguity may persist and indeed, "employers have often been keen that a larger group (or other establishments) should also be involved"[19] in the determination of the appropriate segment of the work force to be polled. Clearly, the general interest of employers in this particular matter may reside in the dual objective of limiting the number of unions claiming recognition from the employer and, by expanding the scope of the ballot, weakening the union's chances of claiming that a sizeable percentage of the work force seeks union recognition. In recognition cases that have proceeded as far as an inquiry by the ACAS, a claim by the employer that the scope of the balloting be extended is not at all unusual; a similar claim by Black & Decker is not, therefore, anomalous within the context of British industrial relations.[20]

---

[17]"Review of ACAS reports, 51–75," *Incomes Data Service*, Brief No. 125 (January 1978), p. 2.

[18]Jason Crisp, "Black & Decker image polished for the battle ahead," *Financial Times*, July 2, 1979, p. 9.

[19]"18 months of Section 11 produce sixty ACAS reports," *Incomes Data Service*, Brief No. 117 (September 1977), pp. 8–9.

[20]The most controversial union-recognition case in recent years, the London-based Grunwick Film Processing Laboratories' refusal to recognize the Association of Professional, Executive, Clerical and Complex Staff (APEX), isolates the paradoxical position in which the ACAS occasionally found itself. In Grunwick's case, this was the ACAS' initial recommendation that APEX be recognized despite the fact that 87% of Grunwick's employees voted against the union. The predicament in which ACAS finds itself results from its statutory ability to disregard the wishes of the majority of the workers when making a recognition recommendation. Not only has ACAS recommended union recognition when only a tiny minority of workers has favored it, but ACAS has also refused to recommend that a non-TUC union be recog-

A distinguishing feature of the British "voluntarist" system is that to have a majority of employees in favor of the union is not necessarily a prerequisite of union recognition. "In the absence of statutory requirements ACAS has avoided laying down any general rule on the kind of support the union must be shown to enjoy before a recommendation can be made in favor of recognition."[21] Thus, in the first twenty-five cases to have been decided by the ACAS, as small a favorable response to the union as 21 percent of employees balloted was in one instance sufficient for the ACAS to recommend recognition. More generally, however, the ACAS appears to base its recommendation for recognition on a majority or near-majority response to the question of whether the individual whose opinion is polled wishes the applicant union to bargain for him.[22] That some application of the majority-rule principle prevailed in these cases further locates an employer's claim that the balloting should be extended within the British context. It has been observed, moreover, that "union claims for full collective bargaining recognition were only turned down where ACAS inquiries revealed a low level of support for the applicant union."[23]

Two final features of the British system and the conduct of the ACAS in recognition inquiries are worthy of mention. The first is that the ACAS occasionally recommended "partial recognition"—a status unknown in the American context where union recognition rights are more in the nature of "all or nothing." Partial recognition provides that the employer recognize the union to the extent that it consults with union officials at the plant. Such recognition would appear implied in Black & Decker's stated willingness to consider all matters raised by elected shop stewards on behalf of their members. Typically, partial recognition has been granted by the ACAS in instances where the union did not make up a sizeable percentage of the work force, as in the case of Black & Decker. A second feature that would appear curious in the context of American industrial relations is the fact of individual employee's union membership even when such membership does not convey bargaining rights with the employer. At Black & Decker, for example, "the reason most of the skilled craftsmen at B and D hold union membership is apparently

---

nized when 90 percent of the workers supported that union. Some Conservative members of Parliament view favorably the American system whereby a simple majority of the workers decide by secret ballot whether or not a specified union shall represent them.

[21]"More law changes being discussed," *Incomes Data Service*, Brief No. 122 (December 1977), p. 3.

[22]*Ibid.*

[23]"18 months of Section 11 produce sixty ACAS reports," p. 8.

to retain the option of moving jobs."[24] In a country where the closed shop is allowed, such membership may be seen to convey the possibility of individual mobility.

The statutory powers granted the ACAS in 1976 were removed in the summer of 1980, following the repeal of Sections 11 through 16 of the EP Act.[25] New legislation in 1980 constituted a return to the voluntarism that has traditionally characterized British industrial relations. Relinquishing its statutory powers in the matter of recognition, the role of the ACAS reverted to one of conciliation. In reviewing the reports on recognition issued by the ACAS during those years, one observer noted that

> some patterns emerge . . . . In the 90 cases before the House of Lords' decision on Grunwick, ACAS recommended recognition in 78% and 18 (26%) of these resulted in an agreement. In the period between the Lords decision and the general election in 1979, recognition recommendations fell to 56% but in 27% of these agreements were signed. After the general election, although 64% of the reports were for recognition, only 15% resulted in agreements perhaps because it was known the end of statutory powers was in sight.[26]

As the numbers suggest, a rather broad disparity existed between the ACAS recommendations for recognition and the actual agreements concluded between management and the unions.

Under the statutory powers of the ACAS, however, further remedies were available to the applicant union in the event of employer noncompliance:

> An ACAS recommendation becomes operative for the purpose of the EP Act 14 days after it is received by the employer. If he has failed to comply after a further two months the union can make a complaint under (Section) 15 to ACAS, who then try to produce a conciliated settlement. If this proves impossible the union is free to make a claim under (Section) 16 to the Central Arbitration Committee (CAC) for improved terms and conditions; CAC first has to determine whether the employer has complied with the ACAS recommendation, if it is decided that he has not then CAC can award the union all or part of the improved terms and conditions they have claimed.[27]

Some union officials have therefore concluded that "although (Section) 11 did not help them to gain recognition, the Central Arbitra-

---

[24]Crisp, "Black & Decker image polished," p. 9.
[25]"Statutory recognition: the final chapter," *Incomes Data Service,* Brief No. 188 (September 1980), p. 1.
[26]*Ibid.*
[27]"Results of ACAS recommendations in reports 26–50," *Incomes Data Service,* Brief No. 127 (March 1978), p. 2.

tion Committee's powers under (Section) 16 enabled them to get substantial improvements for their members."[28]

Summary of the Issues

Over 200 reports were finally issued before the ACAS' statutory powers in the area of recognition were dismantled; several times that number had been submitted to the ACAS by unions seeking recognition. The majority of these were either still at the inquiry stage or had been settled without a final report, either because an agreement had been reached between employer and union or because the union had withdrawn its claim for lack of support among the work force.

Some have argued that U.S.-owned subsidiaries in particular have run afoul of local practice in not recognizing unions.[29] One such view holds, moreover, that resistance to a union by a U.S. employer based on the claim that a majority of its employees do not want the union constitutes a transplant of American practice into the United Kingdom.[30] Neither view is entirely justified. Indeed, the sheer bulk of the case load that came before the ACAS during its four years of statutory powers in this area indicates that both the issue of union recognition and an employer's defense based upon a concept of majority rule are not at all unusual in the context of British industrial relations. This finding corroborates that of Gennard and Steuer who note that United States and British companies in the United Kingdom differ little in the matter of union recognition.[31]

Comparison with an IBM Subsidiary

The voluntarism of the British system does not in every case imply that trade unions be granted recognition. Union attempts to organize IBM's 13,000 United Kingdom employees received a resounding rebuff when the employees voted overwhelmingly against union recognition.[32] The margin of victory surprised even

---

[28]"Statutory recognition: the final chapter," p. 1.

[29]ILO, *Multinationals in Western Europe,* p. 4.

[30]*Ibid:* "Some American corporations have inappropriately transferred their home-grown convictions about union recognition and union security to overseas environments."

[31]John Gennard and M. D. Steuer, "The Industrial Relations of Foreign Owned Subsidiaries in the United Kingdom," *British Journal of Industrial Relations,* Vol. IX, No. 2 (July 1971), pp. 143–59.

[32]Article originally published as "Rejection of Unions by IBM British employees," (Philadelphia: Industrial Research Unit, The Wharton School, University of Pennsylvania, 1977).

the company; 95 percent of its employees voted against having a union, and only 102 employees were already union members.

Commenced in early 1976 shortly after the enactment of the EP Act, the drive to unionize IBM was spearheaded by the Association of Scientific, Technical and Managerial Staffs (ASTMS). The ASTMS focused its recruiting efforts on IBM's Greenock, Scotland, manufacturing plant which for historical reasons was deemed to be the most receptive candidate for unionization. Joined by TASS, the white-collar section of the AUEW, and the white-collar section of the Electrical, Electronic, Telecommunication and Plumbing Unions (EETPU-EESA), the ASTMS referred the recognition issue to the ACAS under Section 11 of the EP Act.

Denying allegations that the company was antiunion, IBM took the position that staff employees were free to belong to unions if they so chose. IBM does recognize unions in West Germany, Sweden, France, and Italy. The company, however, refused to recognize unions in the United Kingdom on the grounds that the level of union membership was too low to merit formal union recognition. With conciliation between the parties out of the question, the ACAS undertook a recognition inquiry.

From the outset, IBM challenged the limited scope of the recognition reference, which was confined to the 2,000 employees at Greenock. Pointing out that industrial relations were conducted on a companywide basis and that terms and conditions were uniform throughout the company, IBM insisted that the recognition inquiry had to be expanded to cover all its United Kingdom employees. The unions bitterly opposed this attempt to widen the bargaining unit. A compromise was finally reached whereby the ACAS agreed to survey the opinion of all IBM's employees with the results from Greenock being identified separately. IBM also took umbrage with the wording of the ACAS's proposed questionnaire, claiming that it had a definite prounion slant. After negotiating with the company, the ACAS put forth a revised five-point questionnaire for the March 31, 1977, ballot.

To combat union propaganda, IBM engaged in an intensive internal publicity campaign designed to alert its employees to the facts. Relying on its excellent record in terms and conditions of employment and its history of no strikes and no layoffs in its twenty-five years in the United Kingdom, IBM contended that there was no need for union representation.

The contest at IBM generated widespread interest since many people thought it would reveal whether any company could withstand a determined union's recruitment drive in the aftermath of such prounion legislation as the EP Act. Even IBM, which was always confident that a majority of its employees would vote against unions, was uncertain of its ability to stave off union inroads. It will be recalled that, in some cases, when a minority of employees has voted for the union, the ACAS has not recommended bargaining rights but has awarded some other form of recognition. As a result, IBM feared that the ACAS might recommend that the ASTMS be given the right to accompany a member through the company's highly developed grievance procedure.

IBM's decisive victory graphically demonstrated that a company could successfully resist a union organizing drive despite the 1975 legislation and general economic factors which made the white-collar (salaried), nonunion sector a particularly attractive target for unionization. The level of union support at IBM, which the unions grossly overestimated, might have encouraged other employers to demand a ballot of employees rather than to concede bargaining rights.

In the United States, as in the United Kingdom, the issue of union recognition is subject to challenge from both sides of industry. With respect to both Black & Decker and IBM, then, one could rephrase the issue in the form of a question: does a company have the right to withhold union recognition? The British experience would appear to supply an affirmative answer. In light of the many cases to have come before the ACAS, a far more interesting question is why the not unusual case of one foreign subsidiary, Black & Decker, was, among several hundred similar cases, the only one to be catapulted into prominence before an international body. Reference to another alleged violation of Paragraph 1 aids in answering this question.

CITIBANK U.K.

On March 30, 1977, the International Federation of Commercial, Clerical, Professional and Technical Employees (FIET) and the National Union of Bank Employees (NUBE), a British white-collar union, submitted through TUAC to the CIIME a charge against the U.K. subsidiary of the U.S.-owned Citibank–Citicorp:

> It is the contention of FIET and NUBE that the international management of Citibank-Citicorp conducts a world wide anti-union policy. Wherever possible, it avoids recognizing trade unions and negotiating with them. To conduct this policy, there is evidence that instructions are given to their local management about the tactics to be used in local situations.[33]

―――――――
[33]Roger Blanpain, *The OECD Guidelines for Multinational Enterprises and Labor*

The evidence submitted by the two unions to back their claim of an antiunion policy was a guide book published by Citicorp headquarters in New York addressed, according to the union, to company managers in the United Kingdom. The guide purportedly outlined company policy in the area of employee relations and included a statement of the company's policy toward unions: "The management of Citibank firmly believes that the best interest of all Citibankers are served without the presence of a union. To that end management commits its effort to the maintenance of an environment which renders unnecessary the intervention of a third party."[34] The unions further charged that, presumably as a result of the application of the policy outlined in the guide, "the Bank's opposition effectively stopped the recruitment of members by NUBE and the hostile environment undermined the support of those who had become members."[35]

There is regrettably scant evidence that either confirms or denies the unions' allegations that the bank "effectively stopped" a recruitment drive by the NUBE or that a "hostile environment" undermined exisiting support for the union. If indeed the bank did prohibit its employees from joining the NUBE this would be a clear violation not only of ILO Convention No. 42 and Paragraph 1 of the OECD guidelines, but of British law as well, which guarantees freedom of association. The unions' allegation belies such clarity and focuses the reader's attention instead on the meaning of "effectively stopped"—words which in this context do not necessarily imply any specific activity on the part of the company to the detriment of the union. Such a reading, moreover, is supported by the fact that the Citibank case was never pursued through legal channels at the national level. This fact alone suggests that there was little to pursue, if not the presentiment of a "world wide" negative attitude toward unions.

The Company's View

The company's position on the affair is somewhat different. To begin with, the booklet in question appears to have been an outdated guide bearing specifically on the United States, with little relevance to other countries. The booklet, therefore, was never intended as a guide to the behavior of managers in the British sub-

---

Relations, 1976-1979: Experience and Review, English text rewritten by Michael Jones (Deventer, The Netherlands: Kluwer, 1979), p. 174.
[34]*Ibid.*
[35]*Ibid.*

sidiary and to assume so, based on the presence of a copy of this booklet in the United Kingdom, is, from the company's point of view, to draw both a broad and erroneous conclusion. More compelling is the fact that the unions' charges before an international body did not stem from any similar charges at the national level. Indeed, the ACAS came into the bank to review the bank's employment policies and pronounced them to be satisfactory.[36] Lastly, the unions' charge that the company is antiunion on a global scale is clouded by the fact that Citibank recognizes unions or some other form of employee representation in thirty of the ninety-six countries in which it has subsidiaries.

The Citibank case is expressive of the more general phenomenon of white-collar unionism, which is on the rise in several industrial countries. In the context of the United Kingdom, it is useful to note, some researchers have found that nonrecognition of white-collar unions "is not particularly a symptom of foreign-owned companies since domestic firms have shown a dislike of white-collar unions."[37] The banking industry, in particular, seems to have been one locus of organizational effort by unions, especially the NUBE: "On only one occasion has a direct complaint been made to the ILO Governing Body Committee on Freedom of Association from the United Kingdom. This was by the National Union of Bank Employees in November 1962 and led to the setting up of an official inquiry in the United Kingdom which made suggestions for the improvement of trade union recognition by the Banks."[38]

Prior to legislation of the 1970s which sought to encourage freedom of association and collective bargaining in all sectors, attempts to discourage white-collar unionism were apparently rife. One account from the 1960s noted that

> most big banks and insurance companies still maintain a prohibition against their workers' joining a union and will dismiss employees for advocating a union. Although the ILO Convention of 1949, which condemned the "yellow dog contract," was ratified by the British government, there was no legal prohibition against such contracts between employers and employees, and in many small U.K. firms such contracts still exist.[39]

---

[36]Author's telephone interview with Citibank executive, March 1982.

[37]Gennard and Steuer, "The Industrial Relations of Foreign Owned Subsidiaries," p. 155.

[38]B. A. Hepple, "Great Britain," in *International Encyclopaedia for Labor Law and Industrial Relations*, Vol. III, Roger Blanpain, ed. (The Netherlands: Kluwer, 1979), p. 137.

[39]Seyfarth *et al.*, *Labor Relations and the Law*, p. 23.

That times and practice have changed is evidenced by trends in both labor legislation and union membership in the United Kingdom during the 1970s. At Citibank U.K., moreover, some employees are union members, and the unions' allegations do not extend to the charge that these employees have been discriminated against. Quite the opposite impression emerges from the findings of the ACAS review of the bank's policies.

CITIBANK AND BLACK & DECKER: SUMMARY OF THE ISSUES

A similarity binds these cases together. In each, the behavior of the subsidiary has been neither illegal nor foreign to the conduct of domestic employers. Why, then, have these companies been offered up for international public scrutiny with the implication that their conduct amounts to what one observer describes as "notorious exceptions" to the generally good record enjoyed by multinationals?[40] If the answer is not to be found in the specific allegations lodged against these subsidiaries by the unions, the allegations may nevertheless provide a clue. In both submissions to TUAC, the unions charge the companies with "world wide" infractions of Paragraph 1 of the guidelines. One view would contend that the underlying motive of the International Trade Secretariats (ITSs) is to enhance their own status through suggesting a role for the CIIME that the latter clearly does not have—that of an "international court."[41]

Curiously, such an effort is not served by allegations relating to a single national context. The submissions by TUAC, instead, beg the question of the relationship of the provisions of the individual guidelines to the "chapeau clause" which calls for conformity to the national environment. That there may be tension between these two is apparent, particularly with regard to Paragraph 1. The discussion of these two cases was premised on the observation that countries may be grouped (in a general sense) along the lines of those where union recognition is less of an issue and those where it is more of one. This disparity becomes more apparent in interpreting the CIIME's remarks with regard to Paragraph 1 on the occasion of the committee's 1979 review.

Commenting on the meaning of Paragraphs 1 and 2, the CIIME observed that the thrust of these "provisions of the Guidelines is

---

[40]Blanpain, *The OECD Guidelines for Multinational Enterprises*, p. 18.
[41]See Chapter I for background.

towards having management adopt a positive approach toward the activities of trade unions and other bona fide organisations of employees of all categories and, in particular, an open attitude towards organisational activities within the framework of national rules and practices."[42] To one commentator, the CIIME's remarks suggest that an "antiunion attitude, policies or instructions to go nonunion are contrary to this approach. The employers should, in fact, take a neutral attitude."[43] Does the duty of employer neutrality imply, as one corporate executive put it, that management should "roll over and play dead" in the face of a union-organizing campaign? The same commentator who observed that employers should adopt a neutral attitude adds that this "does not take away the right of the employer to express his opinion on the matter, but this should not amount to threats or anti-union policies."[44]

Clearly, it is the extent to which an antiunion attitude is translated into discriminatory or illegal employment practices that is the more tangible problem area in the CIIME's review of Paragraph 1. Citibank may well believe that the intervention of a third party, the union, is unnecessary in the conduct of its employee relations in the United States or the United Kingdom, and there is little doubt that the thrust of the booklet intended for U.S. managers is clearly to instruct the manager on legal means by which to discourage unionism. Significantly, the booklet contains paragraphs not only on what may be said to this end—but also on what may not be said under U.S. law.

In the United States and the United Kingdom, such employer tactics appear to be common, and correspond to similar tactics employed by unions in expressing their point of view. This alone suggests that union recognition is something of an issue in each country. If the meaning of Paragraph 1 of the guidelines, specifically the "positive approach" and "open attitude" toward union organizational drives, is actually to remove the right of the employer to express its opinion or otherwise to counter a union's organizational drive, such a meaning would ignore the adversarial basis of union-recognition issues in the United Kingdom and the United States. It is thus to demand that multinational employers behave differently than their domestic counterparts. To enforce this meaning, further-

---

[42]Organisation for Economic Cooperation and Development—Committee on International Investment and Multinational Enterprises, *The Review of the 1976 Declaration and Decisions on International Investment and Multinational Enterprises*, (Paris, 1979), Paragraph 60.

[43] Blanpain, *The OECD Guidelines for Multinational Enterprises*, p. 146.

[44]*Ibid.*

more, is to suggest that a voluntary international guideline should prevail over national law and practice. The international union movement would perhaps favor such an interpretation. International employers would not.

OTHER PROVISIONS OF PARAGRAPH 1

The discussion thus far has focused solely on the interpretation of the first clause of Paragraph 1, "the right of their employees to be represented by trade unions." Most of the cases brought before the CIIME concern this clause, especially in the expanded form of the issues that the clause introduces: union membership and union recognition. Most of the discussion has involved the latter. Union membership, however, is also not free from national variety. In the United States, the National Labor Relations Act (NLRA), governing labor-management relations in the private sector, specifically excludes from its definition of "employee" supervisory staff, which the NLRA views as part of management. The same distinction is not true elsewhere. "In some countries the labor law permits supervisors and even members of higher management not only to organize but also to belong to the same union as production workers. Other legislative systems keep them separate. In some countries unionization of supervisors is encouraged, in others the reverse."[45]

There are, moreover, other passages of Paragraph 1 where potential meaning may be latent. The phrase, "other bona fide organisations of employees" for example, gives rise to differences of interpretation. In the writing of the guidelines, the expression was intended to designate other forms of employee organization, such as works councils, as exist in Germany, the Netherlands, Austria, and France, and may not be synonymous with unions. It is, however, "possible that TUAC and certain other union bodies will insist that the term 'bona fide organisations of employees' includes international union organisations such as the ITSs. Such a position would conform with efforts they are making toward achieving multinational collective bargaining."[46]

The possibility of this meaning was perceived by TUAC, and prior to the 1979 review of the guidelines, TUAC had attempted to render explicit such a meaning. The ITSs, it argued, "are trade unions, certainly bona fide organizations, and that they should be recognized

---

[45]USA-BIAC CIIME, *A Review of OECD Guidelines for Multinational Enterprises*, p. 18.
[46]*Ibid.*, p. 19.

by the multinational enterprises on the basis of Guideline 1."[47] The Business and Industry Advisory Committee (BIAC), while considering that ITSs "have a role to play within the overall trade-union system itself,"[48] nevertheless doubted that it was the intention of the guidelines to suggest recognition of ITSs on the part of multinationals, as at no time during the negotiations of the guidelines had the subject of the ITSs been discussed. The opinion would probably concur with TUAC's statement that ITSs are "bona fide organisations"—they are not, however, "bona fide organisations of employees." Strictly speaking, then, they are not trade unions, but federations of trade unions. The report of the CIIME, in its 1979 review, does not help clarify the issue:

> The question has been raised, however, whether the Employment and Industrial Relations Guidelines could put obstacles in the way of recognition by the management of an MNE, in agreement with the national trade unions it has recognised and consistent with national laws and practices, of an International Trade Secretariat as a "bona fide organisation of employees" referred to in paragraph 1 of the Guidelines. It is the Committee's view that no such obstacle exists or was intended in the Guidelines.[49]

Removing an obstacle to meaning, however, is not an assertion of meaning, and differences in views will no doubt persist. Such differences will be further explored in the upcoming discussions of Paragraphs 2 and 9.

The phrases that follow in Paragraph 1: "and engage in constructive negotiations, either individually or through employers' associations, with such employee organisations with a view to reaching agreements on employment conditions" have, implicitly at least, been touched upon in previous pages. The issue of union recognition implies as well the logical end of that recognition, the bargaining arrangement. Paragraph 1, however, makes no mention of the level on which bargaining should occur, whether national, regional, industrywide, or companywide, and clearly, examples of each are plentiful depending upon the country. It was noted earlier, for example, that membership in an employer association may both confer automatic union recognition and determine the level on which bargaining is to occur.

On the matter of employer association membership, here again, national practice varies, "with many European nations tending to favor bargaining through employer associations. Even there, local

---

[47]Blanpain, *The OECD Guidelines for Multinational Enterprises*, p. 186.
[48]*Ibid.*
[49]OECD-CIIME, *Review of the 1976 Declaration*, Paragraph 62.

bargaining often supplements the industrywide contract. Nothing in the guidelines indicates a preference for bargaining through associations of employers."[50] An ILO study found that multinationals tend to become members of the appropriate employers' associations in countries where such practice is customary.[51] This is all the more true in those countries, such as Sweden, where not to belong to the employers' association is to be isolated from an influential economic and social organization.

The subject of bargaining "employment conditions" is also susceptible to views broadening or narrowing its scope. "The ILO Declaration of Principles (Paragraph 49) reinforces this more limited definition of bargainable matters by referring only to the 'regulation of terms and conditions of employment.' "[52] A tendency to broaden the scope of bargainable issues has more recently emerged as an important union interest, particularly at the European Community (EC) level, and is expressed in such themes as worker participation in such traditionally managerial prerogatives as investment decisions—an area closely related to union interest in information disclosure. The potential for disagreement is expressed in the view of one corporate executive: "Accepted by the unions or not, the prevailing and current management position is to consider basic investment and production deployment decisions as outside the scope of industrial relations matters appropriate for consultation or bargaining."[53] Issues surrounding the content of bargaining will reappear in subsequent pages, particularly in reference to Paragraphs 3, 6, and 9.

The remainder of Paragraph 1: "which should include provisions for dealing with disputes arising over the interpretation of such agreements, and for ensuring mutually respected rights and responsibilities," is echoed in the ILO's Declaration of Principles concerning Multinational Enterprises and Social Policy (Paragraph 53). Great variety exists as to the precise nature of grievance machinery to be used, whether purely internal procedures, as are specified in many U.S. collective bargaining agreements, or greater reliance on external mechanisms, such as the conciliation and arbitration framework of Australian industrial relations. In some European

---

[50]USA-BIAC CIIME, *A Review of the OECD Guidelines for Multinational Enterprises,* p. 19.

[51]ILO, *Multinationals in Western Europe,* pp. 66–67.

[52]USA-BIAC, *A Review of the OECD Guidelines for Multinational Enterprises,* p. 19.

[53]Robert Copp, "Laws of Industrial Relations Decision Making in Multinationals," in *Multinationals, Unions, and Labor Relations in Industrialized Countries* R. F. Banks and J. Stieber, eds. (Ithaca, New York: New York State School of Industrial and Labor Relations, Cornell University, 1977), p. 45.

countries, "union structure often does not provide for distinct tiers of union organization at the work site."[54] In the absence of a well-developed local union structure, grievance procedures may not be directly under union control, but may be established through the existence of works councils as in Germany, Austria, and France.

CONCLUSION

A propensity for overprescription was suggested in the introduction to the present study with regard to the CIIME's review report on Paragraph 1. There it was noted that the broad encouragement for unionization exceeded the customary practice of the United States and perhaps other countries as well, such as the United Kingdom. In 1981, the ILO adopted a convention on collective bargaining which also appeared to go considerably further in promoting collective bargaining as a public good than does the public policy of the United States and probably that of several other Western countries as well.

By way of a single example, the convention states that it applies to all branches of economic activity. This could mean investment, plant closings and sales decisions, appointment of management officials, appointment of union officials to company boards of directors, and virtually any demand put forward by unions that is even remotely concerned with the business or with economic activity in general. Such matters may be voluntarily bargained in the United States, but there is no compulsion for management to do so, and it is an unfair labor practice for a union to insist upon such bargaining.

A major problem with the collective bargaining convention is the attempt to develop in the name of principles what are really required procedures, rights, and duties, and to do so on an international basis when in fact, for collective bargaining, these procedures, rights, and duties vary tremendously not only from country to country, but also often from industry to industry within countries. Such principles, like the "clarifications" of the guidelines, run the risk of becoming rigidly prescriptive and overly uniform. They may ignore that historical development, custom, and legislation vary widely in different countries, as do representation rights and methods, bargaining structure, and consequently, bargaining systems and coverage.

---

[54]Kassalow, *Trade Unions and Industrial Relations*, p. 152.

CHAPTER IV

Paragraph 2-A

Enterprises should:

> provide such facilities to representatives of the employees as may be
> necessary to assist in the development of collective agreements.

The language of Paragraph 2-A opens two areas of potential
ambiguity. Precisely what is meant by the term "facilities" constitutes the first, and is compounded by the variety of laws and practices in effect in the OECD countries. The second area relates more
generally to the employer's obligation to "assist in the development
of collective agreements," assistance that, here too, is variously
defined by different laws and practices.

With respect to the facilities, employers in the United States, for
example, "are very much restricted by law and the NLRB (National
Labor Relations Board), the body that administers the National
Labor Relations Act (NLRA) rulings as to the kind of assistance or
facilities accorded worker representatives."[1] Section 8(a)(2) of the
NLRA states that it

> shall be an unfair labor practice for an employer to dominate or inter-
> fere with the formation or administration of any labor organization or
> contribute financial or other support to it: Provided that subject to
> rules and regulations made and published by the Board pursuant to
> Section 6, an employer shall not be prohibited from permitting
> employees to confer with him during working hours without loss of
> time or pay.

Assistance supplied by the employer to the development of collective agreements depends on the nature of those agreements as
defined in individual, national contexts. In the United States, for
example, ongoing talks between employers and unions through the
grievance mechanism provided for in collective agreements can be

---

[1]USA-BIAC Committee on International Investment and Multinational Enterprises, *A Review of the OECD Guidelines for Multinational Enterprises: Employment and Industrial Relations* (New York, 1978), p. 20.

55

considered part of the collective bargaining process *per se*. In the Federal Republic of Germany, on the other hand, many grievances are resolved through legal channels. As Everett Kassalow observes:

> European collective agreements are generally less comprehensive than American collective agreements, and this is partly because social legislation regulates a great many matters in Europe that in the United States are covered by collective bargaining. And since the scope of bargaining is smaller in Europe, there is less need there for strong grievance procedure systems in industrial relations. In some countries there are labor courts which further reduce the need to include strong grievance provisions in collective agreements.[2]

If the decentralization of collective bargaining constitutes a trend in European countries, it is plausible that the scope and content of collective agreements will also be affected. In Australia, meanwhile, collective agreements are concluded through a third party, the Conciliation and Arbitration Commission, to which unions and employers submit their respective demands for a final decision.

Although the development of an effective collective agreement necessarily warrants cooperation from both unions and employers, in the United States, the NLRA specifically limits the contribution that the employer may make to the process of bargaining.

> Indirect employer support which has been invalidated has included allowing an organization to use company facilities, time, or concessions. And NLRB suspicion has been aroused when an employer has allowed an inside union or other favored organization to use company bulletin boards, company meeting rooms, or company printing equipment to print notices. Employers granting concessions to a favored organization, such as allowing the union officers to handle grievances and other organizational duties on company time and employers paying overtime rates for performing such duties after business hours, have been subjected to remedial orders.[3]

The key factor kept in mind by the NLRB in arriving at its decisions has been the independence of the labor organization in question. The courts have tried to differentiate between support and cooperation. For instance, a history of antiunion activity has been an important factor in the courts' determinations:

> When it has been found that the organization is in fact independent of employer control and that the support given is of a trivial nature, courts have applied the *de minimis* doctrine and have avoided the literal language of the Act. Courts have been unwilling to find unfair

[2]Everett Kassalow, *Trade Unions and Industrial Relations: An International Comparison* (New York: Random House, 1969), p. 151.

[3]*The Developing Labor Law: The Board, the Courts and the National Labor Relations Act*, Charles J. Morris, ed. (Washington: Bureau of National Affairs, 1971), pp. 140–41.

labor practices and to identify labor organization where merely a cooperative spirit, which advanced the industrial stability intended by the Act, was evidenced, particularly if the employees have not been deprived of Section 7 rights to self-organization. This judicial policy of encouraging union-employer cooperation was finally accepted by the Board in *Camo Knitting Mills* where the Board held that "the use of company time and property does not, *per se*, establish unlawful assistance."[4]

In Germany, on the other hand, law requires employers to allow the holding of elections to works councils during working hours. And the employers must rearrange the workload and assign substitutes for employees attending works council meetings. At the request either of 25 percent of the members of a union or of a majority of a group of the works council, "a delegate of a union represented in the works council may participate at the meetings in an advisory capacity."[5] The West German Works Constitute Act of 1972 states that

> the examples resulting from the activities of the works council shall be borne by the employer [and that] the employer shall provide the necessary offices, materials and office personnel for the meetings, consulting hours and normal operations of the works council.[6]

A somewhat similar situation exists in Italy where, for the most part, collective bargaining negotiations *per se* are held at a national level. In local-and plant-level bargaining sessions, the employers are required by the Workers' Statute of 1970 to provide help to the workers' representatives. According to Article 24 of the above mentioned statute, trade union officers "shall be entitled to unpaid leave in order to participate in trade union activity negotiations or to attend congresses or meetings of trade union nature for a period not exceeding a total of eight days a year."[7]

In addition, in production units with more than 200 workers, the employer must provide the employee representatives with a permanent base, such as a room or the like, located near the production unit concerned. Union officers, under certain circumstances, have the right to paid leave for collective bargaining purposes and the right to post notices and collect trade union dues.

Although the situation in France is not as clear cut as in Germany or Italy, employers in some cases are expected to make a certain specifiable monetary contribution to the works councils, according

[4]*Ibid.*, p. 142.
[5]*Martin Peltzer and Ralf Boer, Betriebsverfassungsgesetz: Labor Management Relations Act* (Frankfurt am Main: Fritz Knapp Verlag, 1977), pp. 60–62.
[6]*Ibid.*, p. 86.
[7]International Labour Office, *Legislative Series: 1970–Italy 2* (Geneva, 1970), p. 8.

to Article L432-3 of the Work Code.[8] The various differences notwithstanding, close scrutiny of European and U.S. law and practice
would probably indicate that the spirit of legislation and of common
behavior is similar. The letter of the laws may be quite different, but
the aim, in both America and Europe, is to provide cooperation during collective bargaining without giving the employer the option to
dominate the union and thus the whole bargaining process.

As suggested above, the term "facilities" may connote actual
physical or monetary contributions by the employer. In Belgium, for
example, the unions have no legal status and cannot therefore be
sued by the employer in the event of infringement of an agreement.
"It is for this reason that employers—seeking some guarantees as
to the execution and administration of collective agreements—have
directly linked the payment of 'benefits' reserved to union members
. . . to the faithful performance of the collective agreement and the
maintenance of social peace during the lifetime of the agreement."[9]

On the other hand, the word "facilities" could imply more of an
attitude on the part of the employer toward cooperation with the
unions or employee representatives in the framework of the collective bargaining process, a meaning not very distinct from the wording of Paragraph 1. The general willingness of the multinational
employer to "facilitate" the collective bargaining process has been
noted in the discussion of Paragraph 1, as well as in the introduction
to this study. Here, as elsewhere, nevertheless, the key to compliance with this guideline by the multinational employer would
appear to reside in the decentralization of industrial relations and
adaptation to the local context. As one American automobile industry executive has said:

> Labour relations management is basically an employee problem-
> solving business through the application of collective agreements,
> laws, customs and practices, and by understanding the interplay of
> human reactions present in an industrial environment. Given this
> description of the labour relations function, the only possible way to
> achieve a successful labour relations programme (in any corporation)
> is to utilise the skills, education, social background, motivation and
> awareness of local labour relations managers and their staffs—
> whatever the enterprise and wherever it may be located.[10]

---

[8]"Comité d'entreprise," *Liaisons Sociales,* 1979, p. 61. French labor legislation has,
however, been the subject of several proposed changes recently. See Chap. VI, pp.
89–91.

[9]Roger Blanpain, "Belgium," in *International Encyclopaedia for Labour Law and
Industrial Relations,* Vol. 1, Roger Blanpain, ed. (The Netherlands: Kluwer, 1979),
p. 131.

[10]International Labour Office, *Social and Labour Practices of Some US-based
Multinationals in the Metal Trades* (Geneva, 1977), p. 133.

Many firms have stated that they use local labor relations managers and encourage them to develop good relationships with the local, regional, and national union representatives. This is the case with Caterpillar, Ford, John Deere, and International Harvester.[11] In the petroleum industry, membership and active participation in national employers' organizations or their constituents is common practice, undoubtedly in order to "facilitate" the collective bargaining process.[12] Exxon has recommended to its labor relations specialists that all laws and regulations concerning collective bargaining be rigorously observed and that it is company policy to deal cooperatively with unions.[13]

In Germany, multinational enterprises (MNEs) have abided by the codetermination laws that require employee representation on supervisory boards. In some instances, members of International Trade Secretariats (ITSs) have been elected to supervisory boards (see Table XII-2). As a general rule, however, most multinational subsidiaries deal with unions and employee representatives through the structures determined by the local context in which the subsidiary operates. The freedom of union or employee representatives to engage in their specific activities is defined by the law and practice of individual countries, as are the employer's obligations to "facilitate" or "assist" in the activities of employee representatives. Table IV-1 describes provisions for time off for union or employee representatives in ten countries.

TABLE IV–1
*Time Off for Worker Representatives
in Ten Countries*[a]

Country	Provisions
Belgium	Works councillors (mandatory in all firms with more than 100 workers) and safety representatives (mandatory in all firms with more than 50 workers) are entitled to paid time off for meetings during working hours. Plant-level union delegates have rights (under a legally binding central agreement) to normal pay for time spent on union activities.
Denmark	Safety representatives (mandatory in firms with at least 10 workers) are entitled to "reasonable" paid time off to carry out their activities. Cooperation committee members (with rights stemming from a legally binding central agreement covering firms with 50 or more workers) are granted paid time off for all meet-

[11]*Ibid.*, p. 119.
[12]International Labour Office, *Social and Labour Practices of Multinational Enterprises in the Petroleum Industry* (Geneva, 1977), p. 75.
[13]*Ibid.*, p. 119.

TABLE IV-1 (continued)

Country	Provisions
	ings. Shop stewards (elected by union members in each firm and with distinct rights under industry/company agreements) are generally granted paid time off for union activities. All worker's representatives are usually entitled to "reasonable" unpaid leave on request, in line with agreements or custom and practice.
France	Works councillors (mandatory in firms with at least 50 workers) and safety representatives (mandatory in industrial firms with at least 50 workers and commercial firms with at least 300 workers) are entitled to paid leave for all meetings and, save in exceptional circumstances, up to 20 hours a month on full pay to carry out any necessary duties. Personnel delegates (mandatory in all firms with more than 10 workers) are entitled to up to 15 hours' paid leave a month. Union delegates (appointed by the main unions in firms with at least 50 workers) are entitled to paid leave only in firms with at least 150 workers. The maximum permissible leave ranges, according to work force size, from 10 to 15 hours a month total time for all delegates taken together.
Germany	Works councillors (mandatory in all firms with at least 5 workers) are entitled to certain paid time off although in principle, they must "perform their duties without pay as an honorary function." They are entitled to at least 3 weeks' paid leave to attend State-approved training and education courses; and in firms with at least 300 workers are entitled to be released completely from normal employment on full pay to carry out their duties as representatives. The number of councillors eligible for the latter form of leave varies with work force size, subject to a maximum of 11 in firms with 10,000 workers plus an additional councillor released completely from normal employment for each additional 2,000 workers or fraction thereof.
Italy	Union representatives (in firms with more than 15 workers) are entitled to paid time off to carry out their duties of at least 8 hours a month. They are also entitled to unpaid leave of up to 8 days a year to participate in negotiations and union meetings. In all cases these rights vary according to work force size—e.g. in firms with 201 to 3,000 workers, only one representative per 300 workers (or a fraction thereof) is eligible for leave.
Netherlands	Works councillors (mandatory in firms with at least 35 full-time employees) are entitled to paid time off to attend meetings during working hours. Union workplace representatives (appointed by unions under many collective agreements) are frequently entitled to paid time off to carry out their duties under the relevant agreements. A bill, granting these representatives minimum statutory rights for the first time, is currently before Parliament. In all cases, the precise amount of time off is agreed between the parties at plant level.
Portugal	Works councillors (optional in all firms regardless of size) are entitled to paid time off of 40 hours a month (for actual council duties); 50 hours a month (for duties on a coordinating committee, bringing together councillors in a particular production area); and 8 hours a month (for specific works council subcommittee duties). These entitlements are granted on an individual basis and cannot be accumulated where a worker is a member of more than one

TABLE IV-1 (continued)

Country	Provisions
	committee. In firms with 1,000 workers or more, however, individual entitlements may be reassigned/added together, subject to an individual monthly maximum entitlement of 80 hours. Union workplace representatives are entitled to paid time off "as necessary" to carry out their duties.
Spain	Works councillors (mandatory in firms with at least 50 workers) and workers' delegates (mandatory in firms with 11 to 49 workers) are entitled to paid leave to carry out their duties. In both cases, these rights depend on work force size—with a maximum of 40 hours' leave per month per representative in firms with at least 751 workers. Individual entitlements may be added together and reassigned, in accordance with collective agreements, provided the overall maximum entitlement is not exceeded and payment is guaranteed. Union workplace representatives have no general rights to time off to carry out their duties. Such rights are, however, sometimes granted by collective agreements. Workers performing union duties at provincial level and above are entitled to unpaid leave as required to carry out their duties.
Sweden	Union-appointed employee workplace representatives (with rights deriving from law and central agreements) and safety representatives (mandatory in all firms with at least 5 employees) are entitled to "reasonable" paid time off for union workplace activities—the exact amount of time off being determined by local negotiations. Paid time off is also granted for union training, with the employer required to cover the costs of any course fees.
United Kingdom	Workers who are authorized representatives of independent unions recognized by the employer for bargaining purposes are entitled to paid time off during working hours for industrial relations with their employer and training on union courses. The precise time allowed must be "reasonable in all the circumstances." Further guidance is provided in a Code of Practice. A recent test case has established that such rights may extend to representatives attending national meetings at which general union policy issues are discussed. Workers' representatives are also entitled to "reasonable" unpaid leave for union activities, excluding industrial action.

Source: "International: Special leave in 10 countries," *European Industrial Relations Review*, No. 100 (May 1982), pp. 14–16.

[a]Time off for employee representatives in the United States is a matter of the collective bargaining agreement and is a quite common provision in such agreements with wide variations on the amount and type of time off negotiated.

PHILIPS AND ITS SUBSIDIARIES

Among the original cases submitted by the International Metalworkers' Federation (IMF) to the Committee on International Investment and Multinational Enterprises (CIIME) in 1977 was one that alleged violations of Paragraph 2-A by the Dutch multinational, Philips, and two of its subsidiaries, one in Belgium, the other, PIG-Glass, in the United Kingdom. The charges against the subsidiaries stemmed from their refusal to "grant leave of absence for one convener and two shop stewards by a British trade union and other trade union representatives from a Belgian factory to attend a seminar organized by the Dutch union, Industriebond NKV and supported by the European Metalworkers' Federation (EMF)."[14] The charges against the parent company, meanwhile, referred to the refusal by Philips' management to meet with an EMF delegation that included an IMF member. The company claimed that the participation of the IMF violated an earlier agreement with the EMF to deal only with matters confined to the European Community (EC). Did the company's comportment or that of its subsidiaries frustrate the meaning of Paragraph 2-A in not providing the "facilities"—in this case, leave of absence—to assist in the development of collective agreements?

First, it should be noted that "no company has had more detailed experience in multinational union discussions than Philips,"[15] which has had contact with European trade union federations, especially the EMF, since 1967. Notwithstanding such contact, however, the company espouses a decentralized management philosophy and invests a considerable degree of autonomy in its subsidiaries. Moreover,

> [decentralization] particularly holds true for personnel and industrial relations policies, which have to follow national legislation in the field of labour and social security and have to fit in the national labour market situation, industrial relations structure and climate and take into account national characteristics and preferences.[16]

Philips had expected to gain from informal meetings with the EMF, since it was thought that such meetings would give management's representatives the opportunity to elaborate on the company's view of local autonomy in the decision-making process.

The EMF, however, foresaw the upgrading of these meetings to a point where the company would be drawn into some kind of interna-

---

[14]Trade Union Advisory Committee "Complaints on the policy of multinational companies calling for application of the OECD Guidelines for MNEs."

[15]Herbert R. Northrup and Richard L. Rowan, *Multinational Collective Bargaining Attempts* (Philadelphia: The Industrial Research Unit, The Wharton School, University of Pennsylvania, 1979), p. 145.

[16]P. L. Dronkers, "A Multinational Organization and Industrial Relations: The Philips Case," (Address before the International Industrial Relations Association, Third World Congress, London, September 1973). Cited in Northrup & Rowan, p. 145.

tional collective bargaining agreement.[17] Significantly, collective bargaining had clearly been beyond the scope of these meetings, and indeed, the four meetings that had been held had focused rather on orientation and the exchange of information. Thus, when the EMF sought to include a member of the IMF in these meetings, in an apparent attempt to broaden the meetings' purpose, the company refused to meet with the EMF:

> It is apparent that the EMF feels that Philips is a prime target for a bargaining relationship. It is equally clear that Philips approached these meetings with the idea that it could satisfy the unions with a good faith demonstration of its willingness to provide information, its openness, and the fairness of its wages and personnel policies. This, of course, ignores the drive by unions, whether local or international, to achieve parity of decision making with management and to develop an organization and a framework of operations that require consultation and mutual consent before policies are determined and actions taken rather than after the fact. For union leadership, informational meetings are valuable only as a stepping-stone to what is regarded as a necessary bargaining relationship between parties of at least equal stature.[18]

In refusing to meet with the international union delegates, Philips signaled its objection to an expansion of the original terms under which both the company and the EMF had, however informally, been meeting. The IMF, meanwhile, voiced its objection to the company's behavior in its submission to the CIIME, claiming that

> the attitude of PHILIPS signifies a refusal to enter into discussions with the official international organization which represents trade unions, who are its authentic bargaining partners in various parts of the world, and to examine problems concerned with decisions at central management level. This refusal is considered as an infringement of the OECD code, as it also concerns the union attempt to bring up matters regarding PHILIPS operations in the area of OECD member countries.[19]

The discussion of Paragraph 1 noted that the prevailing management view, and Philips' own, is that the IMF, like other international trade union groups, is indeed an "official international organization." The IMF, however, is *not* the "authentic bargaining partner" of the company. The IMF's wish to "examine the problems concerned with decisions at central management level," furthermore, conflicts with the company's philosophy of decentralized deci-

---

[17]Northrup and Rowan, *Multinational Collective Bargaining Attempts,* p. 147.
[18]*Ibid.,* pp. 149–50.
[19]Roger Blanpain, *The OECD Guidelines for Multinational Enterprises and Labour Relations 1976–1979,* English Text rewritten by Michael Jones (Deventer, The Netherlands: Kluwer, 1979), p. 192.

sion making in matters concerning industrial relations at the subsidiary level.

Both these issues—the nonbargaining status of an international trade union group, and the locus of decision making—converge on a third, with immediate bearing on Paragraph 2–A. The purpose of the proposed meeting between the EMF and the company was not collective bargaining. Can the company, therefore, be alleged to have violated a recommendation "to assist in the development of collective agreements" by refusing to meet with an international union body with which the company does not even negotiate? The IMF clearly believed so, implying that the term "representatives of the employees" applied to itself as well.

The IMF's association of itself with the company's employee representatives and its apparent view of its function as assisting in the development of collective agreements were both rather broader perceptions of the IMF's role than those held by the company. To the company, the IMF's attempt seemed aimed at expanding the international union group's influence in the bargaining structure of the company. A more detailed view of that bargaining structure and the extent of its decentralization was provided by the allegations against two of Philips' subsidiaries.

British and Belgian Subsidiaries

The refusal of the managements of British and Belgian subsidiaries of Philips to grant leave to union personnel for a meeting in the Netherlands was based in both cases on the subsidiaries' conceptions of the terms of the local collective agreements. The parent company argued that both agreements were quite specific in their provisions for time off for the duties of employee representation, and that neither the Belgian nor the British collective agreement specified a leave-of-absence provision for a crossborder meeting. The company, moreover, argued that more extensive provisions in this area are clearly not the norm:

> In the case of the British factory the national management replied that the 'Industriebond N.K.V.' conference concerning Philips glass activities did not meet the requirement that the activity relates to and is consistent with the collective bargaining structure within the company in which the employee operates and his role as a representative of the unions within this structure. Therefore the management could not comply with the request to release the 3 persons concerned to attend on Company time.[20]

---

[20]*Ibid.*, p. 194.

Similarly, the company held, in Belgium:

> Leave may be granted either for training courses or for meetings organized on behalf of co-ordination between trade unions representatives of different establishments belonging to one company in Belgium within the same branch of industry. These various types of leave have been laid down in national collective agreements. Therefore the Belgian management was not obliged to grant leave for a purpose beyond the scope of these agreements.[21]

Neither subsidiary wished to abet what it viewed as an attempt to broaden the context of industrial relations to something beyond its actual, decentralized structure:

> We believe that it is incorrect and contrary to normal practice and agreed procedures for the unions to interpret these as having a border-crossing scope, introducing in this way a principle that has nowhere been established, i.e. that of granting leave for meetings outside the national industrial relations context.[22]

The statement above reflects corporate policy. The decisions not to grant leave, however, were well within the purview of the national managements that made them:

> It is also incorrect to suggest that the decision was taken by the National management on instruction from Central Management in Eindhoven. The decisions were taken by the national managements themselves on the basis of the relevant normal practice and agreed procedures. We are astonished that these unions should not be aware of the actual context of these facilities.[23]

The OECD guidelines themselves do not specifically address the issue of leave of absence for international union meetings, nor do they address the issue of international collective bargaining. Paragraph 46 of the ILO declaration of principles does, however, broach the former subject:

> Representatives of the workers in multinational enterprises should not be hindered from meeting for consultation and exchange of views among themselves, provided that the functioning of the operations of the enterprise and the normal procedures which govern relationships with representatives of the workers and their organisations are not thereby prejudiced.[24]

Similarly, Paragraph 61 of the 1979 review of the OECD guidelines, in language reminiscent of the ILO declaration, counsels a "cooperative attitude" toward such meetings:

---

[21]*Ibid.*
[22]*Ibid.*
[23]*Ibid.*
[24]See Appendix B, Paragraph Forty-Six.

While explicitly not addressing the issue, the Guidelines imply that the management of MNEs should adopt a cooperative attitude towards the participation of employees in international meetings for consultation and exchanges of views among themselves provided that the functioning of the operation of the enterprise and the normal procedures which govern relationships with representatives of the employees are not thereby prejudiced.[25]

Presumably, had the subsidiaries chosen to discipline worker representatives who, on their own time, had elected to attend an international union meeting in the Netherlands, then the subsidiaries would have been guilty of unjust discrimination against those employees and also of "hindering" or manifesting "an uncooperative attitude" against international union meetings. The issue is far less broad, however, and centers more on the provision in collective agreements for granting leave. Thus, in commenting on Paragraph 46 of the ILO declaration, the parent company noted:

> It will be clear the the term 'normal procedures' etc., in this connection refers to the national industrial relations' context in the framework of which facilities for granting leave may have been laid down per country.[26]

In neither agreement did "normal procedures" allow the granting of leave for an international union meeting. Neither the ILO nor the OECD recommendations, moreover, suggest that a breach of normal procedures should occur in order "not to hinder" or to "adopt a cooperative attitude" toward international union meetings. Had either recommendation extended beyond its present wording, the result would have been that companies should actively support international union meetings, an unreasonable recommendation in the view of most multinational employers.

CONCLUSION

The discussion above clearly indicates that neither subsidiary wanted to lend its support (through the granting of paid time off) to a union meeting of international scope beyond the national boundaries within which each subsidiary operates. The question is not whether the subsidiaries' employee representatives could or could not attend an international union meeting—they clearly could. Yet,

---

[25]Organization for Economic Cooperation and Development—Committee on International Investment and Multinational Enterprises, *The Review of the 1976 Declaration and Decisions on International Investment and Multinational Enterprises*, Paragraph 61.

[26]Blanpain, *The OECD Guidelines for Multinational Enterprises*, p. 194.

it is also clear that the granting of paid or unpaid time off to employee representatives wishing to attend international union meetings is by no means "normal procedure." For the subsidiaries to have granted paid time off for attendance at such meetings would have implied not merely the "adoption of a cooperative attitude" on the employers' part but the active support for such meetings as well. Such support would have betokened a rather significant change in normal procedures, a change that would have considerably outdistanced the unfettered neutrality with which the CIIME views the possibility of international union meetings. Far from neutral, the company has elsewhere evidenced its respect for the international trade union movement. Further support than this would be to "prejudice" the "normal procedures which govern relationships with representatives of the employees." The guidelines do not inhibit a company from showing greater support if it so chooses. Neither, however, do the guidelines suggest that greater support should occur, for to do so would render insignificant the meaning of the "chapeau clause" of the guidelines.

The charges brought against Philips by the EMF and affiliated unions stem from the 1970s, a period in which multinational collective bargaining appeared to be a lively prospect in the view of some international union groups. Recent developments, however, provide an interesting footnote to the activity of the 1970s. On April 20, 1982, in The Hague, Professor Herbert Northrup met with Hubert Thierron, general secretary of the EMF, in an interview during which current EMF strategy was discussed. Claiming that negotiations at the European level were impossible, Thierron stated that he was no longer pressing for a meeting with Philips' central management and, moreover, would recommend against such a meeting.[27] Rather, renewed emphasis would appear to have returned to the national and local levels where, according to Thierron, the coordination of demands and contract termination dates should be the objectives defining the unions' interest in multinational collective bargaining.

---

[27]Interview between Professor Herbert R. Northrup and Hubert Thierron in The Hague, Netherlands, April 20, 1982.

CHAPTER V

Paragraph 2–B

Enterprises should:

> provide to representatives of employees information which is needed for meaningful negotiations on conditions of employment.

The scope and timing of information disclosure is among the most vigorous contemporary issues in industrial relations. Indeed, that the duty to disclose information is directly or indirectly the focus not only of Paragraph 2–B, but of Paragraphs 3 and 6 as well bears witness to the central importance of the issue. In principle, the disclosure of information may facilitate the collective bargaining process by enabling worker representatives to make reasonable demands and to perform better their representative function. Management, in turn, may benefit from a better understanding of the company's position through disclosing information and thus increasing chances for industrial peace. Information, however, is a powerful resource, and it is equally true that the safeguarding of managerial prerogatives may conflict with the growing demand for worker participation in decision making. Paradoxically, then, information may facilitate an agreement or constitute a major impediment to reaching an agreement.

A number of current issues bear directly upon the question of information disclosure. The current economic climate has spawned an interest in employment and income security, investment and disinvestment plans, and the effects of technological change, each interest sponsoring its own demand for information. A more sophisticated and better-educated work force, moreover, has, in many countries, shown an interest in participating in present and future decisions affecting employment. Similarly, the interest in rendering the operations of multinationals more transparent and accountable has also been translated into demands for information disclosure.

The wording of Paragraph 2–B reflects these many trends. Because such terms as "meaningful negotiations" and "conditions of employment" are themselves not stably defined, but have evolved, the scope of "information" has also been subject to change.

The great diversity among countries must be added to this historical trend in evaluating the employer's duty to disclose information,
whether by law or through the process of negotiation, and whether
to works councils or in collective bargaining sessions.

NATIONAL DIVERSITY

Unions' or employee representatives' rights to company information vary greatly depending upon the national setting. In its 1979
review of the guidelines, the CIIME noted that "provision of information to employees is usually dealt with under national systems of
labour relations or, more recently, by legislation and is an area where
national diversity is great." Broadly speaking, the information usually provided to employee representatives is of two types: that relating to the company's labor decisions (wages, staffing, promotions,
training, etc.) and that pertaining to the company's financial health.

In the United States, the employer's duty to disclose information
arises out of the statutory duty to bargain in good faith [Section 8
a(5) of the National Labor Relations Act (NLRA)]. The employer is
required to disclose information only on issues that are subject to
bargaining and, therefore, relevant to employees in the bargaining
unit. An employer who counters a union's demand for a wage
increase by claiming an inability to pay, for example, entitles the
union to the financial information that would substantiate such a
claim. In a landmark decision, the United States Supreme Court
noted that

> good faith bargaining necessarily requires that claims made by either
> bargainer be honest claims. This is true about an asserted inability to
> pay an increase in wages. If such an argument is important enough to
> present in the give and take of bargaining, it is important enough to
> require some proof of its accuracy.[1]

James O'Reilly has noted that the National Labor Relations Board
(NLRB) criterion for disclosure of financial information in the context of bargaining distinguishes between an employer's refusal to
pay—a company policy or philosophy—and its inability to do so:

> An employer acts at its peril when it explains its position on a wage
> demand without stating that it is *not* claiming inability to pay. An
> employer's assertion that it would pay "what is right" was regarded
> as a claim of inability to pay when the employer had complained dur-
> ing negotiations about high wage costs. The statement that "the

---

[1] James T. O'Reilly, *Unions' Rights to Company Information* (Philadelphia: Industrial Research Unit, The Wharton School, University of Pennsylvania, 1980),
p. 51.

employees came to the wrong well . . . the well is dry," even though made in the course of hard, good-faith bargaining, resulted in an order for disclosure of substantiation data.[2]

The examples above were interpreted as referring to a present inability to pay. The duty to disclose substantiating information, however, may also befall an employer who expresses doubts of future profitability in response to a wage demand. As O'Reilly observes: "Disclosure orders can be based upon something less than an express statement that the employer would go out of business if the demands of the union are met. Stating that the company cannot pay higher fringe benefits and 'remain competitive' is enough to force disclosure of substantiating information."[3] Similarly, the duty to substantiate is also implied when an employer claims that the company's wage levels are equal to or higher than competitors, or that economic considerations have motivated certain actions during the term of the contract:

> In Puerto Rico Telephone Co. v. NLRB, the company had been subcontracting a major portion of its business because of a massive modernization and expansion program that was then being undertaken. The union filed a grievance when the company began to lay off employees. The employer asserted that the work force reduction was due to an economic reorganization of the company. The union sought data dealing with the volume of business, earnings, and wage savings from the layoffs. The (NLR) Board ordered disclosure. . . .[4]

In this case, the duty to disclose information was upheld during the life of the contract through the grievance mechanism rather than in the context of negotiations.

During collective bargaining in the United States, the employer is under no duty to disclose information unless the union makes a specific request.[5] Usually, moreover, the union must prove that the information it requests "is relevant and necessary to the performance of its function as bargaining representative."[6] Information, however, that bears directly on the mandatory subjects of bargaining as defined in Section 8d of the National Labor Relations Act, ("wages, hours, and other terms and conditions of employment") has been interpreted by the NLRB as "presumptively relevant." Under this rule, union requests for information on wage data, including actual wages, fringe benefits, and how wages are set, and

---

[2] *Ibid.,* p. 52.
[3] *Ibid.,* pp. 52-53.
[4] *Ibid.,* p. 54.
[5] *Ibid.,* p. 11.
[6] *Ibid.,* p. 21.

data on incentive and piece rates, merit increases, bonuses, and premiums, have usually been viewed by the NLRB as relevant.[7]

Also considered presumptively relevant by the NLRB is information on training, unit employee names and addresses, and layoffs: "in layoff situations, the presumptive relevance principle applies if layoffs are presently occurring, have occurred, or are about to occur."[8] It applies as well to the company's rehiring policies.

The basic legislation regulating labor-management relations in the United States has been expanded through interpretation by the NLRB. Since the 1960s, moreover, a spate of legislation in the areas of equal employment opportunity, occupational safety and health, pension and retirement provisions, as well as the Freedom of Information Act (1974), has broadened the scope of information disclosure. In a recent case, for example, an NLRB official "held that plant chemicals' identities and compositions were presumptively relevant. The information had been withheld for protection of a trade secret. The ruling was that the union would be incapable of policing the portion of the contract relating to worker safety unless detailed chemical information was available."[9] The discussion will return below to the conflict between the need to safeguard confidential information and the rights of employee representatives to information.

It is clear from the last example that union rights to company information have grown broader over recent years through the parallel broadening of the scope of bargainable issues. Although legislation in the United States has enhanced union rights to company information, it appears no less true, as O'Reilly has concluded, that "the greatest quantity of information sharing occurs in the context of bargaining between employers and employee representatives."[10] The evolution of information disclosure in the United States confirms a trend apparent elsewhere in the industrialized world: disclosure is "on the increase, for reasons linked with the development of the idea of democratic behavior and participation by workers in management decision-taking."[11] In the United States, the vehicle for participation has remained collective bargaining, aided by the passage of protective legislation. Elsewhere, the structure of information dissemination has been through works councils.

---

[7] *Ibid.,* pp. 23–24.
[8] *Ibid.,* p. 33.
[9] *Ibid.,* p. 35.
[10] *Ibid.,* p. 7.
[11] Jack Peel, *The Real Power Game* (London: McGraw-Hill Book Company, 1979), p. 122.

In Belgium, a Royal Decree of 1973 clearly delineated the type of information that must be made available to works councils. In addition to data relating to personnel matters, the works council is entitled to economic and financial information on the company and, under certain conditions, to information pertaining to the company's competitive position and future investment plans. As one author has noted,

> The royal decree stresses that the objective of providing detailed information on production costs and intended future investments is to help works council members to understand the relationship between the prevailing economic and financial conditions in the enterprise and their effect on work and workers.[12]

The greater disclosure of information is a general trend, and the works council, among other industrial relations structures, is not necessarily privy to more information than would be exchanged through collective bargaining. Nevertheless, in countries where the participative machinery of the works council is well established, as in the Federal Republic of Germany, the provisions for information disclosure do appear to be among the most extensive. Here, the obvious and direct link between information and codetermination has resulted in a broad entitlement to information, as Table V-1 reveals.

TABLE V-1
Rights of Works Councils to Information

Country	Rights
Austria	The powers of the works council are consultative and cover all sectors of management of the undertaking: economic problems, personnel questions, and welfare matters. The council may obtain information on all matters affecting the interests of the personnel and on general management policies, including investment plans and the financial position of the undertaking. It must be notified in advance of recruitments and promotions, and may demand to be consulted on these subjects.
Belgium	The works council consults with management on such matters as training activities, measures which might affect work organization or the organization of the undertaking, conditions of work, and productivity. The employer is required to supply the council with information, in particular, on personnel policy (including the rules for recruitment and selection), productivity, the economic and financial position of the undertaking and operating results, plans and prospects, including those for the structure and development of employment in the undertaking.

[12] *Ibid.*, pp. 125–26.

TABLE V-1 (continued)

Country	Rights
France	The works council must be consulted on all matters concerning the organization, management, and general progress of the undertaking, and it must receive quarterly and annual reports on production, financial results, investments, and plans for the following financial year, wages, conditions of work, and the employment situation in the undertaking. The works committee must be informed of proposed changes in equipment and production or operational methods and of their effect on working conditions and employment, and it must be consulted in advance on those subjects.
Germany	The works council and the employer may conclude undertaking agreements, except on wages and other conditions of employment determined or normally determined by collective agreement. The council receives prior information and is consulted, in particular, on engagements, promotions, transfers, individual, and collective dismissals. It receives prior information and is consulted on the construction and transformation of premises, installations, processes, and workplaces. The council has a right to codetermination in regard to directives concerning selection of personnel for engagements, transfers, and dismissals, and on hours of work and rest and holiday periods, disciplinary matters, determination of the principles to govern selection and remuneration, piece rates, bonuses and other methods of payment by results, the adoption of new remuneration methods, vocational training, and the organization and management of welfare services. The council has the right of codetermination when major changes are contemplated which would lead to unfavorable repercussions for the personnel (such changes must be the subject of a compromise and a "social plan"). The council assists the competent authorities in action relating to safety, health, and occupational accidents.
Luxembourg	The head of the undertaking must inform and consult the committee before taking any important decision on the introduction or changing of equipment, working methods, or production processes. He must inform and consult the committee on manpower requirements and on training measures. The committee must be informed and consulted in principle beforehand on any economic or financial decision which could decisively influence the structure of the undertaking and the level of employment (for instance on the volume and trend of production, investment policy, plans for closure or relocation of the undertaking, the restriction or extension of its operations, mergers, or changes in its organization); the possible repercussions on employment, and on terms of employment and conditions of work, must be examined, as well as social measures being taken or contemplated, such as retraining and resettlement. The committee must be informed and consulted in writing on the economic and financial progress of the undertaking.
Netherlands	The opinion of the works council, which was already required in respect of important decisions such as a major change in the organization of the undertaking, total or partial closure or relocation, considerable reduction or expansion of activity, merger or association, is henceforth also required for major investments or loans, collective recruitment, and the setting-up of new undertakings. The employer must supply biannual reports on the operations and results of the undertaking, including its investments in the Netherlands and

TABLE V-1 (continued)

Country	Rights
	abroad, annual accounts, long-term plans and any financial estimates relating to them, as well as internal manpower forecasts.
Spain	The committee is informed of general economic trends, the production and sales of the undertaking, the production program and probable employment trend. Each quarter it must receive statistics on absences from work and their causes and on occupational accidents and the working environment. It must examine the balance sheet.

Source: International Labour Office, *Workers' Participation in Decisions within Undertakings,* (Geneva, 1981), pp. 205–19.

On the other hand, as concluded in a recent study of worker participation by the International Labor Organization (ILO),

> collective bargaining as a method of workers' participation in decisions within the undertaking also plays a very important part in countries other than the United States. This is, for instance, the case in Canada, where the industrial relations system bears many similarities with that of the United States.[13]

In the United Kingdom, moreover, where works councils are not developed, the shop steward plays an important role. "In practice, shop stewards exert a great influence on an ever-growing number of management decisions."[14] In the United Kingdom, as in the United States, "disclosure is limited to the subject-matter of collective bargaining listed in Section 29(1) of the Trade Union and Labour Relations Act 1974. This excludes information for longer term investment planning."[15] The employer, however, may be required to disclose the latter type of information should the secretary of state for industry support the claim of an independent trade union that requests it. Significantly, British law does impose limitations on the duty to disclose in the event that such disclosure "would cause substantial injury to the employer's undertaking, for reasons other than its effect on collective bargaining."[16] Similar legislation exists in Germany, despite the existence there of highly developed works councils.

---

[13] International Labour Office, *Workers' Participation in Decisions within Undertakings* (Geneva, 1981), p. 171.

[14] *Ibid.,* p. 172.

[15] B. A. Hepple, "Great Britain," in *International Encyclopaedia for Labour Law and Industrial Relations,* Vol. III, Roger Blanpain, ed. (The Netherlands: Kluwer, 1979), p. 164.

[16] *Ibid.,* p. 165.

In addition to legislation and industrial relations structures, union strength in collective bargaining appears to be an important factor in information disclosure. In the Netherlands, for example, works councils "have the right to ask for information relating to the progress of the enterprise and to discuss important decisions before they are taken."[17] But Dutch law also grants to unions in general the right "to be consulted in advance about any measures concerning the transfer of control of the enterprise."[18] The development of collective bargaining in Italy, meanwhile, has extended to unions rights to information that parallel those of employee representatives in many northern European countries. The ILO study referred to earlier observed that

> over the past few years, company collective agreements have included clauses not only on hours of work, work pace and workloads, health and safety problems and job classification, but also on the limitation of subcontracting and homeworking, on transfers within the undertaking, and generally on the employment aspects of all reorganisation and rationalisation measures. Clauses concerning investment became much more frequent from 1976 on, giving the trade unions not only a right to information and consultation on investments, but in practice a right to genuine negotiation on the subject. In addition, the trade unions have tended in their negotiations to put pressure on undertakings to assist the local authorities (communes and provinces) with public works and social services.[19]

At times, Italian unions have been able to shift investment plans to the poor, southern part of the country, an effort sometimes facilitated by the political clout of the Communist Party, often the ally of Italian unions.

Vastly different from the collective bargaining structure of Italy is Australia's system of compulsory arbitration:

> In Australia . . . no data are generally provided to the trade union, since negotiations commence without prejudice to either party and, in the event of recourse to arbitration, formal arguments would be lodged against union claims, covering such points as precedents and standards laid down by the Arbitration Commission, standards existing in industry generally, surveys of practices, wage rates and job classifications, in comparable industries, and questions of public interest.[20]

In recent years, however, the criteria developed by the Conciliation and Arbitration Commission have become subject to increasing ero-

---

[17] Peel, *The Real Power Game,* p. 127.
[18] *Ibid.*
[19] ILO, *Workers' Participation,* pp. 173–74.
[20] International Labour Office, *Social and Labour Practices of Multinational Enterprises in the Petroleum Industry* (Geneva, 1977), p. 84.

sion through challenges by the country's powerful unions. Collective bargaining has become an oft-discussed alternative to central arbitration, an alternative that would likely impose disclosure responsibilities on employers.

As was noted in Table V-1, works committees in France are entitled to receive information pertaining to the economic and financial performance of the company, including quarterly and annual production results. Recent changes in French labor law seek to bolster not only the works committee, but collective bargaining as well. As one commentator noted prior to the laws' passage, both developments would have an impact upon information disclosure:

> One objective of the proposed law is to expand the role of the works committee in reviewing the economic performance of the business. To this end, the economic and financial reports which the committees already receive are to be expanded and their contents more precisely defined: in addition to the information required by existing legislation, employers must now supply in particular details on the division of shareholdings between those entities holding more than 10% of the shares of the company and on the position of the company within the business sector. The contents of the annual and quarterly reports already supplied to works committees will be more closely regulated by the new legislation, which requires the inclusion of information on a number of specific subjects. The works committee is entitled to receive, as well, copies of the same documents that are furnished to shareholders, partners, and directors (or members of the supervisory board) of the company. The list of specific circumstances in which the works committee is to be consulted will be extended, taking into account certain situations identified by prior court decisions, such as the merger of the company, major investments by others in the company, and the acquisition or sale of the subsidiaries.[21]

To enable employee representatives to use the information given them, moreover, the law provides a training period to acquaint representatives with the analysis of economic and financial data.

The French legislative changes appear to be at the very nexus of vigorous trends in European industrial relations. One of these is the growing decentralization of collective bargaining. Indeed, another labor law change in France makes collective bargaining mandatory on an annual basis in undertakings employing over fifty persons.[22] Decentralization itself appears closely allied to the demand for greater decision-making power:

> Collective bargaining proper is increasing at the levels of the undertaking and of the establishment in many market economy countries

---

[21] Cleary, Gottlieb, Steen, and Hamilton, "Memorandum on Current French Labor Law Legislation," May 7, 1982, pp. 16–17.
[22] *Ibid.,* p. 16.

and is covering a much greater number of subjects—including working conditions and the organisation of the undertaking, welfare, and employment and income security—than in the past, when bargaining usually centred on questions of wages and fringe benefits, grading, hours of work and holidays.[23]

Clearly, the vast quantity of information subject to disclosure for whatever initial purpose may ultimately contribute to negotiations and collective agreements between the two sides of industry.

In France, current legislative efforts are aimed at enhancing both collective bargaining and works committees. Elsewhere, however,

the strengthening of the role of works councils by increasing their rights of co-decision and signing more agreements within them has been particularly marked in those countries where, traditionally, collective agreements in the strict sense were signed not at the level of the undertaking but at that of the industry, or regionally or nationally, or even for all occupations; it is current practice today in some of those countries for agreements made in works councils to supplement national industrial agreements.[24]

This tendency bears directly on the disclosure of information. In Belgium, for example, there is no specific obligation to disclose information in the context of collective bargaining, but there are extensive obligations to disclose information to the works councils.

In Scandinavia, the traditional strength of unions and the well-developed machinery of collective bargaining, coupled with the participative nature of social democracy, have resulted in rather extensive rights to information for employee representatives. In Sweden, for example, a 1976 law on codetermination broadened employee representatives' rights. The act introduced "a particularly far-reaching right to information, for instance on production, the financial situation of the undertaking, and the general principles of personnel policy."[25] National legislation in Sweden, as in other countries, has been instrumental in defining disclosure of information duties. Legislative developments at the level of the European Community (EC) have been just as, if not more, significant.

INFORMATION DISCLOSURE
AND INTERNATIONAL REGULATION

Legislation at the EC level has gradually broadened informational rights of employee representatives in specific areas. Thus, in 1975,

[23] ILO, *Workers' Participation*, p. 198.
[24] *Ibid.*, p. 199.
[25] *Ibid.*, p. 172.

for example, the EC Council of Ministers issued a directive pertaining to collective dismissals,[26] which stipulated *inter alia* that notification of projected plant closings or mass dismissals must be made to the appropriate body of employee representatives in advance of the actual closing, accompanied by detailed information explaining the decision. This directive underscores the importance given not only to the type, but to the timing of information in order that meaningful input from employee representatives may occur.

More recently, the ILO has adopted a convention on dismissals that significantly restricts the employer's ability to terminate individual employees. The convention "places on the employer the burden of proof that layoffs are justified."[27] Submitted only recently to national governments for ratification, the convention may have widespread impact: "even if not in force in the United States, the Convention could have an impact on the subsidiaries of American companies in the foreign countries that ratify it."[28] In many countries, therefore, the rights to both collective and individual dismissals compel certain duties of disclosure of information to employee representatives such that the latter may be not only informed of, but influential in, the decision.

Two impending EC directives portend even broader duties on the employer to disclose information. One of these, moreover, the proposed directive on worker information and consultation in companies of complex structure (or Vredeling directive, after the name of the bill's original sponsor in the European Commission), is aimed more directly at multinational companies. The other proposed law, currently nearing the final step of the EC's legislative process, discussion in the Council of Ministers, is the fifth directive on company law. Originally proposed in 1972, the fifth directive seeks to institutionalize worker participation in decision making by compelling companies employing above a certain number of employees to adopt a participatory organizational structure to include employee representatives. Greater information disclosure would therefore be an indirect product of structural change in the company.

It is the Vredeling directive, however, that has the greatest potential of broadening employee representatives' rights to information and consultation. In its original form, the directive would have required the periodic provision of "relevant" information of a prospective nature on the "dominant undertaking and its subsidiaries

---

[26] See Chapter IX, p. 137.
[27] "New I.L.O. rule would tighten layoffs," *New York Times*, June 23, 1982, p. A-17.
[28] *Ibid.*

as a whole."[29] In addition to the regular transmission of information, when the "dominant undertaking" proposed to make a decision that would affect any of its subsidiaries, information would have to be transmitted to employee representatives through the subsidiary prior to the making of the decision. In the event of noncompliance with either the provision of information or the extensive consultation rights contemplated in the bill, the original wording of the bill foresaw granting employee representatives the right to bypass subsidiary management and directly contact the management of the "dominant undertaking." The continued failure of management to comply would result in the right of employee representatives to pursue their request through "tribunals or other national authorities."

Although the fall 1982 sessions of the European Parliament introduced far more flexible language to the directive's original wording (the right to bypass local management, for example, has been significantly curtailed), business organizations in Europe, Japan, and the United States have continued to express their objections to the very need for a mandatory community instrument in the area of information and consultation. The employers argue that the existence of extensive national legislation and practice, as well as of voluntary codes of conduct, obviates the need for the directive. Of particular concern to employers are the protection of business secrets, the provision of prospective information greatly surpassing that given to shareholders, the extensive rights of employee representatives to consult with management prior to a decision's having been made, and, another of the bill's provisions, the creation of a transnational works council having the potential to facilitate transnational bargaining. Employers also question the timing of the proposed law: "Without providing any balancing benefits for employees, the proposal will create delays and difficulties in the planning and implementation of technological changes, which are needed to increase the competitiveness of Community industry. This would have adverse consequences for economic recovery, business confidence, new investment, and, ultimately, growth in employment in the Community."[30]

---

[29] Language proposed by the Commission of the European Communities, OJ No. C 297, (November 11, 1980), p. 3.

[30] "Statement by U.S. Industry Coordinating Group representing these organizations: The Chamber of Commerce of the United States, United States Council for International Business, The National Foreign Trade Council, The National Association of Manufacturers and the American Chambers—Europe (Euromed)," (March 1983), p. 2.

Problems with Disclosure

Addressing a group of American executives in New York, Ivor Richard, social affairs commissioner of the European Commission, under whose jurisdiction the Vredeling directive now lies, echoed a few of the central concerns of multinational employers with respect to the proposed directive. Richard noted: "business concerns for confidentiality and the potential cost burden of the proposals should be addressed. . . . [and] the scope of the consultation and information subjects might be too broad and ill defined.[31] In addition to confidentiality, cost, and scope of information disclosure, a fourth concern may be noted: the very political origin of supranational legislation, and its attendant risk of legislating unworkable solutions on those most affected—labor and management.

All these concerns pose a number of practical problems. In Belgium, the Netherlands, and the Federal Republic of Germany for example, where works councils are highly developed, law allows management to withhold certain information in order to safeguard confidentiality. In these countries and elsewhere, "works council members have to keep information confidential until senior management is able to release it to all parties simultaneously."[32] The obligation to represent employees and, at the same time, to maintain the confidentiality of company information may pose conflicts to employee representatives and union officials because of their dual allegiance, to the union or the work force, on the one hand, and to the company, on the other hand. "The obligation to keep information secret creates a dilemma for the unions. They often feel they cannot participate in a meaningful way in the affairs of the company if the information given to a minority of their representatives must be kept secret."[33]

Conflicts such as these beg the question of to what ends information should be disclosed. In the United States, the purpose of information disclosure is to enable unions to better represent their members in negotiations with management—to facilitate "meaningful negotiations," in the wording of Paragraph 2-B. But management also might benefit from the deeper understanding unions would have of its positions when they were provided with information. Ideally, then, information disclosure could constitute a means of creating a more peaceful industrial relations environment. Such a

---

[31] "Companies in Europe Reel in Wake of Amendments on Worker Information," *Business International*, Vol. XXIX, No. 15 (April 16, 1982), p. 121.

[32] Peel, *The Real Power Game*, p. 128.

[33] *Ibid.*, p. 129.

result, however, will not necessarily ensue. "Paradoxically, while the social and democratic arguments for disclosure of information are well-rooted, there is no firm evidence that disclosure will, in itself, improve industrial relations. Indeed, information disclosed on profit ratios, directors' salaries, job changes, or planned redundancies may well stimulate conflict rather than reduce it."[34]

Clearly, the ideologies of different union movements may also prove to stimulate rather than attenuate conflict. A union such as the communist Confédération Générale du Travail (General Confederation of Labor—CGT) in France, for example, could well perceive the disclosure of information as a means of furthering objectives other than peaceful cooperation and participation with management. More generally, information for the purpose of participation assumes a collaborative rather than an adversarial stance toward management's goals, and this in some cases may require a fundamental change in union strategies.

The ILO study on worker participation observed that "there is now some movement away from the idea of participation seen as collaboration between workers and management representatives on non-controversial subjects towards the idea of participation in dealing with conflict situations, most often involving bargaining in the broad sense of the term, whether formal or informal."[35] The demand for more information, therefore, is not to service passive ends, but is allied with the demand to use that information toward greater negotiation rights.

---

[34] *Ibid.*, p. 130.
[35] ILO, *Workers' Participation*, p. 199.

CHAPTER VI

Paragraph 3

Enterprises should:

> provide to representatives of employees where this accords with local law and practice, information which enables them to obtain a true and fair view of the performance of the entity or, where appropriate, the enterprise as a whole.

The former director of industrial relations of the European Commission has written that "European management faces an explosion of proposed legislation on corporate information disclosure. International bodies like the [International Labour Organization] ILO, [the United Nations] UN, [the Organization for Economic Cooperation and Development] OECD, and [the European Economic Community] EEC, indeed governments everywhere, are scrambling onto the disclosure bandwagon as fast as the legislation procedures will allow."[1] The OECD Guidelines for Multinational Enterprises are composed of seven sections, one of which is devoted entirely to the issue of information disclosure. That section counsels that

> enterprises should, having due regard to their nature and relative size in the economic context of their operations and to requirements of business confidentiality and to cost, publish in a form suited to improve public understanding a sufficient body of factual information on the structure activities and policies of the enterprise as a whole. . . .[2]

The aim of the information disclosure section of the guidelines is to "improve public understanding" of the operations of multinationals, and thus it is addressed to a broader constituency than just the employee representatives.

---

[1] Jack Peel, *The Real Power Game* (London: McGraw-Hill Book Company, 1979), p. 122.

[2] "Annex to the declaration of 21st June 1976 by Governments of OECD Member Countries on International Investment and Multinational Enterprises: Guidelines for Multinational Enterprises," in *The OECD Guidelines for Multinational Enterprises: A Business Appraisal,* P. Coolidge, G. Spina, and D. Wallace, eds. (Washington, D.C.: Institute for International and Foreign Trade Law, Georgetown University Law Center, 1977), p. 256.

The recommendations of Paragraph 3, however, provide for disclosure to employee representatives, rather than to individual governments or to the public at large. But as one commentator has remarked: "Presumably, what is disclosed to improve public understanding will be available to employees and their representatives. Does [Paragraph] Three imply that the latter are entitled to something more insofar as the enterprise as a whole is concerned? If so, what? This is left obscure."[3] Despite this ambiguity, the major difference between Paragraphs 2–B and 3 resides in the implication of different types of information to be disclosed.

The discussion of Paragraph 2–B dwells upon the subject of how different national laws and practices provide variously for the disclosure of information that would enable employee representatives to engage in "meaningful negotiations," or for the "development of collective agreements." There it was noted that the various rights of employee representatives to information are increasingly extensive, owing in part to the expansion of issues subject to negotiation.

A review of Table V-1 shows that information enabling employee representatives "to obtain a true and fair view of the performance of the entity" is provided in a number of countries, both in the context of the works council and through collective bargaining. Quarterly and annual reporting on operating results, employment, and training trends, and forecasts and investment plans are more often than not within the purview of employee representatives' rights to information, whether or not such information serves the specific end of negotiation. Further elaboration of these provisions in their national variety is not required for the present chapter.

Noted also in the discussion of Paragraph 2–B are instances in which national law limits the disclosure of certain types of information. These include "information which might affect national security, (or) harm a company's competitive position."[4] Paragraph 3, as well, limits the provision of information to those countries "where this accords with local law and practice."

Although there may be some ambiguity surrounding the word "entity," (does this signify the plant alone or the whole subsidiary?), there is little doubt that the "enterprise as a whole" refers to the multinational corporation. This language, therefore, constitutes the first, more or less explicit reference in the OECD Guidelines on

[3] USA-BIAC Committee on International Investment and Multinational Enterprise, *A Review of the OECD Guidelines for Multinational Enterprises: Employment and Industrial Relations* (New York, 1978), p. 23.

[4] *Ibid.*

Employment and Industrial Relations to the duties of the corporation as a whole, rather than to the subsidiary, a significance, as will be seen, that has not been lost on the international trade union movement.

DISCLOSURE OF INFORMATION IN THE UNITED STATES

Precisely where it is "appropriate" to disclose information on the enterprise, what information to disclose, and to whom to disclose it, are all undefined in the wording of Paragraph 3. National laws do, however, compel a broad range of information disclosure, if not specifically to employee representatives, then to public authorities. Moreover, it is possible that the provisions of the disclosure of information section of the guidelines constitute an indication of the type of information on the enterprise that ought to be disclosed. Among the OECD countries, U.S. law and practice on disclosure approximate most closely the recommendations embodied in the disclosure of information section of the guidelines. Table VI-1 illustrates the extent to which these recommendations already form standard practice for most U.S. multinationals.

The fundamental vehicle of corporate disclosure in the United States is the annual stockholders' report. As one business spokesman has commented: "With its substantial disclosure of information, (the annual report) would seem to be an ideal vehicle for making these (new) disclosures even though these annual reports may have been oriented more to shareholders and relevant investment communities than to a worldwide 'public' of diverse economic and social interests."[5] In addition to the annual report, corporations in the United States are required to file performance reports (Form 10-K) with the Securities and Exchange Commission (SEC), in which detailed information on corporations' individual lines of business is recorded. The Federal Accounting Standards Board (FASB), moreover, a government agency that regulates the form and content of corporate information disclosure, requires companies to disclose a broad range of information. Indeed, the disclosure requirements are so broad that, for the most part, as Table VI-1 reveals, "the information disclosure guideline provisions for reporting revenues by line of business is well covered by our own national reporting standards."[6]

---

[5] *The OECD Guidelines for Multinational Enterprises: A Business Appraisal*, p. 56.
[6] *Ibid.*, p. 59.

TABLE VI–1

The Disclosure of Information Section of the Guidelines Versus Information Disclosure Legislation in the U.S.

Disclosure of Information Section of the Guidelines	U.S. Law and Practice concerning Information Disclosure
Multinationals should publish information on:	
1. the structure of the enterprise, showing the name and location of the parent company, its main affiliates, its percentage ownership, direct and indirect, in these affiliates, including shareholdings between them;	Generally provided in the annual report.
2. the geographical areas where operations are carried out and the principal activities carried on therein by the parent company and the main affiliates;	Generally provided in the annual report.
3. the operating results and sales by geographical area and the sales in the major lines of business for the enterprise as a whole;	FASB statement 14 requires the disclosure of profits as well as sales revenues by lines of business. Line of business disclosure also required by Form 10-K.
4. significant new capital investment by geographical area and, as far as practicable, by major lines of business for the enterprise as a whole;	FASB statement 14 calls for disclosure by appropriate geographic areas of (a) sales to unaffiliated customers and inter-group sales or transfers among the geographic area, (b) operating profit or net income, and (c) identifiable assets held within those geographical areas.

TABLE VI–1 (continued)

5. the sources and uses of funds by the enterprise as a whole;	Covered by statement of changes in financial position required since 1971 by the Accounting Principles Board.
6. the average number of employees in each geographical area;	Generally provided in the annual report.
7. research and development expenditure for the enterprise as a whole.	Required since 1974 by the FASB Statement 2.
8. the policies followed in respect of intra-group enterprise;	FASB Statement 14 calls for disclosure of the basis of accounting for inter-segment and inter-geographic area sales or transfers. Changes in the accounting basis from period to period must also be disclosed.
9. the accounting policies, including those on consolidation observed in compiling the published information.	Covered by Accounting Principles Board Opinion No. 22.

Source: P. Coolidge, G. Spina, D. Wallace, eds., *The OECD Guidelines for Multinational Enterprises: A Business Appraisal,* Proceedings of the Workshop on the OECD Investment Declaration and Guidelines, March 16, 1977 (Washington, D.C.: Institute for International and Foreign Trade, Georgetown University, 1977), pp. 55–62.

Other sources of corporate information in the public record are the Census Bureau statistical reports, and the reports of the Bureau of Labor Statistics, which provide data on the general health of specific industries and levels of employment. Moreover,

> by the use of the published services and generally available library sources, a union knows the employer's financial position, the general health of its market, its record with union elections, the existing and new contracts governing its workers, and the sites at which particular union successes or failures have occurred.[7]

It is worth noting, in addition, that U.S. corporations are legally bound to disclose the vast majority of this information. It seems, therefore, that U.S. law imposes broader disclosure duties than do the voluntary guidelines.

A few examples, even though not comprehensive, provide testimony to the availability of information from multinationals. The United Automobile Workers (UAW), for instance, reports that "no difficulty has been experienced in receiving from the managements of Deere and Caterpillar pertinent information requested."[8] Ford's operations in the United Kingdom provide extensive information on the state of the automobile market as well as "production and material costs, productivity levels and anticipated price increases. Information is also given on the anticipated effect of wage increases in prices and sales."[9] DuPont, lastly, has been disclosing information in several areas since well before the existence of the guidelines:

> this includes basic information concerning enterprise structure; location, owernship, and nature of operations of affiliates; geographical areas of operations and principal activities. Sales and investment by geographic area also have been disclosed for several years and, of course, we have reported the sales and income of the major lines of business on a consolidated basis in accordance with SEC requirements.[10]

Taken together with the broad duties to disclose information to the unions, as noted in the discussion of Paragraph 2–B, it appears that extensive information is available from U.S. corporations.

---

[7] James T. O'Reilly, *Unions' Rights to Company Information* (Philadelphia: Industrial Research Unit, The Wharton School, University of Pennsylvania, 1980), p. 5.

[8] International Labour Office, *Social and Labor Practices of some U.S.-based Multinationals in the Metal Trade* (Geneva, 1977), p. 133.

[9] *Ibid.*, pp. 80–81.

[10] *The OECD Guidelines for Multinational Enterprises: A Business Appraisal,* pp. 69–70.

INFORMATION DISCLOSURE IN
THE EUROPEAN COMMUNITY

A survey conducted in conjunction with several European research institutes "found that simply to detail all proposed laws on disclosure in 10 countries covered 32 closely-typed pages."[11] A discussion of proposed—as well as actual—legislation on disclosure in these countries would be an undertaking of far greater length. Illustrative of existing structures of information disclosure to employee representatives, however, are the following two national examples of works council structures.

New rights to information for the works committees in France were discussed in Chapter V.[12] In other French legislation, meanwhile, the rights to information *on the enterprise as a whole* are granted to the *comité d' établissement* ("establishment committee"), an elected body composed of employee representatives in works committees of the individual plants.

> In numerous instances enterprises have several establishments, for instance in the case of a multi-plant enterprise one may consider that the various plants plus the head office constitute so many different establishments. In such case an establishment committee must be created in each different establishment. . . . When separate establishment committees do exist, a central enterprise committee must be constituted.[13]

The central enterprise committee is endowed with the same rights as the individual establishment committees, rights which include disclosure of the same information that is given to shareholders (in the case of a publicly held company).

In addition, the central enterprise committee has access to information on the general condition of the enterprise (mergers, concentration, decentralization, costs), the volume and structure of employment (including advance notice of anticipated collective layoffs), and global data relating to production schedules, profits, equipment changes, methods of production, and the effect of these on employment conditions. Finally, the committee must receive information on the evolution of wages and investment plans for the following year.[14] Such information would seem adequately to ensure

---

[11] Peel, *The Real Power Game*, p. 122.

[12] See Chapter V, p. 77.

[13] M. Despax, J. Rojot, "France," in *International Encyclopaedia for Labour Law and Industrial Relations*, Vol. III, R. Blanpain, ed. (The Netherlands: Kluwer, 1979), p. 150.

[14] *Ibid.*, p. 149.

the provision of a "true and fair view of the enterprise" to employee representatives.

In Germany, a similar works council structure exists:

> If the enterprise comprises several establishments, the central works council shall be established composed of the members of the establishment works councils. The central works council is competent to deal with matters affecting the enterprise as a whole or various establishments which the establishment works councils are unable to settle.[15]

Individual undertakings in Germany employing over 100 persons, moreover, must have an economic committee whose members are appointed by the works council and one of whom must be a works council member.[16] This committee is charged with receiving "information from the employer each month on production methods and plans, the financial situation of the undertaking, production and sales. It must be informed of investment plans, structural changes and any project appreciably affecting the interests of the personnel."[17]

With regard to obtaining a true and fair view of the enterprise as a whole, however, it is clearly the existence of employee representation on the *Aufsichtstrat,* or supervisory board, that would also ensure access to information:

> A supervisory board, elected by the shareholders' general meeting, has the duty of general policy guidance for, and supervision of the activities of, the company concerned; in accordance with the articles of association, it approves decisions of major importance such as the closure of establishments, the opening of new factories, major production changes or investments above a certain volume. It does not meet more often than four or five times a year, and elects the management board, which is the top management body responsible for the conduct of current business.[18]

Therefore, in addition to the existence of a central works committee, it is the participation of employee representatives on the supervisory board that allows not only access to information, but also the power to use it: "While works councils operate at the level of the production unit . . . the right of participation in management is exercised at the level of the undertaking or of the industrial group,

---

[15] Ramm, "Federal Republic of Germany," in *International Encyclopaedia for Labour Law and Industrial Relations,* Vol. III., p. 169.
[16] International Labour Office, *Workers' Participation in Decisions within Undertakings* (Geneva, 1981), p. 212.
[17] *Ibid.,* p. 213.
[18] *Ibid.,* p. 86.

whichever is the responsible legal entity. This right applies both in private companies and in public undertakings."[19]

The existence of a hierarchy of works councils as noted in the two examples above, however, does not mean that many countries' legislation on works councils does not already endow these plant-level industrial relations structures with the means of obtaining a larger view. Disclosure of information to the works council is intended very often to provide a true and fair view not only of the entity—but of that entity's situation within the enterprise. In Belgium, for example, information on productivity, the general state of affairs, and data "which enable the works council to ascertain the results being obtained" by the entity must be given periodically.[20] Significantly, the purpose of "this information is, according to article 3 of the Decree [1973], to give employees a clear and accurate view of the overall situation."[21]

The overall situation of the entity, however, includes "the position occupied by the (entity): in the economic or financial group to which it belongs, and, in the local, national, or international economy."[22] Similarly, in France, the new law on works committees would allow this information not only on the entity itself, but data "on important capital transfers between the parent company and its subsidiaries . . . By 'important capital transfers' is to be understood most notably . . . 'significant operations such as those that entail the gain or loss of control of a company by another.' "[23]

It is also through the works council in the Netherlands, for example, that employee representatives have access not only to information allowing them to gauge the financial status of the firm, but also "to annual financial statements relating to the individual firm itself and to any group of which it may form a part."[24] Recent legislation in the Netherlands, moreover, extends the obligation to form works councils to firms employing fewer than 100 workers: smaller firms are therefore now provided with the structure from which to obtain a larger view. Less clear, however, are the rights of employee representatives to information on parent companies not located in the country of the subsidiary.

---

[19] *Ibid.*

[20] Roger Blanpain, "Belgium," in *International Encyclopaedia for Labour Law and Industrial Relations*, Vol. I, p. 148.

[21] *Ibid.*, p. 149.

[22] *Ibid.*

[23] "Les comités d'entreprise," *Liaisons sociales*, No. 81/82 (July 8, 1982), p. 3.

[24] "Netherlands: Works Councils for smaller firms," *European Industrial Relations Review*, No. 101 (June 1982), p. 18.

WHEN THE PARENT COMPANY IS
A FOREIGN MULTINATIONAL

With reference yet again to new French legislation, lawmakers in that country have envisioned the creation of a *comité de groupe* ("group committee"), whose role it will be to "receive information on the activities, financial situation and employment trends in the group and in each of the companies of which it is composed."[25] When proposed, however, the bill attracted debate, over the very meaning of "group," a concept only loosely defined under French law. The law now defines a "group" of companies as comprising "a 'dominant' company and all subsidiaries of the dominant company (the latter constituting the 'parent' company of the subsidiaries) and all companies of whose capital 10–50 percent is held by the 'dominant' company when the enterprises committees of these latter companies have demanded and obtained inclusion within the group."[26]

A major exclusion to the new law's coverage are foreign multinationals. According to the law, a "group committee" would be formed by a "dominant company . . . whose headquarters are situated on French territory."[27] Prior to the law's passage, one legislator summarized problems that the proposed law's coverage would pose:

> 1. The dominant company is headquartered in France, certain subsidiaries are located in France whereas others are not. . . . A group committee would be formed, but will it be informed of the situation of foreign subsidiaries?
> 2. The dominant company is headquartered in a foreign country, certain subsidiaries are located in France whereas others are not. Will a group committee be formed?
> 3. The dominant company is headquartered in France and its subsidiaries in foreign countries. Can one, in this case, envisage the creation of a group committee?[28]

When passed, the scope of the law excluded employees in foreign subsidiaries included within the group. The issue, however, of obtaining information from an enterprise headquartered beyond national boundaries is currently being discussed in a forum above that of a national legislature, a subject to be explored later in the present chapter.

---

[25] "Les comités d'entreprise," p. 7.
[26] *Ibid.*
[27] *Ibid.*
[28] *Ibid.*

THE SOCIAL BALANCE SHEET

The performance of the enterprise as a whole may be gauged by other than purely financial data. In 1977, a French law established the *bilan social*, or social balance sheet, which was intended to display a wide variety of quantitative data on social aspects of the firm as a sort of appendix to the firm's annual report. Although addressed to the employee representatives, it is clear that the disclosure of information contained in the social balance sheet has been motivated as well by the objective of greater public understanding:

> Historically, the United States appears to have been the country of origin of the initial research undertaken on the social accounting of the firm. In reaction to criticism addressed to large corporations, certain among these were led to justify their activity on society. Paralleling this approach, an internal practice of the firm was developed toward the quantification of social aspects similar to financial accounting.[29]

The French law, whose coverage was progressively greater, was extended in 1982 to companies employing over 300 persons. The social balance sheet appears yearly, and is communicated to the enterprise committee fifteen days in advance of a special meeting during which the enterprise committee may discuss its findings with management. The yearly document presents information on "employment, wages, conditions of health and safety, other conditions of work (time and organization of work, etc.), industrial relations, living conditions of employees and their families which depend to a degree upon the enterprise (lodging, transportation, social activities of the enterprise committee, etc)."[30] The document contains information on the year and two preceding ones, and thus presents its data along evolutionary lines.

The publication of social information is not confined to France, of course:

> European companies are doing well in publishing social reports. Within Europe, German companies are in the lead, 25 companies having published such information during the last two years. Moreover, 300 German reports are in various stages of preparation.... These reports, which are published separately from annual reports, are long and immensely detailed, covering health and safety analyses, pollutant emissions, and even supplier dependency, as well as wage and salary structures. The assessments within the reports stress the com-

---

[29] "Le bilan social," *Liaisons sociales*, No. Spécial 8639 (December 1981), p. 9.

[30] "France," in *International Encyclopaedia for Labour Law and Industrial Relations*, Vol. III, p. 146.

pany's commitments to the needs and welfare of the various groups, and the way the company's activities affect the different groups is shown through indicators.[31]

Many authors have remarked that the growing demand for public understanding of multinational companies has spurred more extensive information disclosure. This particular social force—the interest in public understanding and "accountability" or "transparency" of multinational operations—would therefore seem as vital a trend as the more specific one of worker participation. They are clearly related and, together, their strength is reflected in the formulation of a series of proposed directives at the European Community (EC) level.

PROPOSED EUROPEAN COMMUNITY LEGISLATION

Chapter V introduced the discussion of the Vredeling directive, briefly summarizing the provisions of the proposed directive.[32] The significance of the proposed directive with specific regard to Paragraph 3, however, resides in the perception of a potential gap in disclosure duties between a subsidiary in one country, for example, and a parent company headquartered in another. The international union movement has been the most outspoken proponent of this perception. Indeed, the European Trade Union Confederation (ETUC) recently released an eighty-page document outlining eighteen alleged instances of the withholding of relevant information by multinationals.[33] The timing of the publication was deemed crucial by the ETUC in its effort to influence the course of the Vredeling directive through the European Parliament (EP). Accordingly, the document

> cites cases where workers were informed about the closure of their factory two weeks before the decision was to take effect, where national or local management themselves were unable to provide information because they were uninformed, thus rendering information and consultation agreements concluded at the local or national level inoperative, and where regular information given to workers was too general or merely contained details of final decisions which had already been taken by central management.[34]

---

[31] Peel, *The Real Power Game,* p. 124.
[32] See Chapter V, page 79.
[33] "Survey and Documentation of Cases of Conflict Involving European Subsidiaries of Multinational Corporations," *Multinational Service Fortnightly,* No. 133 (June 3, 1982), p. II-1.
[34] *Ibid.*

The ETUC contends that instances such as these are not isolated, and that they illustrate the need for legislation at the supranational level.

Employers, however, have argued that no such need exists, and that the costs of such sweeping legislation are potentially several, extending well beyond the financial burden that the disclosure responsibility would impose. As was noted in Chapter V, of particular concern to employers' groups is the issue of confidentiality incident on the disclosure of information to several groups, a problem aggravated by different views of what constitutes adequate safeguarding of business secrets, or indeed, of what those secrets are:

> One problem that arose in the discussion on this issue [in the European Parliament] was that in the original Commission text, the English version requires the employees' representatives, etc. to "maintain discretion" and the German version requires them to "maintain secrecy."[35]

A spokesman for the Confederation of British Industry (CBI), however, has noted that, "unfortunately not everyone is always discreet especially about confidental information. The imposition of penalties after secrets have been leaked is no redress to the employer even if the culprit can be identified."[36] The duty to maintain discretion within the context of an individual subsidiary can and has already posed some difficulties in practice.[37] It would seem ineluctably true that as the numbers (and interests) of those who are to share confidential information grow, control of that information is likely to diminish.

It is, moreover, unclear that the disclosure of information in itself will improve industrial relations in the multinational subsidiary— indeed, the opposite is easily imaginable. What, for example, might be the effect of a generalized disclosure of the multinational's investment priorities? It is possible that employee representatives in one subsidiary would not react with complacency to the investment projects of another subsidiary. Along with disclosure, the extensive consultation duties contemplated by the directive may, in the opinion of the CBI spokesman cited earlier, constitute an impediment to the competitiveness of European industry:

---

[35] "The Vredeling Proposal: The Ongoing Debate," Aegis Group (April 1982), p. 8.
[36] Confederation of British Industry document in the author's possession.
[37] Peel, *The Real Power Game,* p. 128.

> If strategic decisions are delayed, the competitive edge of Community industry blunted ... there will be less wealth created to pay for improving social affairs and less, not more employment.[38]

The directive provides that the information "shall be given in writing supported by documents and explained at a meeting with the subsidiary's employees' representatives .... [In addition,] the employees' representatives shall at all times be entitled to ask questions and receive answers."[39] A critical provision in the original wording of the proposed directive was the so-called "by-pass amendment," by which

> if the management of the subsidiary is unable or unwilling to communicate the information, (general information) the employees' representative may submit a written request to the management of the subsidiary, who then has four weeks (28 days) to provide the information. If the management of the subsidiary fails to provide the information after the 28 days, the employees' representative may nominate representatives to approach the management of the dominant undertaking directly, which is obliged to provide the information requested.[40]

The by-pass amendment was viewed both by the European Parliament and by employers with considerable concern, for it risked interrupting the process of industrial relations on a national, decentralized level. "Use of the by-pass option will not only undermine the authority and credibility of local management, but will also reduce the existing legally recognized autonomy of the national company."[41] It would have potentially, moreover, "extend[ed] industrial relations beyond the national context into a new dimension, the consequences of which cannot be foreseen."[42]

In a significant sense, therefore, the Vredeling directive in its original form would have furthered the dismantling of structures and remedies at the national or local level in favor of strengthening international solutions to industrial relations problems. The employers' minority opinion on the report of the Economic and Social Committee of the European Commission on the Vredeling directive summarized the risks inherent in the proposed directive:

> For reasons stemming more from history and collective mentalities than from law, the [socio-economic] context differs considerably from

---

[38] Confederation of British Industry document in the author's possession.

[39] "Proposal for a Council Directive on procedures for informing and consulting employees of undertakings with complex structures, in particular transnational undertakings," Text as amended and adopted by the European Parliament's Social Affairs and Employment Committee, April 1, 1982, Article 5, Section 3.

[40] *Ibid.*, Article 5, Section 4-a and b.

[41] Confederation of British Industry document in the author's possession.

[42] *Ibid.*

one country to another. There thus exists in each Member State an already vast ensemble of laws and established practices that allow a satisfactory response to the vast majority of problems that may arise. It is for this reason that, in attempting to harmonize Community law, one runs the risk of creating more problems than such harmonization would resolve.[43]

In the discussion of specific cases, subsequent chapters of the present study tend to corroborate the view that the "vast ensemble" of national laws that currently exist, as well as established industrial relations practices, have proved adequate for dealing with industrial relations problems, whether the undertaking is a local firm or a multinational subsidiary.

OTHER EUROPEAN COMMUNITY DIRECTIVES

Two other directives that seek to harmonize company law in the EC also aim at the disclosure and availability of information from the multinational. Of these, the proposed Seventh Directive on Company Law has the most direct bearing on the recommendations of Paragraph 3 of the guidelines. First proposed in 1976, the seventh directive was amended in 1979 following recommendations emerging from discussions in the EP:

> The directive is aimed at filling the gap left by the Fourth Directive ... over the preparation of consolidated accounts by groups of companies. These accounts should be drawn up to give a picture of the corporate group as a whole . . . .It is likely that companies will have to include in the consolidated accounts details of their holdings in affiliates—possibly as low as a 10 percent stake—as well as in companies over which they exert a significant influence, without necessarily having a large shareholding.[44]

Presently, the seventh directive is nearing adoption by the EC's Council of Ministers. As was noted earlier, the obligation to publish consolidated accounts is already legally prescribed under U.S. law.

Unlike the seventh directive, the fourth directive has already been adopted by the EC Council of Ministers. Its coverage extends to individual limited liability companies, although the issue of consolidated accounts for groups of companies was deferred to the seventh directive.

> The fourth directive lays down a detailed list of the information to be provided by companies in the balance sheet and profit and loss

---

[43] "CEE: Information et consultation des travailleurs," *Schweizerische Arbeitgeber Zeitung*, No. 16 (April 1982), pp. 290–91.
[44] "Update on EEC business law," *Multinational Service Fortnightly*, (January 7, 1982), pp. 4–5.

account of their annual accounts and also lays down minimum requirements for information to be contained in the notes to the accounts. The directive stipulates that the accounts must give a true and fair view of the firm's assets, liabilities and general financial position. Various definitions of valuation principles and methods are explained, with the directive sticking closely to the rules which relate to the historical cost accounting system.[45]

The terms and provisions of the fourth directive were to have been incorporated into the national law of the member states of the EC as of the beginning of 1982. Only two countries, however, have so far incorporated the provisions,[46] although the remaining member states are in the process of enacting legislation. Together, then, with the issue and legislative proposals surrounding the disclosure of information, the putting of that information into a homogeneous, intelligible form would appear to constitute a priority of legislation at the supranational level in Europe.

Although the seventh directive is nearing the end of its legislative journey, the Vredeling directive must still encounter obstacles to its passage. European unions however, were lobbying for such legislation well before the publication of the ETUC document outlining their perceived need for information disclosure. Arguably, one form that this lobbying effort has taken has been through the form of case submissions alleging infractions of the OECD Guidelines on Employment and Industrial Relations. The following discussions of individual allegations against two multinationals provide interesting cases in point.

PHILIPS

In 1976, Philips, the Dutch multinational in the electronics industry, announced its intention to close six subsidiary plants in the Federal Republic of Germany within the framework of a rationalization of the enterprise's international plant structure. The reasons, as outlined in the final settlement with the works council of one of the German plants, were several:

> Taking into account that structural market changes in the sector of electronic condensers on the one hand and unfair competition due to the growing import from low wage countries on the other hand, make it no longer possible for Philips Germany to continue its activity in the field of condensers . . . .[47]

---

[45] *Ibid.*
[46] The two countries are Denmark and the United Kingdom.
[47] "Information and consultation with works council and trade unions concerning

The Union's Allegations

The interest of the West German Industriegewerkschaft Metall (Industrial Union of Metalworkers—IG Metall) was in job security, and the union's submission of the case to the Trade Union Advisory Committee (TUAC) through the International Metalworkers' Federation (IMF) alleged a lack of information from the Eindhoven-based parent company to the subsidiaries. The union's charge focused on one plant in particular, a manufacturer of condensers located in Herborn, where, the union claimed, the plant closing would mean the shutting down of modern production facilities and the loss of 300 jobs:

> The closing down of the Philips plant in Herborn is a striking example of the lack of information from a multi-national to the workers and their trade unions in the decision-making process, and even after, concerning the actual employment situation of a whole workforce. It is also an example of rigid decision-making at international level without allowing for any reconsideration of measures to maintain production or to provide alternative employment opportunities in the course of consultations and negotiations with the trade unions on the merits of the whole case.[48]

The allegations above, however, were accompanied by further charges against the company. Claiming that even the management of the German subsidiary opposed the parent company's "rigid decision-making," TUAC's submission further stated that,

> in fact, the works councils and the Metalworkers' Union IG Metall heard, more or less accidentally, about the decision taken by Philips central headquarters in the Netherlands to close down the plant in Herborn. When the rumours became true, the whole matter had already been definitely settled. Furthermore, public authorities were not approached.[49]

The accusations implied that no steps had been taken by Philips either to inform the trade unions or to alleviate the plight of those to be left jobless. Indeed, TUAC's submission further alleged that only at the insistence of the unions were "severance pay and other social provisions" granted to the workers after the plant closure.[50]

---

the closing down of the manufacture at Herborn," statement by management of Philips Germany to the OECD meeting of March 30, 1977.

[48] "Failure of the Philips Company to inform trade unions and cooperate with them on plant closures in the Federal Republic of Germany," Submission by the International Metalworkers' Federation through the Trade Union Advisory Committee, March 30, 1977.

[49] *Ibid.*

[50] *Ibid.*

The Company's Position

The position stated by Philips on the plant closing offers a different view of what occurred. The management of the German Philips subsidiary emphasized the rather stringent requirements of German law in matters of information, consultation, and plant closings. As noted earlier, the Works Constitution Act of 1972 established an economic committee whose duty it is to be kept informed of the economic and financial position of the firm. The committee must therefore also be informed of impending plant closure intentions:

> The law says that information must be given and consultations held the moment the employer has the intention to close the enterprise. The employer is not allowed at that time to implement his intention, since the consultations with the economic committee must leave the possibility open to examine everything and possibly change the employer's intention.[51]

The claim that no information was provided, therefore, as well as the contention that the works council and the union "heard more or less accidentally" about the intention at a stage when the latter had already become a firm decision are serious charges. If true, they are clearly infractions of German law, specifically, of Section 6, Paragraphs 2 and 3.6 of the Works Constitution Act of 1972.

The logical remedy for the alleged infractions would have been through the German courts, a solution that was not taken by the German union. The alternative point of view is that the Philips subsidiary had behaved in conformity with German law, and that the allegations in the TUAC submission were either incorrect or misleading. The latter conclusion is implied in the recounting of events given by the management of Philips Germany:

> The management of Philips Germany informed the economic committee about its intention to stop the manufacture of condensers, during a meeting which lasted many hours. All the members of the economic committee participated at that meeting. These members are elected by the enterprise works council and are, consequently the legitimate representatives of all employees of the Philips enterprises as far as economic matters are concerned. Taking the information thus given into account the economic committee decided to hold another meeting for the purpose of seeking the intention of management. All the members of the economic committee were present at that meeting, including a representative of the trade union and management representatives from all plants, who might be concerned with the intended

---

[51] Roger Blanpain, *The OECD Guidelines for Multinational Enterprises and Labour Relations 1976-1979: Experience and Review* (The Netherlands: Kluwer, 1979,) p. 212.

closure (Herborn, Wetzlar . . .) That meeting also lasted for many hours.[52]

Procedurally then, there appears to have been no infraction, as the extensive information and consultation requirements of German law appear to have been undertaken before the decision to close had become definite. Most significant was the conclusion of the economic committee's deliberations:

> On the grounds of that [second] meeting the spokesman of the economic committee informed the management of Philips that the economic committee, even after consultation with the representative of the trade unions, saw no alternative solution to avoid the closure.[53]

Although an alternative to the closure of the Herborn plant did not emerge from the committee's discussion, a joint personnel committee was formed in order to discuss the transfer of some of the Herborn site's employees to the Wetzlar plant. This final step was not obligatory, but was undertaken by the management of Philips Germany in order both to alleviate the plight of Herborn's redundant work force and to fulfill a need for labor at the Wetzlar plant.

In several other meetings between labor and management, in which union representatives, accompanied by a legal advisor, participated, "negotiations prescribed by (German law) to settle the interests of the workers and the establishment of a social plan were initiated."[54] Both the settlement and the social plan were jointly accepted by management and the works council, and agreed to by the representative of the union. In closing down the plant's activities in 1976, the agreement stipulated that,

> in order to avert or to mitigate the resulting economic adverse effects for the employees due to the closure, Philips Germany and the works council of Herborn accepted a social plan. The works council agreed to the interest settlement and the implementation measure under Sections 111, 112 of the Works Constitution Act, notwithstanding the legal and conventional rights of co-determination of the works council.[55]

Conclusion

Of the many issues surrounding plant closure, German law imposes on the employer stringent duties of information disclosure, consultation, and the determination of severance benefits. It is thus

---

[52] *Ibid.*
[53] *Ibid.*
[54] *Ibid.*, p. 213.
[55] *Ibid.*

well within the purview of national law that any allegations or wrongdoing could have found legal remedy, and the absence of any legal claims surrounding the Philips Germany dispute would appear to support the company's claims of legally acceptable behavior. Perhaps more at issue here is a multinational's ability to allocate its resources based on economic, as well as social and legal considerations, without undue constraint, an issue to which attention will be given in Chapter IX.

BENDIX

Included in the submissions to TUAC on March 30, 1977, were allegations brought by unions representing workers at the KIP Kampeerwagenfabriek BV in Hoogeveen, the Netherlands. At that time, the Dutch company was a subsidiary of the U.S. multinational Bendix Corporation, which had purchased the company in 1972.

The Unions' Allegations

Two Dutch union confederations, the Nederlands Verbond van Vakverenigingen (Dutch Federation of Trade Unions—NVV) and the Nederlands Katholiek Vakverbond (Federation of Dutch Catholic Trade Unions—NKV) (which now, after merger, form the Federatie Nederlandse Vakbeweging) (Federation of Dutch Trade Unions—FNV) alleged that an international structural reorganization by Bendix, involving the sale of the Dutch company, KIP, to a Swedish company, CABBY, had involved an infraction of Paragraph 3 of the guidelines. The Swedish company had, until recently, also been a subsidiary of Bendix. Like KIP, the Swedish company had been bought by Bendix in 1972, although Bendix, by the time of the KIP dispute, had divested itself of CABBY.

The union confederations alleged that the proposed sale of the Dutch company to the Swedish one had been attempted without the Dutch unions being able to obtain sufficient information from Bendix on the financial repercussions of the sale. Information that would allow the unions to assess future employment security at the Dutch company was also wanting, the unions claimed:

> Managers of KIP Kampeerwagenfabriek BV had talks with the Industrial Federations of the Dutch Central Trade Union Organizations NVV and NKV. Director Nilsson of the Swedish camping waggon (sic) factory CABBY (which with KIP belongs to Bendix) is to continue KIP operations in Hoogeveen. To that end the KIP caravan factory is separated from the Bendix concern. KIP debts at the bank

are to be taken into the Bendix account. At the same time Nilsson is to take over the Swedish plant of Bendix.[56]

The talks between the managements of KIP and CABBY and the Dutch union confederations were a complicated series of transactions dealing with the sale of the subsidiaries by the multinational parent, Bendix. The unions, however,

> refused to give their approval to this plan; first they wanted insight into all the financial repercussions this would have for KIP. Also they wanted information about employment guarantees for KIP workers and the continued operation of the plant.[57]

The NVV claimed to have documents showing that the KIP financial accounts were "confused," whence the interest in the financial repercussions of the sale.[58] This interest was all the greater, because according to TUAC, in a meeting held at the Dutch Ministry of Economic Affairs between management representatives of KIP and Bendix and the mayor of Hoogeveen,

> it was disclosed that KIP was misusing fl. 1.25 million from the authorities. That money had been loaned to the firm to secure jobs for 151 workers. But meanwhile the personnel at KIP had been reduced to 134 people.[59]

The discussions with the unions and the public authorities appear to have left the impression with the former that Bendix was "slowly withdrawing from KIP; but there is no information from the multinational company on its real intentions."[60] In a summary of its charges, therefore, the TUAC submission read:

> There is a break-off of commitments by the company towards the public authorities with regard to employment security, and there is ignorance in the subsidiaries of management policies and decisions elaborated at the international headquarters, making it practically impossible for the trade unions and public authorities to negotiate in the interests of the workers.[61]

The Company's Position

After acquiring the Dutch and Swedish firms in 1972, Bendix found that it had bought companies that were having great difficul-

---

[56] Blanpain, *The OECD Guidelines for Multinational Enterprises*, p. 201.
[57] *Ibid.*
[58] *Ibid.*
[59] *Ibid.*
[60] *Ibid.*
[61] *Ibid.*

ties, were poorly managed, and in which poor management spilled
over into labor relations. After examining the situation and finding
that it would be extremely difficult to rectify, Bendix decided it
should not be in these businesses and proceeded to sell both firms.[62]

It would appear that the Dutch union confederations concurred
with the parent company's assessment of the management of the
Dutch subsidiary. It is somewhat confusing, however, (and the available evidence does not reveal) why there should have been an expression of doubt by the unions over the parent company's intentions
with regard to KIP. The TUAC submission reveals that Bendix had
divested itself of CABBY and that the latter had undertaken to
acquire the Dutch company. There would appear to have been linger-
ing concern over future employment security which, no doubt, neither the proposed new owners nor the Bendix Corporation may have
been able to assuage. It is equally apparent that the concern over
breach of loan obligations to the public authority was eminently
within the province of Dutch law. Indeed, as subsequent case discussions will show, Dutch employee representatives have unusually
extensive legal rights to challenge through the courts an employer's
management of a company.[63]

Analysis of Events

A new, more exacting law setting forth the provisions of works
councils in the Netherlands was enacted in 1979. Even prior to this
date, however, the works council had the right to be informed of and
consulted about major changes at a plant, including its proposed
sale. The failure to perform this obligation, then, would clearly have
been an infraction of national law, and remedies to such an infraction are available through Dutch legal channels. Such remedies do
not appear to have been pursued, a situation similar to that in the
preceding case discussion.

Unlike the Philips Germany discussion, however, the present
issues do not involve a decision by a foreign multinational to close a
subsidiary. They concern, rather, the proposed sale of a subsidiary,
and the TUAC submission itself indicates that the appropriate notification and consultation procedures preceded these proposed transactions. Parties to these discussions, moreover, included the unions,
the local managements, representatives of the multinational parent,
and the public authorities. Despite these discussions, and the fact
that their purpose was the sale of the Dutch company, it is alleged

[62] Telephone interview with company executive, April 1982.
[63] See Chapter IX, page 141.

that a true and fair view of the entity and its standing in the enterprise was somehow lacking.

The allegation is all the more surprising as the financial details of the proposed sale appear to have been the object of discussion between the managements of KIP and CABBY and the Dutch unions. Rather than ignorance, the NVV claimed cognizance of the "confused" financial affairs of KIP and, indeed, contrasted the situation in the Dutch company with that in the Swedish firm:

> The unions were kept informed about the [Swedish] company's negotiations with Bendix and could in every phase express their opinion. There was union approval of the decision to buy CABBY from Bendix, as well as to acquire ... the Dutch KIP .... At CABBY they are quite aware of the problems in the Dutch company KIP. The situation in the Swedish company is in flagrant contrast to the management methods and confusion and the adverse repercussions on the employment security of the workers in the KIP plant, which still depends on decisions made by worldwide management of Bendix.[64]

Ironically, it was precisely this dependence "on decisions made by worldwide management of Bendix" that the parent company had been seeking to resolve through the sale of the Dutch firm to CABBY.

CONCLUSION

Both cases discussed in this chapter allow the conclusion that interest in information disclosure, and especially that which ensures "a true and fair view of the entity," is intimately related to the interest in employment security. It is likely that the present economic climate enhances the perception held by some unions and governments that the employment destinies of local workers may be controlled by foreign forces over which the employees have little influence. This perception is in turn belied by the existence in many OECD countries of legal means to ensure the proper comportment of management in its duties to disclose information. Although no country has laws making it impossible for multinational or national employers to respond to economic forces, a growing regulatory climate, particularly at the EC level, is imposing ever greater constraints. The central role of information in industrial relations, introduced here and in Chapter V, is further explored in Chapters IX and XII.

---

[64] *Ibid.*

CHAPTER VII

Paragraph 4

Enterprises should:

> observe standards of employment and industrial relations not less favorable than those observed by comparable employers in the host country.

The recommendations of Paragraph 4 have occasioned little controversy either at the drafting of the guidelines or since then. Indeed, were one to consider the contributions of multinationals to the developing world, as some have,[1] one would likely conclude that multinationals have been instrumental in elevating the standards of employment and industrial relations in those countries. During the drafting of Paragraph 4, the Trade Union Advisory Council (TUAC) sought to bind multinationals to a similar role in the developed world. In TUAC's wording, multinationals would have had to provide employment standards "at least no less favorable than those established by good local employers,"[2] implying that multinationals' standards should exceed the average of those set elsewhere in the host country. Such a discriminatory obligation, however, did not appear in the final draft of the OECD guidelines.

Among member countries of the OECD, both law and practice, and a sophisticated labor market have all contributed to the determination of a high level of employment standards in those countries. For these reasons, as well as for fundamentally economic ones, one would expect multinational enterprises to have roughly equivalent standards to those of the local employers, and certainly not inferior. The data that exist in this area confirm this expectation.

Several reasons account for the ability of multinationals to afford standards of employment and industrial relations that are among

---

[1] See, for example, International Labour Office, *Employment Effects of Multinational Enterprises in Developing Countries* (Geneva, 1981).

[2] USA-BIAC Committee on International Investment and Multinational Enterprises, *A Review of the OECD Guidelines for Multinational Enterprises: Employment and Industrial Relations* (New York, 1978), p. 23.

107

the better in the developed world. Multinationals typically are among the more successful companies in the national market, and are found characteristically in industries of higher than average growth, and in industries of greater than average capital intensity.[3] All these factors bear directly on the ability of multinationals to offer wages that are relatively high and fringe benefits that are among the best in local markets.

AVAILABLE DATA: A SAMPLE OF FINDINGS

The conclusions above follow logically from general features of multinational corporations, particularly of those that enter relatively high-paying, high-technology industries. There remain, however, significant limitations on empirical findings for wages and working conditions, details of which are noted in an International Labor Organization (ILO) study on wages and working conditions in multinationals:

> First, considered as a whole the available evidence despite its volume, is quite fragmentary. Official government statistics on wages and working conditions do not separate out foreign-owned from other firms. Therefore, authoritative and comprehensive survey material is rarely available. Also in the mass of literature on multinational enterprises, very little attention has been given to their compensation policies. In the studies that do make some reference to the topic, usually only impressions or illustrations are provided. A second limitation is that when some comparative statistics are available it is not always an easy matter to determine the underlying reasons for the observed difference between the foreign-owned and local firms. These differences may arise because of the multinational character of the companies or they may be due to other differences between the two groups of firms being compared such as location, plant size, capital intensity and market position. . . . A third limitation arises from the fact that there are bound to be great variations between multinationals in the policies they follow not only between economic sectors and countries, but also within the same industry.[4]

These limitations notwithstanding, research that has been undertaken on employment standards of multinationals tends to corroborate the favorable influence of multinationals. Thus, for example, a major study carried out by the United States Department of Commerce attempted to compare wages of foreign and domestic firms in those developed countries that account for 75 percent of employ-

---

[3] International Labour Office, *Employment Effects of Multinational Enterprises in Industrialised Countries*, (Geneva, 1981), p. 97.
[4] International Labour Office, *Wages and Working Conditions in Multinational Enterprises* (Geneva, 1976), p. 2.

ment in U.S. affiliates abroad. It was found that U.S.-based firms paid wages comparable to those of local firms in the same industry and that pay increases through time were also equivalent.[5]

The ILO attempted to extract from United Nations (UN) statistical data average annual wages and salaries (excluding supplementary benefits) for U.S.-owned affiliates in fifteen OECD countries. This study concluded that U.S.-owned subsidiaries paid substantially higher wages and salaries in all but four of the countries surveyed. In only one of these four, moreover, did U.S.-owned firms pay less than local firms in the same industry.[6] Still other studies have shown that multinationals tend to pay higher wages and salaries on average in individual countries, ranging from a 5 percent differential in Belgium to considerably higher figures.[7]

The perception of higher wage and benefit standards among multinational firms is widespread. Ironically, multinationals in the United Kingdom have encountered some union criticism as a result of these higher standards. The argument proffered by unions is that the practice of paying higher wages or providing more generous fringe benefits has the effect of discouraging union organizing attempts.[8]

Another study in the United Kingdom illustrates the institutional constraints that all firms, multinational or local, may face if they attempt to deviate from industry pay standards. On the one hand, if foreign firms were unwilling to match the pay levels of national enterprises, they would be subject to a higher incidence of strikes. On the other hand,

> if the foreign firms follow an unusually high wage policy, they might have a better strike record themselves but be an indirect source of difficulties for national firms. . . .If the high wage policies of foreign firms in fact were an important problem one would expect to find greater strike activity and a relatively high incidence of wage claim disputes in the national firms, . . . it was found that after making adjustments for differences in industrial distribution, foreign-owned firms have fewer strikes. However, there was no difference between the two types of firms in the incidence of wage claims as a cause of strikes. Therefore, it was concluded that the wage policies of foreign firms do not appear to give rise to an unusually large number of industrial disputes.[9]

---

[5] *Ibid.*, p. 8.
[6] *Ibid.*, p. 9.
[7] *Ibid.*
[8] J. Gennard and M. D. Steuer, "The Industrial Relations of Foreign-Owned Subsidiaries in the United Kingdom," *British Journal of Industrial Relations,* Vol. IX, No. 2 (July 1971), p. 154.
[9] ILO, *Wages and Working Conditions,* p. 14.

It is likely that, particularly in the developed world, if multinationals did not provide standards equal to those of local firms, institutional factors would force conformity.

EMPLOYMENT POLICIES: SOME EXAMPLES

In an environment of heightened public scrutiny of multinationals, many corporations have perceived the need to publicize their positions on employment standards. U.S. firms generally feel that their pay scales are either at or higher than the level of other companies in the industry. In response to questions concerning policies on wages and working conditions in host-country operations of U.S.-based multinationals in the metal trades, companies remarked that their compensation packages and working conditions were as good as or better than those provided by local employers.[10] Ford commented that its subsidiaries strove to be "competitive" in their local labor markets, except for Ford Australia, which stated its policy to be in the forefront of Australia's automotive industry.[11] Caterpillar has stated that it seeks to "compensate people fairly, according to their contribution to the company, within the framework of prevailing practices (and to) protect the health and lives of employees by creating a clean, safe work environment."[12] General Motors attempts to rank high in the provision of wages and working conditions where it has subsidiaries. In Southampton, England, for example, the policy is "to provide wages and conditions as good as or better than the normal conditions of the country."[13]

Although these are policy statements and not empirical results, the remarks of these companies *inter alia* tend to corroborate various research findings. Despite, therefore, the several limitations of the available data, there is general agreement that multinational enterprises, in comparison with national employers, tend to take a leading role in providing superior conditions of work.[14]

> This view was expressed, for example, in the recent report of the International Organization of Employers on the social policies and practices of multinationals which maintained that the fringe benefits of those firms are at the top of the scale, especially in the area of pensions. Moreover, as for hours of work and paid holidays multina-

---

[10] International Labour Office, *Social and Labour Practices of Some U.S.-based Multinationals in the Metal Trades* (Geneva, 1977), p. 57.
[11] *Ibid.*
[12] *Ibid.*
[13] *Ibid.*
[14] International Labour Office, *Multinationals in Western Europe: The Industrial Relations Experience* (Geneva, 1976), p. 66.

tionals were said to keep to those generally accepted in developed countries.[15]

The employers' findings parallel those of studies by intergovernmental organizations, such as the ILO. Concurrence in these favorable findings, moreover, comes from trade union groups as well. Thus, "in an OECD meeting of trade union experts on the subject of multinationals, there was general agreement that these firms often provide better fringe benefits than domestic companies."[16]

DIFFERENT EMPLOYMENT STANDARDS?

Multinationals vary in their degree of integration. Moreover, it is not only the production processes that may be integrated, but communication and management systems as well. In general, the size and experience of multinationals may breed efficiencies that serve to distinguish them from local employers:

> Many multinationals tend to live in or create a somewhat special world. Their internal communications are more developed; they must be to operate far-flung companies. Their industrial relations functions, especially in the case of the United States firms, are often more professionalized. Their fringe benefits and sometimes wages they pay are often in the lead, compared to surrounding plants in Western Europe. Their systems of personnel training are often more 'modern' and developed and more inward based than is the case with most national companies ... Their wage systems, job evaluation, performance ratings and the like sometimes reflect their long experience elsewhere.[17]

Thus, if the employment and industrial relations standards of multinationals appear higher on the average than those of the local employer, these standards may also be different. To the extent that progress may be viewed as the result of the interaction of new ideas, the changes introduced by multinationals may be greeted as improvements, drawn from the global experience of the multinational firm. It is, of course, the local environment in which the subsidiary operates that ultimately determines whether multinationals' standards are substantially different from local practice, and, if so, whether these differences are improvements.

---

[15] ILO, *Wages and Working Conditions,* p. 39.

[16] Organization for Economic Cooperation and Development, Manpower and Social Affairs Directorate, "Meeting of Trade Union Experts on Multinational Companies," (Paris, 1970), p. 16.

[17] ILO, *Multinationals in Western Europe,* pp. 64–66.

INSTITUTIONAL AND ECONOMIC CONSTRAINTS

The implied capability of multinational subsidiaries to provide employment and industrial relations standards that are different from those that prevail in the local market is clearly dependent upon economic and institutional factors which vary from country to country, as well as among industries. Of the economic factors that are influential, the subsidiary's competitive position in the market, its size, and its market share constitute the constraints that determine a firm's ability to pay and to attract and retain employees. Obviously, the availability of labor in the local market is also a major criterion of these abilities. Whether the subsidiary is unionized and the level at which bargaining occurs may also be limiting factors in the firm's customary standards.

In many OECD countries, legislation regulates some aspects of working life independently of both the firm's unilateral decision making and the collective bargaining process. The length of the workweek, vacation entitlements, pension contributions, and other employer contributions to the welfare of the work force, as well as working conditions and safety and health standards are among the topics that frequently fall under legislated domains. Taken together, these institutional constraints and economic or market factors constitute powerful forces compelling the conformity of the multinational subsidiary to local standards of employment and industrial relations.

The meaning of Paragraph 4 has been applied not only to general standards of employment and industrial relations, but also to short-term fluctuations in those standards resulting from economic conditions. The following case discussion gives an example of one such interpretation of the paragraph's recommendation to observe favorable employment and industrial relations standards.

Warner-Lambert

The company is a major, U.S.-based multinational that develops, manufactures, and markets an extensive line of pharmaceutical, optical, and consumer products produced in 140 plants around the world, 40 or which are located in the United States. In 1976, the year in which the dispute to be described occurred, the corporation employed over 58,000 persons.[18]

In October of that year, Warner-Lambert announced that it was considering the closure of its Swedish operation for the manufacture

---

[18] Warner-Lambert *Annual Report* for 1976.

of razor blades, with the potential loss of some 240 jobs. The company announced that the decision would be contingent on the outcome of attempts to restructure the Swedish operations. Investments in the operation had been made in 1974. In 1975, however, the subsidiary had shown a loss.[19]

The Swedish subsidiary's management met with the Swedish union and, during consultations, suggested that the union accept a lower wage level than the national average for those grades of work in the industry. Management further argued that the economic hardship faced by the subsidiary, caused in part by high labor costs, compelled management to consider the transfer of its Swedish operation to the Netherlands. The union, however, contended that the subsidiary's wage level was already 12 percent below the national average. The results of the negotiations ended in no agreement and on January 3, 1977, management announced that the subsidiary would close. Notices of dismissal were sent to the work force in December 1976.[20]

The Swedish union was an affiliate of the International Metalworkers' Federation (IMF) which adopted the Swedish union's claims in a submission made to the Committee on International Investment and Multinational Enterprises (CIIME) through TUAC in March 1977. The IMF charged that

> a contemplated transfer of the production facilities was used as a means of grooming union representatives during collective bargaining negotiations, when the subsidiary had already paid wages less favorable than those observed by comparable employers in the region.[21]

The Swedish union had sought the help of the Swedish government. The latter, however, could offer no assistance to safeguard the workers' wages and jobs—and understandably so, as the subsidiary itself was in no position to offer similar assistance.

The request to lower wages constituted management's attempt to attenuate the negative effects of what it considered to be the inevitable closure of the subsidiary. The attempt was to prolong employment (and to forestall layoffs) for the period from October 1976 through June 1977, allowing ample time for negotiations with the union over the prospective closure.

The Opinion of the CIIME. In its review of the issues introduced

---

[19] "Policy of Warner-Lambert to Close Down its Operations in Sweden," Submission by the International Metalworkers' Federation to the Trade Union Advisory Committee, March 30, 1977.

[20] *Ibid.*

[21] *Ibid.*

in the TUAC submission, the CIIME expressed the opinion that Paragraph 4 was not meant to exclude multinationals from reaching less favorable agreements on wages than those observed in their host countries by local employers when economic necessity dictates such agreements. Paragraph 4 would seem only to imply that a multinational subsidiary should aim in good faith at restoring wages and working conditions to a level comparable to that of indigenous firms as soon as the specific circumstances which give rise to unfavorable conditions no longer exist.

In an analysis of the case, Roger Blanpain concurs with the view of the CIIME:

> It seems in the first place that "the standards of employment and industrial relations" referred to in Guideline 4 include wages; and that "comparable" leaves a certain amount of flexibility. In the second place, logic seems to indicate that since a national enterprise is allowed, respecting local law and regulations, to adapt its wages to economic difficulties, that the same must be possible for a multinational enterprise. The Guidelines do not discriminate between national and multinational enterprises and do constitute "good practice for all" . . . .Consequently, the Guidelines do not prevent a subsidiary adapting wages when economic and financial difficulties are experienced by the firm if such conduct, under local law and practice, is accepted in the country for national enterprises under comparable circumstances.[22]

CONCLUSION

An assessment of the performance of multinationals under Paragraph 4 can be compared and controlled with the findings on their performance under other paragraphs of the guidelines. One much discussed subject that such a comparison yields is the issue of the independence of the subsidiary from the parent company. As was affirmed in the Warner-Lambert case, Paragraph 4 does not preclude the short-term, downward adjustment of wages in periods of economic difficulty. That flexibility, allowed the national firm, must clearly also be allowed the multinational subsidiary. The legal and economic autonomy of the subsidiary in the operating context of the host country would seem implied by the CIIME's interpretation of Paragraph 4. On the contrary, however, the freedom to respond to economic conditions has been challenged, as Chapter IX will show, where the co-responsibility of the parent company for the subsidiary has been called into question.

---

[22] Roger Blanpain, *The OECD Guidelines for Multinational Enterprises and Labour Relations, 1976–1979: Experience and Review* (The Netherlands: Kluwer, 1979), p. 218.

CHAPTER VIII

Paragraph 5

Enterprises should:

> in their operations, to the greatest extent practicable, utilize, train, and prepare for upgrading members of the local labor force in cooperation with representatives of their employees, and, where appropriate, the relevant government authorities.

The recommendations of Paragraph 5 have occasioned little controversy, as "agreement on the content of this provision was reached without much difficulty."[1] Such agreement would hardly seem surprising, given, as the International Labor Organization (ILO) has concluded, that "in the industrialised countries, the multinational companies have made a remarkable contribution to employment by creating and maintaining something like 11 to 12 million jobs."[2] Moreover, in addition to creating employment, "one area in which multinationals generally lead most other companies is in the amount and range of training of personnel they undertake."[3] One purpose of training is to enable the "upgrading" of personnel, as the findings of a recent French study on the performance of multinationals makes clear: "Promotion is from within, or at least is endorsed, by all managements of foreign establishments."[4]

The degree of participation in training programs by government authorities and employee representatives, however, varies considerably from country to country. At the drafting of Paragraph 5, "union spokesmen wanted the words to make clear that representatives of employees and governments should be involved in training and upgrading activities 'at all levels of the local labor force, both in

---

[1] USA-BIAC Committee on International Investment and Multinational Enterprise, *A Review of the OECD Guidelines for Multinational Enterprises: Employment and Industrial Relations* (New York, 1978), p. 24.

[2] International Labour Office, *The Impact of Multinational Enterprises on Employment and Training* (Geneva, 1976), p. 20.

[3] International Labour Office, *Multinationals in Western Europe: The Industrial Relations Experience* (Geneva, 1976), p. 38.

[4] ILO, *The Impact of Multinational Enterprises*, p. 21.

basic and advanced skills.'"[5] The final wording of the guidelines does not overprescribe the range of cooperation with employee representatives, and leaves to the national context the determination of participation by government authorities.

Multinationals enjoy a superb reputation in the areas of employment, training, and upgrading of the local labor force. These areas, moreover, constitute perhaps the most tangible and immediate benefit of the multinational enterprise. A conclusion of the French study cited earlier, for example, held that "foreign MNEs' greatest contribution to local technology is undoubtedly through the training of French executives and specialists in new techniques or comparatively undeveloped branches."[6] Despite such acclaim, constraints on available data impose limitations to quantifying the effects of multinationals in these areas have, however, been included in studies undertaken by the ILO.[7]

A survey of the employment effects of multinationals can be found in Chapter I and no more detailed observations of that subject need accompany a discussion of Paragraph 5. A few conclusions may nonetheless be drawn. First and most significant, the job creation afforded by multinationals is undisputed and results both from investment in new plants and equipment and from the acquisition of existing facilities. "Foreign takeovers are considered very beneficial, for they have strengthened the firms concerned, especially if they were in difficulties before being taken over. Since national firms were unwilling or unable to absorb them, some businesses would have closed down but for foreign investors."[8] Some empirical evidence indicates that employment security in multinational companies may be greater than in smaller firms, since the former are often better able to withstand the employment effects of economic cycles.[9] Lastly, the majority of studies pertaining to the job-export phenomenon conclude that multinationals, in providing jobs elsewhere in the world, do not necessarily deprive their home labor markets of jobs. (See Table II–1 for summarized results of studies pertaining to these issues.)

---

[5] USA-BIAC CIIME, *A Review of the OECD Guidelines for Multinational Enterprises*, p. 24.

[6] ILO, *The Impact of Multinational Enterprises*, p. 27.

[7] Among these, International Labour Office, *Social and Labour Practices of Multinational Enterprises in the Petroleum Industry* (Geneva, 1977); International Labour Office, *Social and Labour Practices of Some US-based Multinationals in the Metal Trades* (Geneva, 1977); and ILO, *The Impact of Multinational Enterprises*.

[8] ILO, *The Impact of Multinational Enterprises*, p. 20.

[9] See Chapter II, p. 22.

EXPORT OF PERSONNEL?

An aspect of the employment effects of multinationals with closer bearing on the recommendations of Paragraph 5, is the staffing of the foreign subsidiary. For political, economic, and industrial relations reasons, the foreign subsidiary draws its personnel from the local labor market.[10] At an earlier stage of the development of multinational business, following the Second World War, the presence of expatriate personnel was a more visible feature of multinational employment than is currently the case. Several examples bear witness to the utilization of the local labor force by multinational subsidiaries.

In the mid-1970s, for example, General Motors employed only 374 U.S. citizens out of over 170,000 persons employed in its subsidiaries outside the United States.[11] Similarly, "Otis (a subsidiary of United Technologies) has a policy whereby most subsidiaries are staffed exclusively with personnel locally hired (including the managing director) with no American or third party nationals in senior executive or key technical positions."[12]

The Dow Chemical Company, one of the ten largest chemical companies in the world, has a similar commitment to the local labor market in which it operates. Forty-one percent of the company's 53,000 employees in the late 1970s were based in countries other than the United States.[13] Moreover, "Dow has adopted a considered policy of employing nationals to operate its facilities in the various countries. Thus, in 1975, 99 percent of its employees in Canada, 95 percent of those in Latin America, and 99 percent of those in Europe, were citizens of the countries where they worked."[14]

Although governments can easily control the level of foreign employees in their countries by means of withholding or limiting the duration of work permits to expatriates, the need for such control does not appear strong. In evaluating investment sites, multinational enterprises routinely take account of the available local labor force in terms of both quality and availability. In addition, it is most

---

[10] The potential for industrial relations conflict in mixing home-and host-country personnel in a hierarchical relationship seems clear. Especially in the personnel function of the subsidiary, the staff tends, for reasons of familiarity with the local context, law, and practice, to consist of host-country nationals.

[11] ILO, *Social and Labour Practices of Some US-based Multinationals*, p. 38.

[12] *Ibid.*

[13] Dow Chemical Company, *1978 Annual Report.*

[14] Herbert R. Northrup and Richard L. Rowan, *Multinational Collective Bargaining Attempts* (Philadelphia: Industrial Research Unit, The Wharton School, University of Pennsylvania, 1979), p. 247.

often less expensive to hire locally than to transplant home-country personnel overseas. The propensity to employ expatriate personnel would seem confined to the case of a subsidiary's encountering serious skill shortages or during some initial start-up period. In the latter case, the employment of expatriates is temporary. The general observation would appear true that, "as time goes on, the natural expansion of multinational enterprises appears to make it easier for local staff to reach responsible positions."[15]

TRAINING IN THE MULTINATIONAL

The training provided by multinationals constitutes the most fundamental level of technology transfer, and is thought to be one of the major benefits of multinational enterprises. There are clearly several reasons why training forms a special need for the multinational firm, and some of these would appear to relate to the nature of most multinational firms in manufacturing:

> [Multinational Enterprises] MNEs have been found to constitute a particularly high proportion of activity and employment in industries making relatively intensive use of both technology and capital. Thus, MNEs loom large in industries such as chemicals, pharmaceuticals, petroleum refining, electrical and non-electrical machinery and transport equipment, especially automobiles and parts. The food, drink and tobacco industries also represent an important sector of MNE activity.[16]

Industries of relatively high technology require a highly skilled labor force; and shortages of skilled labor have frequently been cited by multinationals as the cause of a fundamental need for comprehensive training programs.[17] Because multinationals tend to be in industries of higher growth, they may face relatively tighter labor market conditions, which could further exacerbate skill shortages.

Although the industrialized market economies offer relatively sophisticated labor markets, the need for training is by no means obviated. "From the comments given about the plethora of manpower difficulties experienced by the multinational enterprises around the world it comes as no surprise to learn that they have made major analyses of their training needs and have developed very substantial programs to meet these needs."[18] These programs

---

[15] ILO, *The Impact of Multinational Enterprises*, p. 27.
[16] *Employment Effects of Multinational Enterprises in Industrialized Countries*, p. 97.
[17] ILO, *Social and Labor Practices of Some US-based Multinationals*, p. 29.
[18] *Ibid.*

appear to extend from the lowest to the highest levels of the work force. An OECD study of training in multinationals reached the conclusion that multinational corporations "devote considerable attention to training, and proportionately more to vocational and technical training than to executive training."[19]

The Level and Scope of Training

The focus of most training programs, both in the identification of training needs and in the implementation of training programs, is the local subsidiary level.[20] Moreover, the ILO social policy studies in the petroleum and metal trades industries indicate that the purpose of training encompasses both the provision of technical expertise required to perform a specific job and the general training needed to facilitate promotion from within.

> The petroleum industry provides striking examples of comprehensive and continuing training programmes at all levels which are both general or specific, providing courses which may range from on-the-job training at departmental level or plant level and progressing, according to increased specialization, towards company or group organised courses conducted largely by the enterprises' own staff, but also relying, as appropriate, on public facilities.[21]

The ILO research cites the Exxon Corporation's training program as typical of those in the petroleum industry. Exxon's primary emphasis on employee training and development stems from the fundamental need to keep abreast of technological change in an industry in which such change is continuous and where geographical diversity is characteristic. Company policy is to "provide employment on a career basis, to build a solid foundation of qualified people and promote from within."[22] From this policy derives the company's division of training efforts along two separate lines: first is the assurance that "employees have the necessary skills to perform their present assignment and the second to promote their individual development."[23]

A third aspect relates to the scope and level of training. With respect to the former, the program begins with on-the-job training

---

[19] ILO, *Impact of Multinational Enterprises*, p. 29.

[20] The decentralized focus of training would appear to follow from the multinational subsidiary's reliance on the local labor market for its staffing needs and that market's specific qualities.

[21] ILO, *Social and Labour Practices of Multinational Enterprises in the Petroleum Industry* p. 49.

[22] *Ibid.*

[23] *Ibid.*

to which are added "especially tailored training courses and seminars within the company and special training and educational programmes outside the company."[24] The planning for such programs occurs at the local level: "the identification of training needs and actual conduct of training is a local responsibility and therefore most training is provided to nationals of the country where our operations are located."[25]

Fourth and final is the involvement of levels higher than the local one in the training process. Exxon's corporate and regional headquarters become involved in providing assistance and advice for specific program development needs.

Training Efficiencies of Multinationals

As in the example of Exxon, the sharing of information and experiences form the basis of Royal Dutch/Shell's regional training programs as well:

> Their basis is that a group of medium or small operating companies collectively develop a training program, with the duty of hosting the courses rotating among the participants. The value of such a scheme lies in its more efficient deployment of resources and the benefits of interchange between different companies in the same geographical region.[26]

The accretion of experience in different parts of the world may therefore give to the multinational subsidiary an advantage in terms of the content of training: "Multinational companies are almost without exception organizations with substantial operations and long experience in their own countries. Part of their growth and success can be attributed to their handling of manpower and skills as well as technical processes."[27] The multinational subsidiary has, on the one hand, a potentially vast pool of information, experience, and expertise to draw upon at the local level. On the other hand, the higher the level of employment, the broader the individual employee's exposure to training and development at higher than the local level. The examples above, even if in the form of statements of policy, appear to corroborate these conclusions.

The International Organization of Employers cites the example of one multinational "which first seeks to develop the nationals of each

---

[24] *Ibid.*

[25] *Ibid.*

[26] "Training in the Royal Dutch/Shell Group of Companies," April 1980, internal document in the authors' possession, p. 12.

[27] ILO, *Multinationals in Western Europe: The Industrial Relations Experience*, p. 35.

country to fill the majority of its managerial positions . . . thus pursuing a policy of 'localization'. This is then followed by the second step of 'internationalization', i.e., that of mixing nationalities at the top of the subsidiary."[28] Although the internationalization of personnel at the headquarters level may be a growing phenomenon, the development of host country nationals to fill the top spots at the subsidiary level is a more usual objective. Still, the latter policy may have an international dimension in that executives are sometimes rotated among subsidiaries or sent to the home office for training. In general, then, according to a survey by the International Organization of Employers, "training by the various companies takes place mostly in the place of employment, though fairly frequent secondments of middle and other staff to the parent company and in a few cases to other subsidiaries occur."[29]

Participation of Employee Representatives

The amount of participation by unions and other employee representatives in training programs varies considerably from country to country: "in many OECD countries, unions play little or no part in supervisory and management training."[30] The roles played by both labor and management in training at lower grades of the work force are subject to the same variety. The ILO's study of multinationals in the petroleum industry found that the responsibility for the development of training programs was thought by both labor and management to belong to management. Thus, "although the extent of workers' participation in the formulation and implementation of training programmes is limited or non-existent, no major difficulties or disputes seem to have arisen."[31] In many countries, however, participation in training programs by unions and workers' representatives does exist.

In the Canadian petroleum industry, for example, the Oil, Chemical and Atomic Workers' International Union (OCAW) negotiates training programs with the majority of the petroleum subsidiaries. In the U.S. automotive industry, the United Auto Workers (UAW) has a voice in training: "there are joint national safety committees in effect . . . and one of their responsibilities is the raising of safety

---

[28] *Ibid.*

[29] International Organisation of Employers, *Multinational Enterprises: The Reality of Their Social Policies and Practices* (Geneva, 1974), p. 24.

[30] USA-BIAC CIIME, *A Review of the OECD Guidelines for Multinational Enterprises*, p. 24.

[31] ILO, *Social and Labour Practices of Multinational Enterprises in the Petroleum Industry*, p. 53.

consciousness of all the workers generally, and the training of union safety representatives specifically. There are also apprenticeship training programs and, although the company is responsible for carrying out the training programs, the formulation of these programs is the result of collective bargaining."[32] In the United Kingdom, and to a more limited extent in the United States, unions may have a broad say in the employer's hiring decisions through the existence of the closed shop. In both countries the closed shop principally involves craft unions; and these unions through the training mechanism of the apprenticeship program, can also control entrance to a particular trade. In the United States,

> attempts to control entrance to the trade are limited largely to craft unions. Except for a few industrial unions, such as the United Mine Workers, which have been able to utilize license laws in some areas, industrial unions do not find it feasible to control entrance. Their members learn their tasks by experience. The unions permit the employer to recruit the work force, and union control is exerted in other ways. Craft unions, however, have found that control of entrance is an effective method of increasing their bargaining power. Their efforts to achieve such control take two principal forms: regulation of apprenticeship and support of licensing legislation.[33]

Licensing legislation in the United States, ostensibly "enacted in the interest of the safety of the consumer," has as its practical effect "to limit entry into the trade and to increase union bargaining power by making it difficult for employers to employ strikebreakers."[34] Such legislation is, moreover, one means through which both the government and the unions involve themselves in the training of a firm's work force.

In an ILO survey, meanwhile, union participation was reported to varying extents in the United States, the United Kingdom, France, Germany, and Belgium. In France, for example, employee representatives participate in training programs through the works committee, where their role is a consultative one without decision-making power. One French petroleum company noted that "training courses are organized in accordance with company needs, as well as the relevant legislation enacted in December 1972."[35] Such training is diverse and includes basic educational training for migrant workers.

---

[32] ILO, *Social and Labour Practices of Some US-based Multinationals*, p. 51.

[33] Gordon Bloom and Herbert R. Northrup, *Economics of Labor Relations*, 9th edition (Homewood, Illinois: Richard D. Irwin, 1981), p. 227.

[34] *Ibid.*, p. 233.

[35] ILO, *Social and Labour Practices of Multinationals in the Petroleum Industry*, p. 51.

In the United Kingdom, the Amalgamated Union of Engineering Workers, (AUEW) according to one company, "does participate in the formulation of training but not in the carrying out of training."[36] While the union may be involved in the training of shop stewards, however, it was further noted that "shop stewards do not have any influence on training at the local level."[37]

In the British petroleum industry, union voice in training programs is channeled through the national and regional committees of a government agency, the Manpower Services Commission, as well as through the Petroleum Industry Training Board, upon which unions hold one third of the seats.[38] Indirect representation of trade unions through government agencies also exists in Australia, where unions participate in the individual state training authorities of the Apprenticeship Training Commission.[39] In France, similarly, in addition to participation through the works committee, unions are involved in the National Interprofessional Association for the National Training of Manpower "which is managed on a tripartite basis (administration, employers' associations, unions). Workers willing to complement their knowledge or to acquire new professional qualifications are paid compensation allowing them to attend training sessions."[40]

In Belgium, as in France, unions in several industries receive information on training programs through employee representatives on the works council. Moreover, where works councils play a more significant role in industrial relations, as in the Federal Republic of Germany, the involvement of the employee representatives in training programs is greater. A German subsidiary of one multinational in heavy engineering noted that "the union has an important role. By law, the works council has full co-determination on vocational training and further training, which is put to complete use."[41] The ILO study of the petroleum industry notes, however, that "workers' representatives are legally entitled to participate in the formulation of vocational training programs, but not in their implementation, which is a function of management."[42] Table VIII-1 sum-

---

[36] ILO, *Social and Labour Practices of Some US-based Multinationals*, p. 34.
[37] ILO, *Social and Labour Practices of Multinationals in the Petroleum Industry*, p. 53.
[38] *Ibid.*
[39] ILO, *Social and Labour Practices of Some US-based Multinationals*, p. 35.
[40] M. Despax and J. Rojot, "France," in *International Encyclopaedia for Labour Law and Industrial Relations*, Roger Blanpain, ed. (The Netherlands: Kluwer, 1979), p. 45.
[41] ILO, *Social and Labour Practices of Some US-based Multinationals*, p. 34.
[42] ILO, *Social and Labour Practices of Multinationals in the Petroleum Industry*, p. 53.

marizes the works councils' rights to input on training programs in
several European countries.

TABLE VIII-1

Provisions of Works Councils Relating to Training

Country	Provisions
Austria	The works council must be notified in advance of recruitments and promotions, and may demand to be consulted on these subjects. It may participate in inspections relating to on-the-job training. It may participate in the planning and carrying out of on-the-job training and may sign company agreements on training.
Belgium	The works council may present its views and submit suggestions or objections on training activities. It may obtain information on the rules for recruitment and selection and may participate in the determination of rules to be followed in recruitment.
France	The works committee must be consulted on general problems relating to training. It sets up committees on training and its opinion must be solicited by the employer.
Germany	The works council has a right of codetermination on the selection of personnel criteria and on vocational training.
Luxembourg	The works council must be informed and consulted on manpower requirements and on training measures. It has the power of codecision on the establishment or amendment of the general principles governing the selection of workers and their assessment and promotion.
Netherlands	The opinion of the works council is required for collective recruitment. Codecision is required for the establishment or modification of measures concerning training and recruitment, and dismissal and promotion policies.
Spain	The works committee makes a special report before any decision is made on training plans.

Source: International Labour Office, *Workers' Participation in Decisions within
        Undertakings* (Geneva, 1981), 205–19.

With some exceptions, it seems that "as a general rule, workers
do not participate directly in either the formulation or the implementation of training programs at the manufacturing plants of the
multinational enterprises either in the USA or in the overseas countries."[43] This conclusion appears to imply the great role played by
on-the-job training in many firms as well as by more formal training
programs. The conclusion may be qualified, moreover, by the existence of union or employee representative input into training pro-

---

[43] ILO, *Social and Labour Practices of Some US-based Multinationals*, p. 32.

grams either through the collective bargaining agreement, as in the United States, or through the function of the works council in many European countries. In either case, the national context, rather than corporate policy, is the determining factor: variety in worker participation in training programs and their formulation stems more from "the host country environment than [from] policy differences from one multinational enterprise to another."[44]

Cooperation with the Relevant Authorities

Mention has already been made of the various organisms involving government participation on training boards in specific industries in countries such as France, the United Kingdom, and Australia. More generally, the cooperation of multinational companies with government and local authorities in the areas of employment and training is frequently wide-ranging. Such cooperation can and has extended to company assurances of employment creation in return for loans secured by the government or under other favorable terms. Governments of countries in the OECD would, however, be in violation of the "national treatment" provisions of the guidelines, which stipulate the equal treatment of local and multinational firms, were they to impose special employment and training requirements on multinationals alone. It is not surprising, therefore, that "the governments of Canada, UK, Germany, Switzerland, [and] Australia reported [in an ILO study] that there were no special agreements with any of the relevant multinational enterprises concerning employment, training, social and working conditions and labor relations, other than the general provisions of the law."[45]

Facing high levels of unemployment, many European governments are either considering or have already passed into law special provisions that seek, through tax or other economic inducements to companies, to create jobs. Government subsidies of various kinds in return for companies' hiring and training of the local work force are also relatively common.[46]

Tables VIII-2 and VIII-3 describe specific examples of cooperation between governments and multinational companies. These examples were recorded by ILO researchers in the 1970s. It is likely that the high levels of unemployment characteristic of the early

---

[44] *Ibid.,* p. 34.

[45] *Ibid.,* p. 40.

[46] *See, for example,* Robert B. McKersie and Werner Sengenberger, *Job Losses in Major Industries* (Paris: Organization for Economic Cooperation and Development, 1983).

1980s, and the job displacement resulting from technological change, will bring about closer cooperation between governments and corporations in the areas of training or, indeed, retraining for the future's occupational requirements.

TABLE VIII-2

Examples of Multinationals in the Automotive Industry
Collaboration in Training with the Public Authorities

Company	Collaboration in Training
Caterpillar	Collaboration with Belgian authorities results in a reimbursement of the company's training costs in three areas: special skill training of workers; managerial training in the US in specific functional areas; training of nationals which requires importing instructors from other countries. In England, there is cooperation with local training authority objectives by offering full craft training to apprentices rather than just those skills needed in the company. The company's record of cooperation has led to an exemption from the national tax levy.
Deere	The company reports an advantage of collaboration with public authorities in that the employees' training can be duly recognized by a government agency, so that the employees can be more readily hired in the future by another employer. In the Federal Republic of Germany, the company exercises influence in the formulation of training policy through membership on committees concerned with formal training requirements.
Ford	Ford collaborates with public authorities in the U.S. particularly in responding to requests for information for proposed training legislation. In the Federal Republic of Germany, collaboration with the authorities benefits the company in having the training program conform to its future manpower requirements. In Australia, mutual cooperation between the company and the authorities can lead to training courses even of a general nature having a significant orientation toward the automobile industry skill requirements.
General Motors	The company is strongly committed to working with public authorities in providing sound education and training opportunities for the people of their country. This collaboration takes the form of financial support as well as providing courses of study, methodology, and training equipment. In the Federal Republic of Germany, the company maintains a vocational school at its Russelsheim plant that is licensed by the State of Hesse, and run according to government regulations. In Belgium, many company members serve on the examination boards of technical schools.

Source: International Labour Office, *Social and Labour Practices of Some US-based Multinationals in the Metal Trades* (Geneva, 1977), pp. 38–39.

TABLE VIII–3

Host-Country Government Views on Contributions by
Multinationals in the Automotive Industry
to Manpower Training

Country	Opinion
Canada	The government noted that the company is responsible for on-the-job training of its employees, and reimburses employees for job-related training up to 70 percent of the cost. It also gives time off for management training.
West Germany	The multinational enterprises increasingly train their manpower on their own. No observations have been made of any important differences in the training of manpower by the subsidiaries of multinational enterprises from that of local companies.
Switzerland	According to information available to the federal authorities, one subsidiary does not have an apprentice training program. Nevertheless, the company has various programs for internal training of its personnel including language courses and other professional courses. One can consider that to a certain degree, therefore, the company contributes to the amelioration of the qualifications of its personnel.
Australia	Training by multinational enterprises is very closely linked to technology transfer: foreign companies play an important role in Australia in improving the skills of local staff, imparting the "know-how" necessary to operate equipment and in introducing new production techniques. Furthermore, the operation of multinational enterprises in this country involves the importation of advanced personnel and management practices. The development of local management skills is more pronounced in cases where Australian executives have some freedom in the decision-making process.

Source: International Labour Office, *Social and Labour Practices of Some US-based Multinationals in the Metal Trades* (Geneva, 1977), pp. 40-41.

CHAPTER IX

Paragraph 6

Enterprises should:

> in considering changes in their operations which would have major effects upon the livelihood of their employees, in particular in the case of the closure of an entity involving collective layoffs or dismissals, provide reasonable notice of such changes to representatives of their employees, and where appropriate to the relevant governmental authorities, and cooperate with the employee representatives and appropriate governmental authorities so as to mitigate to the maximum extent practicable adverse effects.

Plant closure is the one event that embraces several of the more hotly debated issues in the field of industrial relations in the Western market economies. All sides of industry, moreover, have a stake in the event. Employees are concerned, as they may be directly affected through loss of their jobs. Employers view plant closures as a sometimes necessary, even though painful, step toward the continuing profitability and general health of their enterprise. For unions, a plant closure may mean a loss of membership and thus a loss of dues revenues, in addition to the hardships created for their members. A plant closure, finally, may pose political and economic problems for local and even national governments.

All sides of industry feel strongly about their position on the issue of plant closure, and are often willing to go to great lengths to exact the most favorable concessions by way of collective negotiation or even legal means in an effort to protect their constituencies. Often, therefore, unions are unwilling to examine the global picture of a firm and are thus unmindful of the economic rationale behind some plant closures and reorganizations. Employers, on the other hand, may sometimes have to subordinate the social and economic consequences of their actions in a particular geographical area to the continued economic health of other areas.

It is sometimes claimed that multinational corporations add another dimension to plant-closure problems by being able to invest and divest in a given country according to purely economic motives.

130

Such a view, however, is somewhat oversimplified as studies have
shown that multinational corporations are remarkably stable in
their investment plans and, indeed, may be even more capable than
smaller domestic companies of weathering the impact of cyclical
downturns.[1]

Nevertheless, public attention has often been captured by well-
publicized occasions on which multinationals have allegedly proceeded to close a plant without prior notice or concern for social
consequences. Such events form the focal point for discussion of a
wide range of issues that include the disclosure of information, the
duty to consult with employee representatives, as well as the locus
of decision making in a multinational enterprise and whether investment decisions are part of the collective bargaining process *per se*.
It is thus that the language of Paragraph 6 makes implicit reference
to other paragraphs of the guidelines.

Paragraphs 2–A, 2–B, and 3 seem implied in a discussion of Paragraph 6 to the extent that the disclosure of information, and the
provision of a true and fair view of the subsidiary or of the subsidiary's place in the enterprise as a whole are oft-evoked issues surrounding plant closures. Paragraph 9 of the guidelines implicitly
enters a discussion of Paragraph 6 in that the locus of decision making is frequently brought into question in the closure of a subsidiary.
While reserving the latter issue for later discussion, it should be
noted that in no member country of the OECD must the decision to
close a plant be made jointly by labor and management. On the
other hand, in several countries, the decision to close a plant is not
the unconditional, unilateral prerogative of management. Rather,
specific consultative duties, often involving the search for alternatives to closure, must be undertaken. As one U.S. executive has
noted, "decisions about new or redeployed production facilities" are
not in themselves industrial relations questions. However, the
"effects or impact of those decisions on employees . . . are the concern of management industrial relations executives, and in most
firms these effects are an appropriate subject for consultation and
bargaining with recognized representatives of designated groups of
employees."[2]

The unions' view is, of course, somewhat different. In many of the
instances of alleged infractions of Paragraph 6 of the guidelines, the

[1] See Chapter II, note 25.
[2] Robert Copp, "Locus of Industrial Relations Decision Making in Multinationals," *Multinationals, Unions, and Labor Relations in Industrialized Countries*, R. F.
Banks and J. Stieber, eds., (Ithaca: New York State School of Industrial and Labor
Relations, Cornell University, 1977), p. 44.

unions' claims revolve not only around the brevity of the notice and failure to disclose information, but especially, and perhaps more significantly, around the failure of the company to explore all possibilities and alternatives to closure and layoffs.[3] The implication of this latter charge relates to union interest in participation in decision making and job security, issues which have emerged in various ways in several market economies, hence, for example, the inclusion of a "no-layoff clause" in some U.S. collective agreements. In many other countries, meanwhile, participative mechanisms extending even to economic decisions of the firm are in place.[4] Moreover, the interest in job security and participation is independent of industrial relations structures, the issues emerging through works councils as well as through collective bargaining.

In the drafting of Paragraph 6, the Trade Union Advisory Committee (TUAC) attempted to obtain the inclusion of language that would have granted a greater degree of employment security and have ensured compulsory cooperation among the firm, the unions, and the government "so as to plan manpower requirements, envisage measures for employment security and to mitigate to the maximum extent practicable adverse effects, avoiding social hardship."[5] Had such been the wording of Paragraph 6, further constraints on plant closure would have resulted.

TUAC also bid for the inclusion of language such that management would have been required "to enter into negotiations with the representatives of employees and their trade union organizations for the maintenance of employment and the provision of a social plan for the protection of any workers who might be affected."[6] Such wording appeared to the Business and Industry Advisory Committee (BIAC) as unrealistic and too restrictive on the ability of management to adapt to ever-changing economic environments. The elaboration of a "social plan" is nevertheless required in some countries, as a discussion of national diversity in the area of plant closures will illustrate.

[3] USA-BIAC Committee on International Investment and Multinational Enterprise, *A Review of the OECD Guidelines for Multinational Enterprises: Employment and Industrial Relations* (New York, 1978), p. 26.
[4] See Chapter VI, pp. 114–118.
[5] USA-BIAC CIIME, *A Review of the OECD Guidelines for Multinational Enterprises*, p. 26.
[6] *Ibid.*

NATIONAL DIVERSITY

Legislation on collective dismissals in countries within the OECD tends to fall into one of two categories. In the United States, Canada, Australia, and New Zealand, for example, there is no legislation on notice or consultation prior to mass layoffs, although in some of these countries, legislation affecting collective agreements can make mandatory the provision of some notice. In the countries of the European Community (EC), however, laws do provide for notification and consultation procedures.

The United States

In the United States, the National Labor Relations Act (NLRA) imposes legal responsibilities on both sides of industry through the structure of collective bargaining. Although the United States is often contrasted with countries in the European Community (EC) as a country in which plant closures constitute an unchallenged managerial prerogative imposing few duties of notification and discussion of the decision on the employer, three brief examples will clarify this impression.

First National Maintenance Corp. v. NLRB. The most recent doctrine concerning plant closures in the United States arose from a Supreme Court decision in 1981 (*First National Maintenance Corp. v. NLRB*), in which the court ruled that a decision to close a facility is not a mandatory subject of bargaining between the employer and the union.[7] The Court recognized that although an employer's decision to close a plant "had a direct impact on employment,"[8] the decision itself to close was nevertheless not amenable to the collective bargaining process. The Court, however, had considered whether the closure decision ought to be a mandatory subject of bargaining:

> After balancing the costs and benefits of making a closing decision a mandatory subject of bargaining—(the Court) stated unequivocally that "the harm likely to be done to an employer's need to operate freely in deciding whether to shut down part of its business purely for economic reasons outweighs the incremental benefit that might be gained through the union's participation in making the decision . . ."[9]

The ability to take economic decisions freely thus emerged from the

---

[7] Philip A. Miscimarra, *The NLRB and Managerial Discretion: Plant Closings, Relocations, Subcontracting, and Automation* (Philadelphia: Industrial Research Unit, The Wharton School, University of Pennsylvania, 1983).

[8] *Ibid.*

[9] *Ibid.*

Court's review of the case as a more compelling need than that of worker participation. That need was further explained by the Court:

> There is strong language in parts of the Court's opinion that defends managerial prerogatives generally, not just total or partial plant closings. The Court stated: "management may have great need for speed, flexibility, and secrecy in meeting business opportunities and exigencies. It may face significant tax or securities consequences that hinge on confidentiality, the timing of a plant closing, or a reorganization of the corporate structure. The publicity incident to the normal process of bargaining may injure the possibility of a successful transition or increase the economic damage to the business. The employer also may have no feasible alternative to the closing, and even good-faith bargaining over it may be both futile and cause the employer additional loss."[10]

It is no less true that, although the decision to close is not itself a mandatory subject of bargaining, the *effects* of that decision, including notification and severance pay, among other subjects, may be bargainable subjects. Two other recent cases illustrate the extent to which collective bargaining agreements may impose constraints on management's unilateral ability to close down operations and terminate employees.

The Singer Company. In 1981, the Singer Company, a major U.S. manufacturer of sewing machines (and a major multinational company since the nineteenth century) announced its intention to close its sewing machine manufacturing facility in Elizabeth, New Jersey:

> The company's employees now sue to compel Singer to keep the plant open. Plaintiffs contend that in exchange for millions of dollars for union "givebacks," the company agreed to keep the Elizabeth facility open for the length of the agreement by investing $2 million to restructure the plant and by using best efforts to keep the plant open, at least in part by securing defense contract work to supplement the manufacture of sewing machines. Plaintiffs claim that Singer has neither spent the $2 million nor used best efforts to secure defense work.[11]

The union's attempt to seek an injunction to keep the plant open was thus based on the terms of a collective bargaining agreement that, the union alleged, management had violated. The application for an injunction was, however, denied by a United States district court on May 21, 1982:

> The Court finds that the agreement, which is clear and unambiguous,

---

[10] *Ibid.*

[11] "Decision of U.S. District Court for District of New Jersey in I.U.E. Local 461 and District III v. the Singer Company," *Daily Labor Report* No. 101, (May 25, 1982), p. D-1.

contains no promise that Singer will refrain from discontinuing operations in Elizabeth. Therefore the Court will not enter an injunction
restraining defendant from closing the plant if it chooses to do so.[12]

The court's reasoning in refusing the injunction is significant, for
presumably, had the language of the agreement committed the company to keeping the plant open as a result of the givebacks, the
outcome of the union's suit might have been different. Resulting
from an interest in job security, instances of collective bargaining
agreements in which no-layoff clauses are specified, while not legion,
are nevertheless apparent in the United States. For example:

> In 1977, the United Steelworkers developed a proposal for a "lifetime
> guarantee" of work: essentially, this involves an extension of supple-
> mental unemployment benefits to provide payments for laid-off work-
> ers until an early retirement date. Since most senior employees do not
> suffer unemployment, such a program's cost is highly dependent
> upon the number of years of seniority that are required for eligibility.
> Moreover, if requirements for seeking employment are not included,
> workers involved in a plant closure could be paid many years for not
> working—an expensive proposition indeed.[13]

The implications of such an agreement on the growing fixity of
the labor factor in production are apparent. It is, moreover, the vehicle of the collective bargaining agreement, accompanied by individual National Labor Relations Board (NLRB) decisions, that has
been used in altering the rights of employees to their jobs. In the
Singer case, the language of the agreement appears to have been
equally unambiguous with regard to Singer's proposed use of the
$2 million giveback, as well as to the company's obligation to seek
defense contract work. The court thus ruled that the company was
in breach of this portion of the agreement, stating that although it
would "not compel Singer to stay in business . . . (it) will award
plaintiffs monetary damages in an amount to be measured either by
the value of the union 'givebacks,' which will be determined at trial,
or by the $2 million Singer promised, but failed, to spend, whichever
is greater."[14] This financial claim by the union against the company
was thus in direct response to the company's decision to close.

The Printing Industry. Mass layoffs short of plant closure may
also result from technological change that alters the conditions
under which an agreement has been signed. This case, involving the

---

[12] *Ibid.*
[13] Herbert R. Northrup and Gordon Bloom, *Economics of Labor Relations*, 9th Edition, (Homewood, Illinois: Richard D. Irwin, Inc., 1981), p. 241.
[14] I.U.E. Local 461 and District III v. the Singer Company, p. D-1.

printing industry, recounts such a conflict. As a United States Court of Appeals summarized in this case:

> By the late 1960s, new computer technology was beginning to work dramatic changes in traditional relationships between publishers and printers in the newspaper industry. Computers that could "scan" typewritten scripts and directly typeset their words without retyping by printers made it possible for highly skilled linotype operators to be replaced by less skilled employees and computerized equipment.[15]

Mindful of the impact of these technological changes on their jobs, representatives of a typographical union and a Cincinnati, Ohio, newspaper publishers' association signed what the parties termed the "Scanner Agreement" in 1974. The agreement appeared to guarantee lifetime job security to full-time employees ("situation holders") in return for the latter's acceptance of new equipment:

> The Post and Times-Star agrees that all regular situation holders and apprentices who will become regular situation holders, as listed in the Post's priority list dated May 1, 1974, *will be continuously employed for the remainder of their working lives by The Post as printers*, subject to voluntary terminations, voluntary retirements, disability retirements: as prescribed and defined in F.I.C.A. (Social Security Act) and involuntary terminations for just cause, as provided in Section 21 of the Contract.[16]

The court of appeals, in view of the wording of the Scanner Agreement, held the particulars of the case to be the following:

> In this case we are called upon to decide what effect should be given to an agreement in the newspaper industry guaranteeing lifetime job security for printers. The newspaper terminated the workers covered by the agreement following a partial reorganization and merger. We reverse the decision of the District Court which declined to give full effect to the job security agreement.[17]

The reversal of the district court's decision, and the upholding of a job security agreement by the appeals' court, is especially significant because the former's decision upheld the layoffs in part because of the expiration of a collective agreement—a criterion that was not held valid by the appeals court. The district court upheld the company, which

> (did) not challenge that language [of the Scanner Agreement] on its own terms. It [the company] argues, rather, that the apparent guarantee of lifetime employment is now ineffective for two reasons. It argues first that because the Scanner Agreement explicitly incorpo-

---

[15] "Decision of Sixth Circuit in Heheman v. E. W. Scripps Company," *Daily Labor Report*, No. 209 (October 29, 1981), p. D-1.

[16] *Ibid.*

[17] *Ibid.*

rates terms of and is otherwise dependent on collective bargaining agreements between the newspaper and its printers, it therefore expired when the collective bargaining agreement expired, in March 1981.[18]

The appeals' court disagreed, arguing that "nothing in the Scanner Agreement indicates that the parties intended its guarantees to expire when underlying collective bargaining agreements lapsed."[19] The appeals' court thus laid aside the district court's ruling, even though the appeals' court claims to have been "not unconscious of the traditional reluctance of courts to construe employment contracts as life-time guarantees."[20]

The few cases above are presented not as a comprehensive overview of the legislation surrounding plant closures and collective bargaining in the United States, but as illustrative of the extent to which the collective bargaining agreement can and increasingly has imposed constraints even on management's economic decision making. Examples are increasingly numerous of collective bargaining agreements that stipulate management's responsibility to provide several months' notice of prospective plant closures. Such agreements already exist in the rubber and printing industries in the United States, as well as in some major corporations, such as General Electric. Although the decision to close operations for economic reasons is not a mandatory subject of bargaining in the United States, other provisions of the collective agreement do impose obligations and constraints on both parties. Because of these, plant closings in the United States, as elsewhere, entail responsible economic and social planning and behavior.

The European Community

In the countries of the EC, legislation exists that supplements collective agreements with regard to collective dismissals for economic reasons. Specific provisions obviously vary from country to country, although the EC Council of Ministers has passed legislation tending to harmonize laws on collective dismissals in the member states. "As part of its social action programme, for instance, the Community drew up a draft directive on collective dismissals which was adopted by the Council of Ministers in 1975."[21] Employers who

---

[18] *Ibid.*, p. D-2.
[19] *Ibid.*
[20] *Ibid.*, p. D-3.
[21] Jack Peel, *The Real Power Game* (London: McGraw Hill Books [UK], 1979), p. 136.

plan collective dismissals within the EC must consult with the representatives of the employees about "the possibility of avoiding or reducing the redundancies and of mitigating the consequences of those which seem unavoidable. Redundancy plans must also be notified in advance to the competent public authority."[22]

Collective dismissal is defined by the EC directive to mean a layoff involving 10 or more employees in a firm employing under 100, or involving 10 percent of the work force in a firm employing 100–299, or 30 or more employees in a firm employing 300 or more workers—if the dismissal is scheduled to occur within 10 days. Where an employer contemplates dismissing more than 20 employees, he must give the employees' representatives at least a ninety-day notice and must consult with them concerning the impact of the collective redundancy. In addition, the directive requires that a government authority, such as the minister for employment or the office of manpower planning, be notified.

In 1979, the EC Council of Ministers passed a directive relating to the rights of employees in mergers, acquisitions, and takeovers of companies. The language of this directive recalls the issues raised by TUAC in the drafting of Paragraph 6 of the OECD guidelines in that employers, under this directive, are compelled to comply with the provisions dealing with prior notice, consultation, and cooperation with the relevant authorities in the event of mergers or takeovers.[23]

EC directives, however, set only minimum standards, and several member states have more stringent terms. In Denmark, for example, law places an obligation on the employer and the employee representatives to negotiate in an effort to find a means by which the planned dismissals can be avoided or kept to a minimum. In the Federal Republic of Germany, the law on codetermination compels prior discussion with the economic committee and the works council before a plant closure or collective dismissal may proceed. Despite the strictness of German law, it does not prohibit the closure of facilities for economic reasons. As they are economic matters, however, the economic committee must be informed in a "timely and thorough manner" about *inter alia* manpower-savings plans, cutbacks, or shutdowns of facilities or parts of facilities, any change in the

---

[22] *Ibid.*
[23] The Third Directive on Company Law, Directive No. 78/855, adopted by the EC Council of Ministers on October 21, 1978.

organization or purpose of works, and other matters and plans which could vitally concern the interest of the employees.[24]

In Belgium, a 1978 law on individual labor contracts "explicitly declares that failure and insolvency do not automatically terminate the individual labor contract. If the decision is made to close down a failing enterprise the employees will have to be dismissed with the appropriate term of notice or the corresponding compensation."[25] An "approach term of notice" must be given employees in Belgium, otherwise damages can be claimed. In principle, such financial awards would correspond "to the length of the term of notice which should have been served, or else that part of the term of notice which had not yet expired."[26]

The length of the term of notice is varied and extensive for plant closures in Belgium. Blue-collar workers must be given twenty-eight days notice if they have less than twenty years of service, and fifty-six days if they have more than twenty years of service. For white-collar workers, the situation is somewhat more complicated. The term of notice cannot be shorter than that given to blue-collar workers earning less than BF250,000 per year. But the term of notice for these employees is not specified by the law. The courts have determined that two criteria must be respected. First, the term of notice must give the employee the possibility to find a job comparable to his terminated one, and thus is determined as a function of his age, the situation in the labor market, and the importance of his functions within the firm. Second, the notice must be both an expression of, and a reward for, the loyalty of the employee to the firm. The length of service of the white-collar employee thus entitles him to a longer term of notice.[27]

For a firm to determine the length of the different notices to be given to different employees on the basis of such a complex system is impossible, and therefore, Belgian law and rules amount to a system of job security, an issue to which this discussion will return. The complexity of employers' obligations in the event of plant closures in Belgium illustrates the diversity of national law on the issue of plant closure. The apparently greater degree of job security afforded the Belgian worker renders it likely that something akin to the Belgian model was sought by TUAC in the drafting of Paragraph 6

[24] Martin Peltzer and Ralf Boer, *Betriebsverfassungsgesetz* (Frankfurt: Fritz Knapp Verlag, 1977), pp. 240–41.

[25] Roger Blanpain, "Belgium," *International Encyclopaedia for Labour Law and Industrial Relations*, Vol. I, R. Blanpain, ed., (The Netherlands: Kluwer, 1979), p. 95.

[26] *Ibid.*, p. 101.

[27] *Ibid.*, pp. 96–99.

in TUAC's attempt to ensure a fairly high degree of job security among employees of multinational firms.

Countries outside of the EC

Laws relating to collective dismissals in European countries outside the EC are similar to those of the EC countries. Employers in Austria, for example, must confer with the works councils when contemplating collective dismissals. In Sweden, meanwhile, employers must give at least 6 months notice if 100 or more employees are to be laid off. In Norway and Finland, statutes also require consultation and advance notice. In both countries, the dismissal of an employee will be deemed unreasonable if other work was available within the plant when the employee was laid off, unless the work is clearly incompatible with the person's training and experience. It should be noted, lastly, that many European countries provide collectively dismissed workers with severance payments in addition to those that the firm must provide. These payments, moreover, vary depending upon the period of notice given laid-off employees.

LIMITED RESPONSIBILITY

The status of a subsidiary—its relative autonomy as a legal and economic entity—is clearly a crucial subject in plant closures. In the event of bankruptcy, employees may join with other creditors of the company in making claims on the company's remaining assets. These assets, moreover, may be insufficient to satisfy the claims of all creditors. Although greater attention will be given this issue in the discussion of the Badger (Belgium) NV case below, it should be noted that here, too, national laws vary considerably, even though the principle itself of limited responsibility is well established in Western market economies.

With respect to the guidelines, it is obviously the extent to which the parent company may be held responsible for the debts of a subsidiary that is of interest. As Blanpain observes:

> German law provides for direct company responsibility in two instances: Creditors of a subsidiary can request the parent to offer security or to guarantee their claims when a contract involving the transfer of profits is terminated; in the case of the closest form of connection between enterprises, the integration of one company into another, the parent company is liable jointly and severally together with the subsidiary for the obligation of the latter. According to Article 101 of the French Bankruptcy Act which confirms an earlier judicial practice, courts may extend the subsidiary's bankruptcy to the parent company if the latter has abused the bankrupt enterprise as a

cloak or facade for conducting its own operations or abusively dis-
posed of the subsidiary's assets. In Belgium and Italy, case law provides for a similar approach.[28]

In England, Wales, Scotland, and Northern Ireland, on the other
hand, the principle of limited responsibility is more strictly defined.
The parent company in these countries is a separate legal entity
from the subsidiaries. Each can only be declared bankrupt separately, and not as part of a proceeding against another company.
Generally, the United Kingdom provides no remedy for claims
against the parent company if the latter is located outside of the
United Kingdom. Parent companies have no responsibility toward
employees who have contracted to work for a subsidiary. Clearly, the
laws uniting—and separating—parents and subsidiaries are considerably more complex than the present discussion allows and, moreover, have garnered a vast amount of attention with regard to multinationals. These issues are touched upon again in the following
analyses of individual charges of infractions of Paragraph 6 brought
by TUAC before the Committee on International Investment and
Multinational Enterprises (CIIME).

PLANT CLOSURE CASES

In the Netherlands, unions and works councils have the right to
challenge plant closure decisions through the courts. Not surpris-
ingly, therefore, a few of the most publicized recent plant closure
decisions have occurred in the Netherlands, and have been characterized by disagreement among the parties concerned and lengthy
court battles. Political support for unions seeking to preserve their
members' jobs has also been forthcoming, although Dutch Economics Minister Jan Terlouw has said that "we don't want international companies to think that when you invest in the Netherlands
you can never get out again."[29] Appendix C contains a discussion of
the ten-year history of the closure of Akzo-Enka's Breda facility;
and of the following four case discussions, two involve recent plant
closure decisions in the Netherlands and the remaining two, in
Belgium.

[28] Roger Blanpain, *The OECD Guidelines for Multinational Enterprises and
Labour Relations, 1976-1979: Experience and Review*, English text rewritten by
Michael Jones (Deventer, The Netherlands: Kluwer, 1979), pp. 143-44.
[29] Michael Van Os, "Foreign firms in the Netherlands seek jobs for workers that
they have let go," *Wall Street Journal*, September 9, 1981, p. 16.

The Plant Closure Issue in the Netherlands: Two Examples

Two multinationals with operations in the Netherlands have recently found their freedom to terminate employees or to close plants seriously constrained by the Dutch unions and courts. Both have become the object of accusations of infractions of Paragraph 6 of the guidelines before the OECD, while at the same time attracting considerable attention at the national level. In both situations, pieces of Dutch legislation that bear particularly upon the company's rights to terminate employment, and which, through the sponsorship of former European Commissioner Vredeling, have become models for legislation at the EC level, impeded the subsidiaries from proceeding toward closure. One of these laws provides rights to the works council, entitling it to challenge a company's decision with which it did not concur in the court of appeals. Another piece of legislation, the "Rechte van Enquete," endows trade unions with rights normally associated with stockholders by allowing the union to demand an inquiry into the management of the company in the event, for example, of the company's decision to close a plant. Both laws have been used effectively to block plant closures in the Netherlands.

This case involves two of a multinational's subsidiaries, both manufacturing plants.[30] One subsidiary, in the Netherlands, is 100 percent owned by the parent. The second facility, in another EC country, is majority-owned by the Dutch subsidiary with the remaining shares held by the parent, itself located in a third EC country.

Although distinct corporate entities, the two plants have constituted a single economic unit for over a decade. A committee was established to oversee the operation of both plants. The financial statements of each subsidiary were and remain consolidated for both accounting and managerial purposes. Research and development and the supply of raw materials are centrally located in the plant outside the Netherlands which supplies the Dutch plant with all of its export product requirements and 50 percent of the Dutch plant's domestic market product.

The company's market forecasting had noted a decline in the consumption of the product it manufactures and anticipated a further decline in the years to follow. Reasons for the diminishing market appeared twofold: evolving consumer tastes; and the necessity to increase the retail price of the product owing to a rise in government

---

[30] Information from company documents in the authors' possession.

excise taxes. For both reasons, the company foresaw little growth in the market for its product in either country. Taken together, both plants had been operating at a loss. Viewed separately, however, it was the non-Dutch facility that had been losing money, whereas the Dutch plant had been consistently turning a profit.

When the company chose to rationalize its operations by transferring production to just one facility, it chose the non-Dutch over the Dutch plant site. The principal reasons for the choice seemed compelling: the non-Dutch plant was modern, much larger and fully capable of absorbing the Dutch operation, whereas there was little room for expansion within the existing Dutch facility or at the plantsite, located in a residential area of a major city. In making its choice, the company was mindful of the social costs of a plant closure. Closing the non-Dutch site would entail over twice as many layoffs as at the Dutch plant. When the conclusion of a report recommending the closure of the Dutch plant was made known to the unions and the works council, their reaction was immediately against the move. The unions claimed that they had not been properly consulted in the discussions about the future of the Dutch plant, and that the decision to close the plant had in effect been taken several years prior to the announcement, again without the participation of the unions. The unions also claimed that the Dutch subsidiary should be viewed as an independent economic unit, and that the company had no reason and little right to close a profitable subsidiary.

A viability study on this matter, undertaken at the request of management and performed during 1976 and 1977, was released sometime later. In view of the declining market, the existing overcapacity, and the resultant loss of revenue, the report recommended that operations be rationalized and that the Dutch subsidiary be closed. The conclusions of that report were made known to the works council, an obligation consistent with the company's labor agreements and Dutch law. The Dutch Works Council Act provides that the works council be consulted before a final decision with regard to a plant closure is made. The act does not, however, stipulate that the works council actually make the decision or agree with the decision once it is made. A further meeting between management and the works council took place at the latter's request during which management further explained aspects of the above mentioned report.

The unions replied to the report in a document addressed to management, which management found to constitute a statement of the unions' unwillingness to further discuss the conclusion of the report. Management, therefore, responded to the unions' letter stating that, in view of the unions' unwillingness to discuss the report further, management would view the main conclusion of the report, the closure of the Dutch plant, as final. Management offered at that time to discuss any further details of the report, as well as the elaboration of a "social plan" concerning the prospective layoff of the Dutch plant's personnel. On the same day, management received a letter from one of the unions' lawyers, in which it was threatened to seek a court injunction against closure of the plant unless the company acceded to the demands put forth in a letter by the trade unions.

Sometime later, the unions sought and obtained an injunction barring the closure of the plant until differences between the unions and management had been resolved. The injunction was not to exceed the period of one year from the date issued. The company appealed the court's decision. The appeal, however, was subsequently dismissed.

The Issue in the Courts. In the meantime, two separate court cases had been brought against the company: one appealing the decision of the company to close down the plant, and the other accusing the company of mismanagement.

A Dutch court set up an inquiry into the management policy of the company, and from the standpoint of business economics, it cleared the company of the charge of mismanagement. Finding the company guilty of mismanagement on social grounds, however, the court annulled the company's decision to close the plant.

With respect to the charge of business mismanagement, the court upheld a fundamental claim of the company that the two subsidiaries be viewed not as separate entities, but as a single economic unit. The operating results of both plants were thus seen by the court to influence the economic decisions of the company. Specifically, the decision to close one plant because of the insufficient profitability of both plants did not, in the court's view, constitute mismanagement. It followed from the court's logic that even the decision to close a profit-making plant to increase capacity and revenue in a loss-making plant was not necessarily economic mismanagement.

The court found, however, that the company had mistakenly interpreted the unions' letter. The company had wrongly concluded that the unions and the works council were unwilling to participate in further discussions with regard to the findings of the report that had recommended the closure of the Dutch plant. The court interpreted the meaning of the unions' letter as less final: the letter had criticized the report and management's actions, and in addition, it had requested further information on several aspects of the report.

The court found apparent a willingness on the part of the unions to take part in further discussions when the general manager of the Dutch subsidiary met with a union representative. Both agreed to meet again to discuss the conclusions of the report. Despite this, charged the court, the company made known in another letter that it viewed the decision to close the Dutch plant as final. Such finality was premature, the court found. That the company had acted wrongly in breaking off discussions with the unions was further apparent in that, for many years, there had been a history of openness between management and the unions and works council in discussions over the Dutch plant's future. The company, the court further held, had been aware of the heightened level of employee concern with regard to the subject of closure.

The court found that the company made reassuring remarks to the employees which had led them to believe that their positions were, if not secure, at least not subject to elimination on such short notice. Supporting its view, the court cited that a senior manager of the Dutch plant, unaware of the conclusions of the report, had said to a union leader that he knew of no plans to close down the plant. As chairman of the works council, the court held that the manager's remarks were rightly perceived as endowed with authority, and wrongly raised employee expectations. Lastly, the court cited the company's adherence to the OECD guidelines as a final measure of the company's social mismanagement:

> The Guidelines . . . indicate that in a case like the one in question the employees' representatives should be consulted. Under these circumstances, [the company's] breaking off of the prescribed consultation with the unions and the works council constitutes a grave dereliction of its duty to conduct such consultation. Thus the company contravened elementary principles of responsible enterpreneurial activity. The decision to close the [Dutch] factory, which the company took contrary to these principles, accordingly constitutes mismanagement and should be annulled.

TUAC's Submission to the CIIME. TUAC, acting on behalf of the Dutch unions, requested that the Committee on International Investment and Multinational Enterprises (CIIME) interpret the guidelines in light of the allegations against the company. Of particular interest to TUAC was an interpretation of Paragraph 5 of the guideline's general policies section, in which multinationals are advised to

> allow their component entities freedom to develop their activities and to exploit their competitive advantage in domestic and foreign markets, consistent with the need for specialization and sound commercial practice.

Interpretation was also requested on Paragraph 6 of the guidelines on employment and industrial relations.

From the context of the Dutch court's decision on the union's charge of mismanagement, it is clear that the relevant section of the guidelines is the Paragraph 6, particularly whether "reasonable notice" of the company's intention to close the plant had been given. It is unclear what purpose—aside from that of broader publicity of the issue—could have prompted the submission of this case to the CIIME. Indeed, the Dutch court found that the company had abrogated its duty to consult with employee representatives, a failure held all the more blameworthy by the court since the company had espoused its adherence to the guidelines. It had clearly been within the competence of national law and practice that the company's actions had been legally evaluated—and a remedy at that level had been imposed.

Curiously, with regard to the recommendations embodied in Paragraph 5 of the general policies section, the Dutch court appeared to rule otherwise. TUAC held that Paragraph 5 was inconsistent with the company's attempt to close a profitable subsidiary in order to maximize profits elsewhere. The Dutch court, however, in considering both plants a single organizational entity, held that it was indeed permissible to support one plant to the detriment of the other. If there is to be any meaning to the "chapeau clause" that precedes the guidelines on employment and industrial relations, it must be seen as supporting the interpretation of the Dutch court. Although obviously not an indication of such explicit support, the CIIME, in its clarification of Paragraph 6, appeared similarly to uphold the freedom of multinationals to operate:

> The Guidelines, and in particular paragraph 6 of the Section on Employment and Industrial Relations, do not support the view that multinational enterprises should maintain existing employment levels or continue activities they wish to terminate, nor that they should guarantee re-employment for personnel dismissed as a result of closure of an entity.

Clearly, plans to close a profitable subsidiary in a period of rising unemployment were sufficient to attract the attention of the press and senior politicians. Moreover, the several issues involved in this case, especially those that appear to relate to the OECD guidelines have contributed to a sociopolitical debate from what initially had been an economic decision.

An agreement between the company and the unions and works council was finally reached, and the company appeared to have bowed both to the adverse publicity that had been directed against it and to the generally sensitive public and political climate. The principal points of the agreement were: the promise to suspend for the moment the company's decision to close down the Dutch plant; the guarantee of employment for some who would have been laid off; a joint study between management and the works council of alternatives to plant closure; and the unions' acceptance of the two plants as one organizational and economic unit.

Ford Nederland NV: Closing an Unprofitable Subsidiary

The most recent addition to the submissions of TUAC to the CIIME occurred on March 22, 1982, involving an alleged infraction of Paragraph 6 of the guidelines on employment and industrial relations by a subsidiary of the Ford Motor Company, the largest automobile manufacturer in the world. The allegations centered on the closure of production facilities at Ford's Amsterdam subsidiary:

> On 24 November 1981, the subsidiary of Ford Motor Company in Amsterdam, the Netherlands, was closed. Ford Amsterdam employed some 1,400 workers and was more than 95 percent owned by the parent company. The closure meant the dismissal of some 1,200 workers. Ford was to maintain only limited activities in the Netherlands, including a sales office and a credit facility for dealers.[31]

The closure of the plant came after more than a decade of unprofitable operations, prolonged by two occupations of the plant by striking workers and the outcomes of three court cases. Perhaps most significant, however, was the timing of TUAC's submission to the CIIME, occurring after the plant closure dispute had been settled at the national level, and after the courts' had found no wrongdoing on the part of the company. In its allegations against the subsidiary, TUAC has been placed in the position of challenging the principle "that if national legislation exists on items covered by the Guidelines, and if the enterprise has not violated this legislation, it has automatically respected the Guidelines."[32] Therefore, the issues surrounding the plant closure of Ford Amsterdam embrace far more than the closure itself.

Summary of Events.   TUAC notes that local management first announced the decision to close the Ford Amsterdam plant on January 13, 1981. After several months of consultation with the works council, management announced on April 24, 1981, its intention to

---

[31] "The Closure of Ford in Amsterdam and questions relating to the OECD Guidelines for Multinational Enterprises and their Implementation," Submission by the Trade Union Advisory Committee, March 22, 1982, p. 1.

[32] *Ibid.*, p. 4.

cease truck assembly operation as of September 30, 1981. Management was prepared to discuss a "social plan" that would determine benefits for the 1,300-plus employees to be terminated. The announcement, however, was met with mass picketing. Discussions in the works council, meanwhile, continued, and the picketing ceased when the works council and management reached a new accord, by which the parties would recommence consultation on the subject of possible alternative uses for the assembly plant. By June 24, 1981, however, no viable alternatives had been found, and management reiterated its decision to close assembly operations on September 30, 1981.

One basis of the unions' allegation of a violation of Paragraph 6 grew out of the failure to find alternative uses for the assembly plant. TUAC's submission alleged that

> the negative attitude of local management to alternative solutions which had been developed by the works council, the trade unions and a team of outside experts shows that there was no readiness to cooperate with the employee representatives and appropriate governmental authorities so as to mitigate to the maximum extent practicable adverse effects. The activities of management representatives were thus contrary to paragraph 6 of the Employment and Industrial Relations Guidelines.[33]

Clearly, however, another point of view would hold that, far from being unready or unwilling to cooperate, local management, in discussions of the alternatives to closure, held that none of them were, in fact, practicable. Subsequent attempts to mitigate the adverse effects of the closure could thus not find actual alternatives to closure, although the exclusion of this possibility was not an *a priori* stance, but rather the fruit of discussion.

In any event, as a result of the June 24, 1981, announcement, the picketing resumed, preventing the entry of senior management into the plant. On July 7, 1981, a court ordered the picketers to end their obstruction of the plant. At the same time, the court ordered the company to take no action to cease assembly operations pending the outcome of an inquiry into the management of the company in a suit filed by the unions. As in the previous case discussion, a legal inquiry was invoked to establish or disestablish the validity of management's decision to close.

The salient difference between the previous case discussion and the Ford Amsterdam situation would appear to be the economic health of the subsidiaries involved. In the former instance, the clos-

---

[33] *Ibid.*, p. 2.

ing of a profitable subsidiary proved to be a difficult political and
legal move. In Ford's case, the company had estimated that the subsidiary had lost over $117 million on its truck assembly operations
since 1969—and over $19 million in the first half of 1981 alone. More-
over, the company argued that only by closing the unprofitable
assembly operation could it preserve a sales and service operation
that had, until recently, been profitable.

The company attributed its losses to underused capacity, rising
costs of raw materials, and the appreciation of the British pound.
(Many of the subsidiary's assembly components were purchased
from the United Kingdom.) In bringing their charge of mismanagement, the unions claimed that among other things, Ford Amsterdam had exaggerated its losses by overstating transfer prices
between the United Kingdom and the Netherlands. Moreover,
TUAC charged:

> It should also be considered that for many years, the mother com-
> pany extracted large sums from the Dutch subsidiary by a system of
> excessive dividend payments to the parent company as well as by
> unwarrantable capital movements. The works council and the trade
> unions also had evidence that Ford Motor Company artificially
> depressed the financial results of the Amsterdam subsidiary.[34]

Presumably, a finding of mismanagement by the Dutch court of
inquiry would have upheld the unions' charges. The fact that no
such finding resulted, and that the subsidiary was cleared of the
charge, compels the conclusion that the charges themselves were
excessive and unwarrantable.

The injunction of July 7, 1981, of course, proved costly to the subsidiary, since it was forced to remain open. Management's response
was to claim that it would declare bankruptcy. Then, the parent
company announced that it would stop subsidizing the Dutch firm's
losses as of November 30, 1981. It was announced that the assembly
operation would close late in November 1981, and dismissal notices
were sent to the redundant employees one month in advance.

On October 28, 1981, a Dutch court removed the injunction
against the company and announced that the company could proceed with its closure plans. On November 24, 1981, the Ford Amsterdam assembly facility was closed. Finally, on December 10, 1981, the
Industrial Enterprise Chamber of Amsterdam dismissed the
union's charges of mismanagement against the company.

TUAC's Submission to the CIIME. The Federation of Dutch
Trade Unions (Federatie Nederlandse Vakbeweging—FNV) formu-

---

[34] *Ibid.*, p. 3.

lated its objections to the plant closure on the basis of alleged infractions of Paragraphs 1, 2, and 4 of the general policies section of the guidelines and Paragraphs 3 and 6 of the employment and industrial relations section. The company, the allegations read:

—did not take into account key policy objectives of the host country;

—did not co-operate wth the local community;

—did not provide the representatives of the employees information which would have enabled them to obtain a true and fair view of the performance of the subsidiary and the enterprise a whole;

—did not provide reasonable notice of its plans to the representatives of the employees although these plans had a major effect upon their livelihood; and

—did not co-operate with the employee representatives and appropriate governmental authorities in order to mitigate to the maximum extent practicable adverse effects.[35]

Paragraphs 1 and 2 of the general policies section of the guidelines recommend that multinationals "give due consideration" to the policy objectives and priorities of the host government. The FNV noted that Ford failed to consider such objectives: "The closure of the Amsterdam plant (a loss of 800 jobs) is not in line with these principles, since the Dutch Government is making every effort to prevent a rise in unemployment."[36] Clearly, however, to create or maintain employment at a loss-making subsidiary would foreshadow an unsound means of ensuring employment stability.

It was partially owing to the interest in employment stability that the Ford Amsterdam subsidiary originally undertook its truck assembly operation,[37] conforming in this way both to the employment objectives of the Dutch government and to the wishes of the employees. The question thus becomes one of how long such consideration should be maintained. That there may ultimately be overriding economic constraints to sustained employment seems implied by the CIIME's earlier review of issues surrounding plant closure:

> Paragraph One of the Section on General Policies recommends that multinational enterprises should fully take into account established general policy objectives of the Member countries in which they operate. Paragraph 2 of the same section brings forward some principal objectives of this nature including, *inter alia*, the creation of employment opportunities. Therefore, in case this latter objective forms indeed part of the host government's objectives, the multinational enterprise should give full weight to it, *inter alia* when it considers closing down an entity or diminishing the number of employees.

---

[35] *Ibid.*, p. 2.

[36] "The OECD Code is being eroded," *FNV News*, No. 16 (January 1982), p. 4.

[37] According, at least, to TUAC submission, p. 2.

These paragraphs, however, are not meant to prevent a multinational enterprise from closing down an entity.[38]

Interestingly, TUAC concedes in its submission to the CIIME that the company fulfilled its obligations with respect to information and consultation under Dutch law:

> If an enterprise respects national law and practice, it seemingly cannot act contrary to the Guidelines. However, it is possible that even if a subsidiary of a multinational enterprise has lived up to national legislation e.g. in terms of information and consultation with the representatives of the employees, the enterprise as a whole has not fulfilled its obligations under the Guidelines.[39]

As was noted earlier, these obligations included even the discussion of alternatives to closure. Obviously, the "maximum practicable mitigation" of the "adverse effects" of a closure would have been the decision to maintain operations and not close, a decision that the company viewed as economically infeasible.

The implication of the last sentence of the citation above, however, that "the enterprise as a whole has not fulfilled its obligations," is the most crucial allegation against the company. TUAC's view is that: "the closure of Ford Amsterdam appeared to be part of a broader reorganization plan which concerned the European activities of the enterprise."[40] TUAC recounted that the Dutch unions and works council had requested that information on the company's European plans be handed over to them. Local management refused, stating that these strategic plans were neither in the possession of local management nor in a form that would be insusceptible to grave risks to confidentiality and secrecy.[41]

The Dutch courts, particularly the one charged to review the management of the subsidiary, do not appear to have viewed such disclosure as obligatory in the Ford Amsterdam case. TUAC's allegation is no less significant, however, for the principal issue at stake is the potential confrontation between the economic integration of some multinationals and the role of individual subsidiaries in that integration. Curiously, the solution (to date) of the previous case discussion was that, in return for keeping the Dutch plant open, the unions have acknowledged the economic interdependence of the Belgian and Dutch subsidiaries. To so acknowledge is to recognize as well that subsidiaries may be integrated units.

---

[38] Blanpain, *The OECD Guidelines for Multinational Enterprises*, pp. 171–72.
[39] "The closure of Ford in Amsterdam," p. 5.
[40] *Ibid.*, p. 3.
[41] *Ibid.*

In Ford's case, it is unclear how the disclosure of the company's Europewide strategic plans could have possibly *not* conflicted with the different objectives of local or national constituencies. It is unreasonable to assume that disclosure of the "full picture" would have made any more palatable the closure of a loss-making subsidiary. Nevertheless, it is the "international perspective" that, TUAC insisted, should be the focus of this closure occurring in national context.[42] Ultimately, however, and especially in times of economic contraction, there would seem to be an inherent conflict between the full autonomy of the subsidiary, on the one hand, and the worldwide profitability of the enterprise, on the other. It is just this issue, rather than the behavior of a multinational in a national context, that appears in part to have motivated TUAC's submission to the CIIME.

New Rationale for Submission of Cases to the CIIME. Through legal and contractual means at the national level, the plant shutdown case of Ford Amsterdam has been closed. That the issues have been explored and solutions found through reference to national law and practice, however, begs the question of why the case has now been submitted to the CIIME. A possible answer appears to be that it is not so much a clarification of individual passages of the guidelines that is being requested, but a review of the machinery for implementing the guidelines. The FNV recently wrote:

> The FNV is far from satisfied with the observance of the OECD code for multinationals in the case of the closure of the Ford plant in Amsterdam. The FNV holds the view that the Dutch contact point for control of observance of the code has functioned unsatisfactorily.[43]

It appears that the Dutch contact point failed to involve the contact points of other European countries in which Ford subsidiaries operate. Rather, the Dutch contact point appears to have given greatest weight to the existence of national means of resolution to industrial disputes, and thus appeared to uphold the language of the "chapeau clause." Again, as TUAC observed:

> The contact point seemed to imply that if national legislation exists on items covered by the Guidelines, and if the enterprise has not violated this legislation, it has automatically respected the Guidelines.[44]

TUAC disagreed with this logic and, in so doing, appeared to imply that national legislation is inadequate in its treatment of items cov-

---

[42] *Ibid.,* p. 2.
[43] "The OECD Code is being eroded," p. 4.
[44] "The Closure of Ford in Amsterdam," p. 4.

ered by the guidelines. Rather, TUAC appeared to propose an expanded role—that of mediation—for the contact point:

> The national contact point should go beyond only making references to either OECD documents, such as the 1979 Review Report, or national legislation, and should engage itself actively in assisting the parties concerned to find solutions.[45]

Arguably, in its recent submission to the CIIME, TUAC is lobbying to expand the authority of the voluntary guidelines and, to this end, to develop further the role of the national contact point:

> The CIIME should focus on the ways in which the Guidelines can function as a valuable supplement to established procedure and national law in situations where international restructuring of operations take place. In addressing this question, the CIIME should also give a view on what could or should be the contribution of governments, employers and trade unions in implementing the provisions of the Guidelines in such cases.[46]

Multinational employers view the implementation of the guidelines as the usual result of good business practices. It is clear, however, that a view of the guidelines as a "supplement to established procedure and national law" is inimical to the spirit of "national treatment" of multinational subsidiaries, the "chapeau clause" of the guidelines, and the guidelines' voluntary status.

Badger (Belgium) NV

Of all the cases to have come before the CIIME, the closure of Badger (Belgium) NV has undoubtedly received the broadest attention in public fora, to the extent even of having become something of a *cause célèbre* to those who favor stricter international controls on multinationals.[47] Part of the reason for its publicity is supplied by the Belgian trade unions themselves, who viewed the Badger case as a test of the effects of the guidelines on multinational enterprises.[48]

Badger Belgium was a wholly owned susidiary of the Badger Co., Inc., which, in turn, is wholly owned by the Cambridge, Massachusetts-based Raytheon, Inc. Badger is a major construction and engineering firm, a builder of processing plants for the chemical, petrochemical, petroleum, and fertilizer industries, employing a worldwide staff of 2,500, of which 800 are professional engineers.

---

[45] *Ibid.*

[46] *Ibid.*, p. 5.

[47] The critical role of the Badger Case surrounding the implementation of the guidelines is discussed in Chapter I, p. 5.

[48] TUAC's submission to the CIIME reads: "Test case of the Effectiveness of the Guidelines."

Formed in 1965, Badger's Belgian subsidiary employed, at the time of its closure in January 1977, 250 highly skilled professionals, approximately 50 percent of whom belonged to the Landelijke Bedienden Centrale (LBC), the Christian Union for White Collar Workers.[49]

Summary of Events. On September 17, 1976, management of Badger Belgium was informed of the company's intention to close the Belgian subsidiary. Management informed the employees of this intention on October 13, 1976. Low levels of investment in the areas serviced by Badger Belgium for two years prior to the fall of 1976 were cited as the principal reason to close. The company further commented:

> The decision taken by Badger to close Badger (Belgium) N.V. was necessary because of continuing poor prospects for orders in Belgium and in other areas served by Badger (Belgium) N.V. Although Badger (Belgium) N.V. had all the capabilities to generate its own workload, on some occasions in the past it had been necessary for it to perform work for other Badger companies in a subcontracting capacity. Because of rapidly increasing costs of personnel services in Belgium in comparison with other countries and because of client and government restrictions, it became increasingly difficult or impossible for Badger (Belgium) N.V. to qualify as a subcontractor to other Badger companies.[50]

The years prior to the decision to close were characterized by peaceful relations between management and the unions. The LBC, it was noted, had never undertaken a salary drive against Badger Belgium, as in the words of the LBC's national secretary, "labour laws were strictly implemented and high wages were paid."[51]

During the fall of 1976, negotiations with U.S. and Belgian companies were undertaken in an effort to sell Badger Belgium. "The Belgian government authorities were notified and were requested to assist in the sale of the company or by other means to preserve the employment of its personnel and to mitigate the effects of the closing."[52] Throughout the negotiations, Badger Belgium's employees were kept abreast of developments. The attempts to sell the subsidiary were unsuccessful, and on December 23, 1976, the employees were informed of the imminent closing of the subsidiary. On January 14, 1977, the employees were individually given notice. Wages for

---

[49] Roger Blanpain, *The Badger Case* (The Netherlands: Kluwer, 1977), p. 85.

[50] "The Badger Case: The company's side of the story," *Commerce in Belgium*, No. 316 (October 1978), p. 17.

[51] Blanpain, *The Badger Case*, p. 79.

[52] "The Badger Case: The Company's Side of the Story," p. 17.

the whole month of January were paid in addition to the legally due
vacation pay and the premium for group insurance.

Term of Notice and Severance Pay. Under Belgian law, the
length of the term of notice of dismissal for white-collar employees
is determined by salary level and seniority, and limited by the time
that it takes for the employee to find a new job. The criteria leave
much flexibility to the courts, the arbiters of dismissal terms,
which, in deciding the actual length of the term of notice required,
may take into consideration such details as the employee's age, the
situation of the labor market, and the importance of the employee's
job functions.

It is precisely this flexibility that became a major source of dispute in the closing of Badger Belgium. In the company's words:

> Severance settlement formulas in Belgium are the most extensive in
> Europe and are fixed by negotiation or by the courts. In recognition
> of that fact, the entire assets of Badger (Belgium) N.V., approxi-
> mately 100 million Belgian francs ($2.8 million), were left in Badger
> (Belgium) N.V., which represented an average termination salary of 8
> months per employee on the closing date. Since operations started in
> 1965, all earnings and profits of Badger (Belgium) N.V. have remained
> in Badger (Belgium) N.V. No dividends were ever paid.[53]

These terms were held as unsatisfactory by the Belgian unions,
which demanded an additional 100 million Belgian francs. The
unions refused, moreover, to allow this supplemental sum to be paid
out of a special fund especially set up by the Belgian government
to pay the indemnity due employees in case of the employer's
insolvency.

The Parent Company's Responsibility. The obligations of a parent company to its subsidiaries may be viewed from both a legal and
an economic point of view. These points of view, moreover, may conflict, for although the status of the subsidiary as a separate, legal
entity would seem well established, subsidiaries may be characterized by greater or lesser economic integration:

> Legal reality is such, that headquarters and affiliates are constituted
> as separate legal entities. Being separate means that each one has a
> separate responsibility and that each entity is, as already indicated,
> only liable to the extent of its assets. Economically, however, head-
> quarters and subsidiaries are part of the same group, which acts as a
> unit, controlled and managed by headquarters, which means that
> headquarters are, in fact, responsible for a number of decisions . . .
> this raises the question whether this economic responsibility should
> also be legal . . . which conflicts with the legal principle of limited

---
[53] *Ibid.*

responsibility, meaning that headquarters are not legally responsible for the consequences of its decisions versus the affiliates.[54]

The Belgian unions demanded that the parent company contribute to severance payments in excess of the remaining assets of Badger Belgium. Such a demand roundly conflicted with the separateness of the subsidiary as a legal entity.

The conflict was all the more apparent in that Badger Belgium had never, in the years since its formation, paid dividends or repatriated profits and earnings to the parent. A considerable degree of economic autonomy thus appears to have characterized the subsidiary along with the fact of its legal autonomy. Arguably, therefore, it was not specifically the issue of the parent's responsibility in the closing of a subsidiary that was central to the unions' claim, but rather the controversial fact that the parent was a multinational headquartered outside of Belgium. Such a view appeared to be suggested by the "test case" status accorded the Badger Belgium closing. One commentator noted that:

> The OECD regulations specifically state that there shall be equal treatment between nationals and multinationals. Of the several bankruptcies of Belgian national companies within the recent past, I am not aware of any accusation or pressure put on the shareholders of these companies to be responsible for debts over and above the net worth of the company. . . . Is it because the major shareholder of BBNV is a multinational company that it is being attacked in the OECD?[55]

That the unions refused to accept additional payments from a national fund specifically designated for that purpose may have further suggested that the Badger closing had been singled out. The submission of the case to the CIIME in March 1977 was thus seen by the company to have less to do with the closing of Badger Belgium than with the furtherance of other union objectives:

> Despite Badger's efforts to comply with the voluntary guidelines of the [OECD] formulated in June 1976, attempts were made by the unions and the Belgian government to bring the Badger (Belgium) N.V. situation before the OECD as a test case to impose on multinationals extensive obligations far beyond those applicable to national companies.[56]

Resolution at the National Level. As has been noted, the original demands of the unions outstripped the value of the subsidiary's assets by the same amount again:

---

[54] Blanpain, *The OECD Guidelines for Multinational Enterprises*, p. 143.

[55] Blanpain, *The Badger Case*, p. 109.

[56] "The Badger Case: The Company's Side of the Story," p. 18.

The Belgian unions demanded from Badger a supplemental payment of over 100 million Belgian francs. The unions demanded full payment for all employees, irrespective of when the employees succeeded in finding new employment.[57]

Initial demands were subsequently scaled down. Also, senior executives from the parent company agreed to join in negotiations with the unions and the Belgian government over the terms of the closure. With the Belgian government acting as mediator, a meeting between Badger executives and government officials on March 22, 1977, resulted in a positive breakthrough. The company recorded the settlement as follows:

> Since Badger and the Belgian unions were willing to come to a reasonable solution, negotiations were reopened after the Belgian government decided to act as mediator. This occurred prior to the meeting in Paris on 31 March 1977, of the [CIIME] established by the OECD Council. The tripartite discussions with the Belgian government and the unions were satisfactorily concluded. To meet its social obligations in full, Badger agreed in April 1977 to increase the assets of Badger (Belgium) N.V. from 100 to 120 million Belgian francs.[58]

Clearly, the most significant outcome of the Badger Belgium settlement was the involvement, both financially and through its personnel, of the foreign parent in a national legal event, the plant closing. The parent's involvement, moreover, was at its own initiative, encouraged by national pressure groups and the publicity resulting from its having been a test case.

The CIIME's Clarification. The CIIME's clarification of the meaning of Paragraph 6 implied a "shared responsibility" by the subsidiary and the parent in the event of a plant closing:

> On the main question "whether a parent company which, through its ownership exercises a significant influence over the activities of a subsidiary, should have a responsibility of its own for the subsidiary's giving reasonable notice of an imminent shutdown and whether it should share responsibility for mitigating the adverse effects of a shutdown on the employees dismissed, one may equally conclude that parent and subsidiary share the responsibility for giving employees 'reasonable notice' when operational changes which would have a major effect upon their livelihood are being contemplated as well as for termination indemnities to the employees of the subsidiary. As to the amount of such indemnities or how early notice must be given, the Guidelines give no guidance other than a general reference to local law, regulations and prevailing labour relations and employment practices. And for good reason, since there are considerable differences between OECD countries in this respect."[59]

---

[57] *Ibid.*
[58] *Ibid.*
[59] Blanpain, *The Badger Case*, pp. 118–19.

The Badger Company had never argued that the closure of its Belgian subsidiary was not its responsibility. Indeed, the company's actions from the moment the intention to close the subsidiary was announced were characterized by involvement in the search for a buyer, negotiations with the unions, and discussions with the government, until a final settlement was reached.

Although "reasonable notice" and the amount of severance payments are nationally determined, the status of the subsidiary as a separate legal entity would seem inadequately resolved. In the three cases discussed thus far, the precise legal and economic status of the subsidiary would appear to have occupied a central position of concern in each—although from conflicting points of view. Thus, for example, the Dutch unions in the first case discussion argued that the Dutch subsidiary be viewed as an autonomous, profit-making subsidiary, whereas, in the Badger case, it was clearly the subsidiary's dependence upon the parent (and thus the parent's responsibility) that was argued by the unions. In the latter case, moreover, it was apparently in large part the contentiousness of the severance pay issue that involved the parent in the dispute to the degree that it was. As the following example illustrates, other multinationals have encountered problems similar to those of Badger in their operations in Belgium.

General Telephone and Electronics

General Telephone and Electronics (GTE), headquartered in Stamford, Connecticut, was formed by the merger of the second largest telephone communications company in the United States and Sylvania Electric, a manufacturer of electrical and electronics products. In 1981, GTE had sales of $11 billion and 227,000 employees.[60]

Like other manufacturers of televisions, GTE's manufacturing arm, known as GTE-Sylvania, has sold facilities that have become unprofitable. Early in 1980, it sold its television manufacturing facilities in the Federal Republic of Germany (Saba) and France (Videon) to the French group, Thomson-Brandt. Excluded from the sale was GTE-Sylvania's color television plant at Tienen, Belgium, because Thomson needed no additional tube production. This meant that a plant employing 880 employees would have to be closed in Belgium where, as has been noted, extraordinarily high dismissal

---

[60] Annual Report, General Telephone and Electronics, 1981.

compensation is required for plant closings, where unions are encouraged to seek even greater dismissal allowances, and where the issue of plant closings, in a climate of high unemployment, receives considerable political and public attention.

GTE scheduled the plant closure for September 19, 1980. The probable closing of the plant was discussed with the Belgian unions, but the unions claimed that GTE had violated the OECD guidelines by not disclosing the information that the agreement with Thomson contained an option for Thomson to purchase most of the plant's manufacturing equipment by the end of 1980. GTE noted, however, that it had adhered to Belgian law. The company undertook to provide jobs for redundant tube plant employees by expanding incandescent lamp production in two of its other plants in Tienen and announced further expansions for early 1981. For those employees for whom no work could be found, GTE offered the full legal dismissal pay required by law and added benefits that varied in amounts according to the individual's seniority and salary. In addition, the company cooperated with the unsuccessful government efforts to sell the facility to the Japanese firm, Toshiba.

All this would seem to have met not only the requirements of Belgian law, but also any possible interpretation of the guidelines. The unions, however, sought even more generous dismissal allowances including three-year salary guarantees, during which GTE would pay the difference between unemployment benefits and a worker's last salary.

It is clear that the Belgian union viewed the GTE situation as another "Badger," and an attempt was made to bring the dispute before the Belgian national contact point, despite the fact that no procedure recommending this existed. GTE, for its part, appears to have complied with both the spirit and the letter of Belgian dismissal legislation, in addition to having attempted to mitigate the job impact of the plant closure. GTE's continued presence in Belgium, and its ability to absorb some of the otherwise redundant employees, thus appeared to distinguish it from Badger Belgium's predicament.

The GTE closure was finally settled with promises of dismissal allowances surpassing those required under Belgian law. After a strike, a sit-in, and threats of legal action and possible action at the OECD level, GTE agreed to supplement state unemployment benefits so as to provide workers with 95 percent of their termination salary for three months after the dismissal. The payments would gradually be reduced to 75 percent of the salary for the final six months of the two-year agreement.

CONCLUSION

The discussion above clearly does not exhaust the repertory of alleged infractions of Paragraph 6 to have come before the CIIME.[61] The underlying issues surrounding plant closures and collective dismissals by multinationals are no less apparent. Among these is clearly the economic moment, a recessionary climate of slow growth and high unemployment to which plant closures serve as a most poignant reminder. When the *multinational* subsidiary closes down, moreover, the local or national public has a ready and foreign target against which to vent criticism for their economic malaise, a target that may furthermore appear to control vast resources.

As the cases discussed here have shown, the continued profitability of the multinational enterprise as a whole may rudely conflict with the poor economic health of a subsidiary. Paragraphs in the general policies section of the guidelines would appear to pit government objectives of employment stability against the decision to close a plant. References *inter alia* to Paragraph 6 of the employment and industrial relations section of the guidelines seemed aimed at eliciting, at best, an alternative to the closure and, at least, adequate income security. The claimants named in all these paragraphs are those in the context of plant closure, not those whose automatic acceptance of a multinational's contraction or restructuring can be assured.

Governments and unions may therefore remind multinationals of their competing claims on the latters' limited resources. In this way, the status of the subsidiary, its apparent dependence upon or independence from the parent company, becomes an issue. As was noted in the discussion of Ford Nederland NV, it was largely the unions' perception of an overly great dependence of the subsidiary upon the parent that appeared to motivate TUAC's call for the guidelines to serve as a "supplement to national legislation."

Noted earlier in this chapter were the legislative and collective bargaining trends toward increasing job security, the ramifications of which include ever higher employment and income guarantees. Greater employment security means increasing fixity of the labor factor, and decreasing management's ability to respond to economic changes and opportunities. Trends such as these could conceivably have an influence not just on multinationals' disinvestment plans, but on their investment planning as well.

---

[61] Allegations were also made by TUAC *inter alia* against the U.S.-based Litton Industries, and the German Siemens Corporation on March 30, 1977.

CHAPTER X

Paragraph 7

Enterprises should:

> implement their employment policies including hiring, discharge, pay, promotion and training without discrimination unless selectivity in respect of employee characteristics is in furtherance of established governmental policies which specifically promote greater equality of employment opportunity.

The antidiscriminatory recommendations of this guideline were "the least disputatious of the nine provisions found in the section headed Employment and Industrial Relations."[1] As noted in the discussion of Paragraph 5, multinationals tend to hire locally, and hiring and promotion decisions are guided by both government policies and employee representatives, either through collective bargaining or through the works council.[2]

The language of Paragraph 7 focuses more specifically on the areas of discrimination and affirmative action. As to the former, the guideline does not "define discrimination or list characteristics often found in claims dealing with discrimination."[3] An earlier wording of the guideline would have recommended that employers not "discriminate on the basis of sex, age, religion, color, ethnic origin and political activities."[4] Two of these bases, age and political activities, encountered some disagreement among OECD negotiators; and "without much disagreement" a final version of Paragraph 7 omitted any reference to specific discriminatory criteria.[5]

The more general wording of Paragraph 7 means that it is the national context that will define discrimination, rather than an over-

---

[1] USA-BIAC Committee on International Investment and Multinational Enterprise, *A Review of the OECD Guidelines for Multinational Enterprises: Employment and Industrial Relations* (New York, 1978), p. 27.

[2] See Chapter VII.

[3] USA-BIAC CIIME, *A Review of the OECD Guidelines for Multinational Enterprises*, p. 27.

[4] *Ibid.*

[5] *Ibid.*

prescription of criteria in a voluntary guideline. With respect to "age," for example, the United States is virtually the only country that bans age discrimination through its legislation. The problem of overprescriptive language would have conflicted with the fact that many OECD member countries have relatively homogeneous populations. In these countries, discrimination based on race and/or religion is less often the subject of legislation. Countries with heterogeneous populations, meanwhile, such as the United States, Australia, Canada, and the United Kingdom, do have legislation banning race and national origin as bases for discrimination.

TYPES OF ANTIDISCRIMINATION LEGISLATION

Although the explicit public policy of most OECD countries is toward the provision of equal employment opportunity and equal treatment at the workplace, there remains a variety of actual and potential categories of "protected persons" that each country's law and practice defines according to its own circumstances. It is, moreover, true that the source of discrimination (and its remedies) may lie not only in the hiring practices of the employer, but also in the exclusionary practices of unions.

Right to Union Membership

If a member state of the OECD is effectively to guarantee freedom of association and the right to join a trade union, it must also take action to penalize employer discrimination on the basis of trade union membership. In the discussion of Paragraph 1 (Chapter III), laws pertaining to freedom of association were mentioned for several of the OECD member states.[6] Nearly all countries, in legislating to protect this right, take action to protect the right of a person not to be discriminated against on the basis of union membership.

Sometimes, such legislation is explicit. For instance, in the United States, it is an unfair labor practice for an employer to discriminate on the basis of union membership. In the United Kingdom, a dismissal is unfair if it is motivated by a person's union membership. In other countries, the right not to be discriminated against on the basis of union membership is implied from the positive right to join or not to join a union. Chapter I also noted that freedom of association and the promotion of collective bargaining form the basis of International Labor Organization (ILO) Conventions Nos. 87 and

---

[6] See Chapter III, pp. 36–39.

98. Thus, a recent ILO tripartite meeting on multinationals and social policy recommended that workers employed in multinational enterprises have the right to join unions and that "they should also enjoy adequate protection against acts of anti-union discrimination in respect of their employment."[7]

It is also true, on the other hand, that the history of trade unionism in Western market economies has included a major chapter on discriminatory practices by unions. Legislation protecting the individual from discrimination by the union exists, for example, in the Labor-Management Reporting and Disclosure Act of 1959 (Landrum-Griffin Act) in the United States.[8] Nevertheless, some aspects of unionism such as the closed shop (in the United Kingdom) or the elaboration of seniority systems, constitute by definition discriminatory practice—the former in regard to hiring, the latter in regard to promotion and dismissal policies. As will be seen, these institutional structures of discriminatory practice can conflict with other legislative provisions.

Equal Employment Opportunity in the United States

Discrimination on the basis of several factors is broadly prohibited by the legislation of OECD member countries. Among the most extensive of these laws is Title VII of the Civil Rights Act (1964) which provides that discrimination on the basis of race, color, religion, sex, or national origin with regard to any employment condition, including hiring, firing, promotion, transfer, compensation, and admission to training or apprenticeship programs is prohibited in the United States.[9] As with other legislation regulating labor-management relationships, U.S. law far surpasses other countries' provisions against discrimination on the basis of a variety of criteria. So much so, in fact, that U.S. law has often formed the model for other countries' statutes in the area of antidiscrimination.[10]

Title VII of the Civil Rights Act as amended foresaw as well the establishment of a federal authority to administer the act's provisions—the Equal Employment Opportunity Commission (EEOC). The EEOC has had a significant impact on the eradication

---

[7] "Reconvened Tripartite Advisory Meeting on the Relationship of Multinational Enterprise and Social Policy," Geneva, 4–7 April 177, (MNE/1977/D.6), p. 10.

[8] Gordon Bloom and Herbert R. Northrup, *Economics of Labor Relations*, 9th Edition, (Homewood, Illinois: Richard D. Irwin, Inc., 1981), pp. 714–740.

[9] *Ibid.*, pp. 792–812.

[10] Janice Bellace, "A Foreign Perspective," *Comparable Worth: Issues and Alternatives*, E. R. Livernash, ed., (Washington, D.C.: Equal Employment Advisory Council, 1980), p. 140.

of discrimination at the workplace, as Professors Gordon F. Bloom and Herbert R. Northrup have noted:

> Although it is impossible to separate the impact of the EEOC from that of other factors, for example, the national concern with civil rights matters in the 1960s and the tight labor market of that period, it seems that the EEOC has had a profound impact on hiring practices and employment patterns, both as to race and as to sex. As a result of EEOC's existence and activities, thousands of women and minorities have had improved opportunities and work status, and thousands more have received back pay because of alleged discrimination by companies or unions. EEOC either directly litigated or supported cases challenging seniority systems which developed the "rightful place" doctrine, thus preventing the impact of past discrimination from continuing unabated.[11]

It is clear, therefore, that the EEOC has been instrumental in furthering equal opportunity at the workplace, irrespective of the source of that discrimination, whether management or labor organization. Moreover, since 1961,[12] the concept of "affirmative action"— the preferential hiring of minorities and women—has been applied to employers doing business with the government.

Application of the concept has introduced potential and actual conflicts with other systems of hiring and advancement already in existence. Seniority systems, most notably, may at times conflict with the corrective goals of affirmative action. Thus, for example:

> Where Kaiser Aluminum and the United Steelworkers established a joint program to increase the number of minorities in skilled trades and in so doing admitted minorities to the trades training program ahead of whites who had greater seniority, the Court ruled that this was permissible.[13]

This and other cases have raised the issue of "reverse discrimination" which, as the expression implies, is a recognition of the fact that, in competition for the same post, special treatment accorded one candidate automatically discriminates against others. One solution is to legitimize such discrimination through the implementation of a quota system, which, as Bloom and Northrup observe, "paradoxically is forbidden by Title VII of the Civil Rights Act."[14] Although some court decisions, such as the one described above, appear to have applied such a solution *de facto*, the solution itself is alien to many features of the American system.

---

[11] Bloom and Northrup, *Economics of Labor Relations*, p. 798.
[12] *Ibid.*, p. 793.
[13] *Ibid.*, p. 803.
[14] *Ibid.*

Antidiscrimination Legislation within the EC

As suggested earlier, the range of antidiscrimination legislation seems to be related to the degree of homogeneity or heterogeneity of a country's population. The homogeneity of European populations is, however, qualified by the free movement of labor among member countries of the European Community (EC) provided for in Article 49 of the Treaty of Rome. Article 49 is significant in the context of Paragraph 7 of the OECD guidelines, as the free movement of labor has been interpreted to mean that workers who are citizens of an EC nation have a right to the same treatment as that accorded nationals of the host country. As a practical result, discrimination on the basis of national origin is to some extent banned within the EC.

With the exception of the United States and New Zealand, all OECD member states have ratified ILO Convention No. 100, which calls for equal remuneration to men and women. In the United States, the provisions of the ILO convention had already been established in law in 1963 when, first among national bodies of law, an amendment to the Fair Labor Standards Act mandated equal pay for equal work.[15] U.S. national legislation in this area served as a model for similar laws, first in the United Kingdom and then on the European continent generally.[16] EC member states are, however, also affected by Article 119 of the Treaty of Rome which provided as well the principle of equal pay for equal work.

The decade of the 1970s in the EC witnessed the passage of three directives relating to equal employment opportunity and emanating from the EC Council of Ministers. The first of these, on equal pay for both sexes, was adopted by the Council of Ministers in 1975. As with all directives, individual national legislatures were to accommodate the provisions of this directive within a given span of time, in this case, of one year.

Two other directives, adopted by the Council of Ministers in 1977 and 1978, related to equal treatment of men and women. The first of these addressed the issue of equal treatment for men and women as regards access to employment, promotion, vocational training, and working conditions. The second regulated the equal treatment of men and women in matters of social security. The former was to have been implemented through national legislation by 1979, while the latter's implementation is to be fulfilled by 1984.[17]

Generally speaking, European legislation is narrower than U.S.

---

[15] Bellace, *Comparable Worth*, p. 140.

[16] *Ibid.*

[17] Chapters IX and XII, in particular, also discuss the wide range of social legislation in the EC.

legislation in matters of discrimination. The concept of affirmative action, moreover, is thus far a distinctly American one. Thus, with regard to the concept of equal treatment at the workplace, West German laws make no provision for equal treatment in relation to the trades, the professions, or vocational education; Italian law applies the equal treatment principle only to certain conditions of employment (pay, age limits, parental leave) rather than to all employment conditions; while Danish law applies the principle to the training and conditions of employment only of those men and women employed at the same workplace.[18]

Governments of OECD member countries do appear to be continually involved in the updating of legislation pertaining to discrimination. In France, for example, a bill seeking to ensure "equality at the workplace between men and women and to promote the integration of all jobs at all levels of responsibilities" has been introduced.[19] The bill would endow trade unions, moreover, with the right to take individual cases of discrimination through the courts.

Interestingly, the French bill contemplates the dismantling of earlier antidiscrimination legislation now thought to have produced the opposite effect of job segregation:

> If a series of measures aiming at the protection of maternity rights is of a necessary and hardly contestable nature . . . certain protective statutes, linked to traditionally perceived roles of women in society are, on the contrary, having the sole consequence of reinforcing discrimination in hiring or at the workplace (notably, the prohibition against women in shift work). The bill seeks to redress certain of these statutes.[20]

In the Netherlands, a proposed law would strengthen and consolidate existing legislation on equal pay and equal treatment through forbidding any discrimination on grounds of sex, marital status, or family responsibilities.[21] The Dutch bill would not include a ban on discrimination on grounds of race which, instead, would be addressed in the country's revised constitution.[22] Although affirmative action, as it is understood in the United States, does not appear to characterize the European situation, legislative activity in the area of discrimination, most particularly as regards maternity and

---

[18] Bellace, *Comparable Worth*, p. 139–159.

[19] "Egalité professionelle entre les hommes et les femmes," *Liaisons Sociales*, No. 17/81 (18 February 1981), p. 1.

[20] *Ibid.*

[21] "Netherlands: Proposed New Anti-discrimination Law," *European Industrial Relations Review*, No. 95 (December 1981), p. 23.

[22] *Ibid.*

paternity rights, seems lively in the EC. Indeed, the EC has recently announced plans for an "action program" designed to place greater emphasis on the application of antidiscrimination legislation in the member states.

The Issue of Comparable Worth

The growing participation of women in the labor force, in conjunction with their entrance into an ever wider range of professions once considered male bastions have combined to shape, in part at least, the emerging issue of comparable worth. Broadly defined, the issue involves equal pay for work of equal value—rather than for the same work. Pay, therefore, would presumably be determined by a finding that a given occupation is comparable to another, rather than by market forces. It is clear that the key problem surrounding comparable worth is the determination of what constitutes "work of equal value." In the United States, "the issue began in litigation in the 1970s and probably the law will not be fully settled until the mid-1980s. Meanwhile, attempts will be made to get specific legislation passed."[23]

Bloom and Northrup observe that should such legislation succeed to passage the result would distort market conditions and prove inflationary:

> The wage structure of American industry, so painfully worked out over the years, will be completely upended and a strong inflationary impact induced. For if job evaluation and wage classification systems are declared void or discriminatory, a push will occur on all sides to raise wages and numerous labor disputes will occur.[24]

In the EC, Professor Janice Bellace notes that considerable ambiguity surrounds the notion of "equal work for equal pay" embodied twenty-five years ago in the Treaty of Rome. Specifically, different governments have answered differently the question of whether equal work means the *same* work or *similar* work. Bellace notes that discrimination between men and women on the basis of pay "was based on the general undervaluing of duties deemed to be predominantly female, the classifying of predominantly female work as 'easy work', and the overvaluing in job evaluation plans of such factors as physical force compared to dexterity and attention."[25] Nevertheless, in the majority of Western European countries, national

---

[23] Bloom and Northrup, *Economics of Labor Relations*, p. 816.
[24] *Ibid.*, p. 816–817.
[25] Bellace, *Comparable Worth*, p. 143.

legislation does not necessarily equate "equal work" with work of "comparable worth." "Of the countries studied," writes Bellace, "four come closest to subscribing to the comparable worth theory: the Netherlands, Sweden, Australia, and New Zealand."[26] In other countries, the issue, however alive, is by no means resolved.

OTHER LEGISLATION AFFECTING EMPLOYMENT POLICIES

It is likely, given the variety of situations that prevail in the OECD member countries, that the guidelines are intended to refer primarily to the most commonly protected categories of persons, such as by sex, race, or national origin. Still other categories of discrimination, however, have fallen under the protection of the law.

In the United States, the Age Discrimination in Employment Act was passed in 1967, originally to protect persons between the ages of forty and sixty-five from job discrimination.[27] In 1978, the age threshold was extended to seventy, and in the following year, 1979, administration of the law was transferred to the EEOC. Bloom and Northrup have observed that the "the Age Discrimination in Employment Act is being especially used by white, middle managers and professionals to protect their jobs in economic downturns."[28]

Curiously, older European workers are being asked to leave their jobs early, and various countries have provided funds to subsidize early retirement programs. In Belgium, for example, three separate early retirement programs exist and are designed to facilitate the departure from the workplace of older workers through a variety of pension subsidies, in favor of hiring young, unemployed persons. Although not age discrimination statutes, the laws are geared at influencing employers' hiring practices through partially subsidizing the cost of those older workers who opt to retire early or subsidizing the salaries of younger workers hired to replace the old.[29]

The Belgian plans join others at the EC level which fall generally under the rubric of "worksharing," the reduction of working hours as a means of job creation, or, as in the case of early retirement plans, the reduction of individual working lives at one end of the age spectrum as a means of opening up jobs for those unemployed at the other end. Worksharing plans of many types and descriptions have

---

[26] *Ibid.*, p. 170.
[27] Bloom and Northrup, *Economics of Labor Relations*, p. 806.
[28] *Ibid.*
[29] "Dossier: La Pré-retraite en Europe," *Intersocial*, No. 62 (July 1980), p. 4.

been the subject of collective bargaining demands in many EC countries. In France, the reduction of the workweek to thirty-nine hours
as a means of job creation was mandated by presidential decree in
1981.[30] Whether worksharing in fact succeeds as a job creation measure is a matter of considerable debate.[31] One major obstacle is that
unions, in demanding shorter working hours, have not tended to
manifest similar solidarity when it comes to their pay for the hours
no longer worked. Far from constituting a job-creation mechanism,
the reduction of working hours under such conditions has raised
labor costs and proven a disincentive to hiring.

Employing the Disadvantaged

Two other pieces of U.S. legislation require affirmative action by
employers doing business with the government. The 1973 amendments to the Rehabilitation Act outlaw employment discrimination
against the handicapped, where "handicapped" is broadly defined
to include both mental and physical disabilities. Under this law,
government "contractors are required to accommodate their work-
places and jobs so that handicapped workers do not have barriers
preventing their working."[32] Similarly, the Vietnam Era Veterans
Readjustment Act, in its 1974 amendments, requires government
contractors to apply affirmative action to this category of protected
persons.[33]

The EC provides a similar array of legislation aimed at protecting
the handicapped worker. Indeed, as Table X-1 shows, many coun-

TABLE X-1
Employers' Obligation to Hire the Disabled Employee in Europe

Country	Obligation
Italy	A minimum quota of 15 percent of job places must be set aside for disabled employees, subdivided according to a specific classification system. For the private sector this includes: disabled soldiers—25 percent of quota; industrial injured—15 percent of quota; deaf and dumb—5 percent of quota.
Netherlands	A minimum quota of 2 percent of job places must be set aside for disabled employees, on the basis of 1 disabled employee per 50 work places. In principle, full quota obligations apply even in

[30] "France," *European Industrial Relations Review*, No. 91 (August 1981), p. 3.
[31] For a discussion of the parameters of that debate, see "Adaptation of Working Time," *European Economy*, No. 5, March 1980, pp. 85–111.
[32] Bloom and Northrup, *Economics of Labor Relations*, p. 806.
[33] *Ibid.*, p. 807.

TABLE X-1 (continued)

Country	Obligation
	redundancy situations. Employers in breach of quota requirements are liable to pay fines of up to HFL1000.
Sweden	There is no quota system as such, but employers are actively encouraged by the public authorities to set aside 5 percent of all new job places for the disabled.
United Kingdom	A minimum quota of 3 percent of job places must be set aside for disabled employees, unless a special exemption is granted by the public authorities on grounds that no suitable disabled persons are available. In principle, full quota obligations apply even in redundancy situations. Employers in breach of quota requirements are liable to pay fines of up to £100 and/or be imprisoned for up to 3 months.
Belgium	A minimum quota of 1200 job places must be set aside for the disabled in Government ministries; 55 in regional and local authority organizations; and a total of 90 in semi-State organizations. There are no sanctions for noncompliance with quota obligations.
Denmark	There is no quota system as such, but every public-sector employer is obliged to accept a disabled employee's 'priority claim on suitable jobs'. There are no sanctions for noncompliance with this obligation.
France	A minimum quota of 10 percent of job places must be set aside for disabled employees. In principle, full quota obligations apply even in redundancy situations. Employers in breach of quota requirements are liable to pay fines calculated in relation to the prevailing statutory minimum wage rate.
Germany	A minimum quota of 6 percent of job places must be set aside for disabled employees according to a predetermined schema of minimum levels: 16 job places—1 disabled employee; 25 job places—2 disabled employees; 42 job places—3 disabled employees. Where the quota cannot be filled, through lack of suitable candidates, the employer must pay into a State fund a monthly "equalization" contribution of 100 DM per unfilled quota place, until such time as the full quota obligation can be met. These equalization contributions are used to promote vocational training and employment of the disabled generally. In principle, full quota obligations continue to apply even in redundancy situations. Employers in breach of quota/equalization contribution requirements are liable to pay fines of 5000 DM per offense.
Ireland	A quota of 3 percent of job places for the registered disabled has been adopted as a target in the public service, to be achieved before the end of 1982.
Spain	A minimum quota of 2 percent of job places must be set aside for disabled employees. There are no sanctions on employers in breach of quota requirements.

Source: "International: The Disabled in Employment," *European Industrial Relations Review*, No. 95 (December 1981), pp. 19-21.

tries impose quota requirements on employers, compelling them to set aside a certain number of spots for the disabled. In some of these countries, moreover, the law substitutes payments to government funds by the employer in the event of noncompliance with the law through the unavailability of handicapped persons in sufficient number in the local labor market.

The economically disadvantaged pose, as well, difficult problems to the wealthy market economies of the West. In the United States, the Comprehensive Employment Training Act of 1973 (CETA) was designed to train and employ the disadvantaged worker until the worker could find unsubsidized employment. The act limited eligibility for CETA-sponsored programs to "any person who is economically disadvantaged, unemployed, or underemployed .... An economically disadvantaged person is defined as a member of a family that receives cash welfare payments or whose annual income in relation to family size does not exceed the poverty level determined in accordance with the criteria established by the Office of Management and Budget."[34] Recently, the Reagan administration has cut back considerably on the funding for CETA, a measure that reflects the program's several deficiencies throughout its nine-year existence. As Bloom and Northrup have noted:

> The training activities of the federal government are based upon theories of human resource planning which ties much unemployment to structural factors. However correct the Department of Labor's theories are, the amount of funds spent seems to yield rather small benefits. One problem is that the CETA programs concentrate on employment in the public sector, whereas the bulk of opportunities are in the private sector.[35]

Where private industry has participated in training programs under the auspices of local CETA agencies, the results have been more promising:

> Some very effective industry training programs were developed in cooperation with local CETA agencies where industry was permitted to assume full charge of the program, train the enrollees in an institutional setting that replicated an industrial one, select the trainees, monitor the progress, and provide flexibility in the training so that enrollees of various abilities and background could be trained at various levels and for various lengths of time. Moreover, the training was the most successful where the training organization was profit oriented and was rewarded for performance and not just for putting enrollees through a set of training activities.[36]

---

[34] *Ibid.,* p. 526.
[35] *Ibid.,* p. 532.
[36] *Ibid.,* p. 531.

Experiences such as these suggest that it is the private sector that is best able to effect the transition of the unemployed disadvantaged to unsubsidized employment.

CONCLUSION

Antidiscrimination legislation, within the relatively short span of twenty years, has likely contributed to the creation of truly equal employment opportunity in many OECD member countries. At the same time, however, the plethora of laws themselves may have introduced some practical problems. In the United States, for example:

> in any meeting, it is often difficult to find anyone who is not a member of a protected class when it is noted that all minorities, women, persons aged 40–70, persons with any mental or physical handicap, and Vietnam Era veterans are among those protected. Employers are especially at risk since the refusal to hire or to promote must be carefully documented and proved when a member of a protected class is involved, lest the action be the basis of a lawsuit.[37]

At base, the issue for the multinational enterprise, as well as for the national employer, is the extent to which hiring and promotion on the basis of individual merit must be constrained to ensure compliance with the laws.

The most vivid example of such constraints on hiring and dismissal policies is in the recent passage of the ILO's Convention on Termination of Employment at the Initiative of the Employer. Under this new convention, the employer must justify grounds for individual dismissal, and moreover, valid grounds for dismissal exclude the following:

1. union membership or participation in union activities outside working hours or, with the consent of the employer, within working hours;
2. seeking office as, or acting or having acted in the capacity of, a workers' representative;
3. the filing of a complaint or the participation in proceedings against an employer involving alleged violation of laws or regulations or recourse to competent administrative authorities;
4. race, colour, sex, marital status, family responsibilities, pregnancy, religion, political opinion, national extraction or social origin;
5. absence from work during maternity leave.[38]

---

[37] *Ibid.*, p. 807.
[38] Text of Convention and Recommendation on Termination of Employment at the Initiative of the Employer, as adopted by ILO, June 1982, Article 5.

The convention has yet to be ratified by individual nations. It is clear, however, that through collective agreement, national law, and international convention, external influence on management's establishment of employment policies is increasingly widespread, and managerial discretion in these areas accordingly reduced.

CHAPTER XI

Paragraph 8

Enterprises should:

> in the context of bona fide negotiations* with representatives of
> employees on conditions of employment, or while employees are exer-
> cising a right to organise, not threaten to utilise a capacity to transfer
> the whole or part of an operating unit from the country concerned *nor*
> *transfer employees from the enterprises' component entities in other*
> *countries* in order to influence unfairly those negotiations or to hinder
> the exercise of a right to organise.[1]

The sole paragraph of the guidelines on employment and industrial relations to have been changed over the six-year history of the
guidelines, Paragraph 8, occasioned considerable debate even at the
guidelines' drafting. At that time, the Trade Union Advisory Committee (TUAC) had strongly supported an initial wording that
would have prohibited a multinational from initiating "a transfer of
operations from a branch of the enterprise to any other country
because a labor dispute which is permissible under a host country's
law is in progress in that branch."[2] This wording, moreover, was
accompanied by a broad definition of "labor dispute" and, furthermore, would have denied one subsidiary's management the right to
import "products from another affiliate during a labor dispute."[3]

The Business and Industry Advisory Committee's (BIAC) objections to the original wording were twofold. Firstly, BIAC held that
"transferring plant units or productive capacity to thwart labor
unions was not current industrial practice and, therefore, the subject should not be introduced in the Guidelines."[4] It was superfluous

---

[1] Words *italicized* constitute the amendment to the original guidelines.

[2] USA-BIAC Committee on International Investment and Multinational Enterprises, *A Review of the Guidelines for Multinational Enterprises: Employment and
Industrial Relations* (New York, 1978), p. 28.

[3] *Ibid.*

[4] *Ibid.*

*Bona fide negotiations may include labor disputes as part of the process of negoti-
ation. Whether or not labor disputes are so included will be determined by the law
and prevailing employment practices of particular countries.

to actual practice, then, to prohibit the transfer of facilities solely on grounds of antiunion animus. A second, more serious objection, however, centered on the implication in original wording of an imbalance in the use of economic weapons by labor and management. Specifically,

> unless trade unions were equally bound by an obligation not to seek support for a strike in one country by sympathetic action elsewhere, this restriction would be an unreasonable discrimination.[5]

The imbalance introduced in the original wording was all the graver as the guideline would have imposed serious constraints on management's ability to ensure the economic viability of the undertaking in the event, for example, of a prolonged strike. U.S. spokesmen, in particular, were mindful of these potential constraints—especially as they conflicted with U.S. law.

U.S. employers have the legal right to transfer all or part of their production facilities for economic reasons resulting from a strike. In a system of free collective bargaining, to deprive the employer of the ability to maintain production would be to leave him defenseless. The union, possessing the potent weapon of the strike, would then dictate terms and the system of free collective bargaining would disintegrate.

The present wording of Paragraph 8 redresses, among other things, the conflict with U.S. law inherent in the original wording of the guideline. Significantly, the present wording distinguishes between the "threat" of transfer and the actual transfer of facilities. In so doing, it focuses the content of the guideline on the conduct of *bona fide* negotiations rather than on resource allocation decisions which, although prompted by labor disputes, may be compelled by economic considerations. Paragraph 8, therefore, implies that "a company faced by a long strike which might threaten its viability is not forbidden under this guideline to transfer a unit in whole or in part to another country, or transfer production to another affiliate, or to import goods from another affiliate to meet customer demands."[6] The distinction between "threat" and actual "utilisation" of a capacity to transfer remains, however, a much contested area.

It is hazardous to attempt a brief summary of the plethora of laws and practices surrounding the issues included in Paragraph 8. Laws and practices in OECD member countries are particularly varied, and the comparative problem is further compounded by the absence

---

[5] *Ibid.*
[6] *Ibid.*

of statutes that would limit employer responses in the face of a labor dispute, or determine whether that labor dispute is legal or illegal. British law, for example, does not distinguish between a "legal" or an "illegal" strike. There, as in some other countries, the courts—as well as customary practice—have developed doctrines defining acceptable behavior.[7] The courts in Germany and the United States view the right to strike as a legally protected economic weapon of employees, with the employer's corresponding weapon being the right to lockout or to maintain production. Still, in the United States, "because of the uncertainty which still surrounds the law of lockout, it is used infrequently by employers, and then only rarely do employers seek to operate with replacements."[8] The complexity of the issues of Paragraph 8 are amply demonstrated by reference to the experience of one country—the United States.

Transfer or Shutdown of Operations during a Union Organizing Campaign: The U.S. Experience

As BIAC observed, in the OECD member countries, it is not common industrial practice to transfer or shut down facilities—or to threaten to do so—during a union's organizing drive or as the result of antiunion sentiment. In the United States, such conduct is also unlawful when the union has obtained a bargaining relationship with management:

> Plant relocation becomes a "runaway shop" when the move is effected for antiunion motives, an action prohibited under the National Labor Relations Act (NLRA). An unlawful relocation can take place if an employer wants to thwart a union altogether or simply to remove unionization's adverse effects on the company's profitability.[9]

In cases where management has closed down the plant or transferred its facilities and a charge of antiunion animus has been brought against it, the National Labor Relations Board (NLRB) has attempted to assess management's true motivation for the action:

> In order to determine whether a relocation has been effected for antiunion reasons, the Board has traditionally considered a number of factors. Primarily, it has attempted to gauge whether the motivating

---

[7] B. A. Hepple, "Great Britain," *International Encyclopaedia for Labour Law and Industrial Relations*, Vol. III, R. Blanpain, ed., (The Netherlands: Kluwer, 1979), p. 170.

[8] Gordon Bloom and Herbert R. Northrup, *Economics of Labor Relations*, 9th Edition (Homewood, Illinois: Richard D. Irwin, Inc., 1981), p. 667.

[9] Robert A. Swift, *The NLRB and Management Decision Making*, Labor Relations and Public Policy Series No. 9 (Philadelphia: Industrial Research Unit, The Wharton School, University of Pennsylvania, 1974), p. 44.

factor behind the relocation was a valid economic reason or whether its purpose was to discriminate against or discourage unionism within the plant.[10]

Such discrimination would be in direct violation of employees' rights to elect representatives of their own choosing, embodied in Section 7 of the NLRA. If the union already exists as the representative of the employees, the potential violation is that of management's duty to bargain in good faith. In practice, however, the determination of the true motives of a transfer of facilities has proven difficult to make, and the NLRB's rulings have not been consistent.

The decision to transfer or to shut down facilities for purely anti-union motives is comparatively rare: "The circumstances of plant relocation virtually prohibit the moving of plants for discriminatory reasons absent economic justification."[11] It would seem no less true, however, that management has not responded in every case to the economic forces that would favor relocation, in part from fear of violating labor laws as they are construed by the NLRB. Relocation for economic reasons, including high labor costs, is nevertheless legal in the United States, although the burden of proof of economic motivation would appear to reside with the employer, and although difficult labor relations may attend the decision to relocate.

A Comparison

As a means of comparison with the U.S. experience, it is worthwhile to recall the details of the shutdown of facilities by Philips Germany discussed in Chapter VI.[12] There, economic factors were clearly the compelling force behind the decision, and these factors included the high cost of German labor. Significantly, employee representatives included on the economic committee and works committee of the plant in question concurred, after lengthy discussion, with the economic justification for shutting down operations.

Clearly, Philips' transfer of facilities was not prompted by a labor dispute, and was only partially prompted, it would seem, by high labor costs in Germany. Thus, it is somewhat outside the wording of Paragraph 8. Nevertheless, it is an instance in which *bona fide* negotiations produced a consensus of the need to transfer facilities— absent any indication of the "threat" to transfer. More recently, in the United States, a company's attempt to relocate for economic

---

[10] *Ibid.,* pp. 47–48.
[11] *Ibid.,* p. 45.
[12] See Chapter VI, pp. 98-102.

reasons was interpreted by the court as a breach of good faith bargaining:

> The company, which manufactures heat transfer coils, suffered business losses shortly after signing a three-year contract with Auto Workers Local 1271 in July 1980. Blaming the losses on high labor costs, the company decided to seek mid-term contract concessions from the union or relocate the heat coil work to another [United Auto Workers] plant in Glasgow, Kentucky, believed to have lower labor costs. Unsuccessful in gaining concessions, the company bargained a contract with the Glasgow local which made mention of the planned relocation of work from Danville. When the company began the actual move of equipment in May of this year, Local 1271 filed charges that the company failed to bargain in good faith before removing work from the Danville plant and that it removed work while Local 1271's contract was in effect.[13]

The injunction sought by the union to halt the transfer of facilities was obtained, according to the union's attorney, in order to "restrain an employer from requiring a union to make mid-term contract concessions under the threat of relocating."[14] The judge granting the injunction held that, "while an employer has the right to close its business without bargaining, it may not relocate or subcontract the bargaining unit work without first negotiating to impasse in good faith."[15]

"Threat" v. "Prediction" in U.S. Law

The recommendations of Paragraph 8 refer to the "threat" to transfer all or part of the operating unit in order to unfairly influence negotiations or to disrupt a union organizing drive. As in the guideline, such threats are illegal under U.S. law and, as in the case of relocations, the practical burden of proof falls on management. In one major case where it was alleged that management's statements to employees on the adverse effects of unionization unfairly influenced the results of a union representation election, the court held that "an employer's prediction of the disadvantages of unionism amounts to a threat if its eventuality is not capable of proof."[16]

Clearly, communications that bear on the future effect of a present cause, *i.e.*, predictions, may quite easily be interpreted as threats. In court rulings, the "objectivity" of the speaker may be a criterion: "a

---

[13] "NLRB uses injunction power to stop mid-term relocation," *Daily Labor Report*, No. 139 (July 20, 1982), p. 1.

[14] *Ibid.*, p. A-1.

[15] *Ibid.*

[16] Swift, *The NLRB and Management Decision Making*, p. 82.

prophecy that unionization might ultimately lead to a loss of employment is not coercive where there is no threat that the employer will use its economic power to make its prophecy come true."[17] Thus, a U.S. employer can express its opinion to its employees on the effects of unionism. Such expression, however, must "be carefully phrased on the basis of objective fact."[18] As the burden of proof that such expression does in fact constitute an objective prediction rather than coercion falls on the employer, the latter is well-advised to obtain competent legal advice prior to such communications.

Operating during Strikes

From the language of Paragraph 8 arises the question of management's response to a union's use of economic weapons. Specifically, must an employer succumb to the adverse effects of a strike and thus to a union's attempt to influence negotiations? Or may the employer attempt to maintain production?

It was noted earlier that a strike in the context of *bona fide* negotiations is variously defined by different countries' laws—or not defined at all. Thus, in the United Kingdom, the strike is neither lawful nor unlawful, as illustrated by the fact that no legal definition of a strike or a lockout exists in British legislation.[19] There is, moreover, "no legal restriction on the right of an employer to replace a striking labour force with 'blacklegs'," in the United Kingdom.[20] In Australia, meanwhile, a strike in the context of *bona fide* negotiations is theoretically illegal, as it is obviated by that country's system of compulsory arbitration in setting the terms and conditions of employment.[21]

Generally speaking, "because of legislation and traditional practice, the right of the union to strike with relative impunity seems to be more absolute in many European countries than in the United States."[22] Whether an employer may respond by attempting to maintain production with impunity is less certain. In Belgium, France, and Germany, laws variously provide, *inter alia*, for employ-

---

[17] *Ibid.*, p. 87.

[18] "United States of America," *International Encyclopaedia for Labour Law and Industrial Relations*, Vol. V, R. Blanpain, ed., (The Netherlands: Kluwer, 1979), p. 127.

[19] *Ibid.*, "Great Britain," Vol. III, p. 172.

[20] *Ibid.*

[21] Brahani Dabscheck and John Niland, *Industrial Relations in Australia* (Sydney: George Allan & Unwin, 1981), p. 67.

[22] Everett Kassalow, *Trade Unions and Industrial Relations: An International Comparison* (New York: Random House, 1969), p. 159.

ers to lock out employees, although a lockout is seldom if ever accompanied by the continued operation of the facility. If not always legally defined, the employer's attempt to maintain production appears to depend, for the most part, on the employer's ability to operate during strikes, an ability which is itself dependent on union solidarity, the nature of the production process, the degree of available police protection, economic factors, and, as the forthcoming discussion of the Hertz Denmark case will illustrate, social and political pressures.

The U.S. Experience

Economic strikes are legally protected in the United States, and although strikers may be permanently replaced in order that the employer may "protect and continue his business," they may not be discharged solely because they are on strike.[23] Federal (and some state) laws do restrict the employer's ability to replace striking workers. These laws, however, are concerned with preventing the use of "professional strikebreakers." Thus, the Byrnes Act provides that

> whoever willfully transports in interstate or foreign commerce any person who is employed or is to be employed for the purpose of obstructing or interfering by force or threats with 1) peaceful picketing by employees during any labor controversy affecting wages, hours, or conditions of labor, of 2) the exercise by employees of any of the rights of self-organization or collective bargaining; or whoever is knowingly transported or travels in interstate foreign commerce for any of the purposes enumerated in this section shall be fined not more than $5,000 or imprisoned not more than two years, or both.[24]

Various state laws, although differing in language, seek to prevent employers involved in a strike, lockout, or labor dispute from hiring replacements through the aid of third parties not directly involved in the labor dispute; recruiting or importing replacements from outside the given state; or hiring "professional strikebreakers" or persons who have "customarily and repeatedly" worked or offered to work in place of employees involved in a strike. It is significant to note, however, that

> Legally, these state acts appear to conflict directly with the right employers have under the NLRA to replace employees and operate during strikes. The constitutionality of such state antistrikebreaking

---

[23] Charles Perry, Andrew Kramer, Thomas J. Schneider, *Operating During Strikes* (Philadelphia: Industrial Research Unit, The Wharton School, University of Pennsylvania, 1982), p. 9.

[24] *Ibid.*, p. 25.

statutes is questionable. Federal labor laws have been held to preempt state legislation dealing with the same matters. Indeed, in the most recent litigation involving such a statute, a New Jersey Superior Court judge ruled that state's antistrikebreaking law to be unconstitutional on the grounds that the NLRA preempted state regulation of the matter.[25]

Employees who are members of bargaining units not involved in a primary strike against an employer may, through a provision in their collective agreement, have the right to honor the strikers' picket line, although not involved in the strike themselves. On the other hand, the employer may replace striking workers or transfer employees from other facilities to replace striking workers in an effort to maintain production. Moreover, supervisory and managerial personnel—not "employees" as defined by the NLRA—may be required by an employer to continue working during a strike whether they are union members or not:

> Moreover, an employer is not restricted regarding the kind of work it may assign these individuals to perform. Thus, an employer does not commit an unfair labor practice by disciplining or discharging managerial or supervisory personnel who refuse to perform work for the employer during a labor dispute, regardless of whether the work is supervisory or non-supervisory in nature.[26]

Other factors of an economic or practical nature will of course determine the employer's ability to operate during strikes. Of significance here is the employer's legal right to continue operating. This legal right includes the employer's ability to transfer all or part of a struck operating unit to other locations for the duration of the strike in order to safeguard the economic viability of the enterprise. Law and current practice in the United States do not, therefore, compel the employer to suffer the economic effects of a legal strike.

Although operation during strikes in the United States is an increasingly common managerial response to a union's legal use of an economic weapon, the United States is not the only country in which such a response is allowable. Indeed, it will be recalled from the discussion of Paragraph 1 that the much-publicized, two-year strike at Grunwick Film Processing Laboratories in the United Kingdom over the issue of union recognition was accompanied by management's continued operation of the facility.[27]

It would appear that factors in other countries, such as the strength of unions and their political influence, may make the actual

[25] *Ibid.*
[26] *Ibid.*
[27] See Chapter III, Note 20.

practice of operation during strikes rare, even when the legal and practical ability to maintain production exists. In the case of Hertz Denmark, management attempted to operate during a strike and brought in employees from subsidiaries in other countries to do so. The practice was no infraction of Danish law. The dispute, however, received intense scrutiny at the international level and occasioned, finally, a change in the wording of Paragraph 8.

THE HERTZ CORPORATION

The Hertz Corporation is the largest car and truck rental concern in the world. Since 1967, Hertz has been a wholly owned subsidiary of RCA, Inc., and, like its parent corporation, is headquartered in New York City. In 1978, Hertz had sales of $938.3 million and employed approximately 14,000 persons.[28]

Hertz's multinational operations are located primarily in Latin America and Western Europe, where it employs approximately 3,500 employees. In other areas and in smaller locations in Europe and the Americas, Hertz uses licensees, which are independent contractors.

The Danish Dispute

Personnel employed by Hertz in Copenhagen were unionized by the Union of Clerical Workers and Shop Assistants in Denmark (Handels og Kontorfunktiioaererners Forbund i Danmark—HK) which demanded wage increases of approximately 30 percent. When Hertz offered much less, the union struck. Hertz countered by bringing in six to eight employees from its companies in the United Kingdom, Italy, and France to operate the facilities at Kastrup Airport and downtown Copenhagen. After several weeks, a compromise settlement was reached, and the strike was terminated on November 24, 1976. Meanwhile, however, Hertz had reorganized its Danish operation, transferred accounting and other functions to its German company, and reduced its complement of unionized Danish personnel from twenty-two to nine.[29] Company officials claim that they had planned to abolish the Danish central office some months before but agreed that the strike and the demand for higher wages made it more advantageous to do so.[30]

---

[28] RCA, Inc., *Annual Report 1978* (New York, 1979). Employment information supplied by the Hertz Corporation.

[29] "Labour Mobility Change after Hertz Dispute?," *Industrial Relations Europe*, Vol. IV (December 1976), p. 1.

[30] Telephone interview, London, May 9, 1977.

The secretary of the HK declared that international union support forced Hertz to concede on the wage matter.[31] The company cited its key reasons for concession as picketing at the airport business location, harassment of potential customers there, and consequent loss of business.[32] It is questionable whether international union pressure had anything whatsoever to do with the company's wage concession, but there is no doubt that this dispute, although it involved at most only twenty-two employees, did generate considerable international publicity. The reason was Hertz's use of its employees from other European countries. They kept the operation running, and this led to widespread attempts on the part of various union bodies to declare this a violation of multinational corporate codes of conduct, as well as to the success of union efforts in the drafting of the International Labor Organization's (ILO) guidelines on multinational enterprises (as discussed below) and to union attempts to have legislation enacted limiting manpower mobility within the European Community (EC) during a strike.

Danish unions also brought pressure to bear on their own government, which demanded information from Hertz as to the number of employees involved, and whether social insurance requirements were being met. Hertz replied that only six employees were involved at the time of the inquiry (formerly there were eight); that they were on loan from other Hertz companies and not on the payroll of the Danish company; that they were fully covered by social security in their own countries; and that such employees remained in Denmark an average of ten days, apparently being rotated.[33] Thus, no violation of Danish law could be charged.

International Action

The unions have used the incident as a *cause célèbre* against the American management tactic of attempting to operate during a strike if at all possible. Mass picketing at Hertz's Copenhagen airport office was dispersed by police.[34] The matter was then raised in the European Parliament (EP) by a Danish member. A unanimous resolution was passed deploring Hertz's action and asking the EC to

---

[31] As quoted in Danish press.

[32] Hertz Corporation, interview in New York City, March 9, 1977.

[33] Letter from general manager, Hertz Biludlejning A/S, to chief of division, Arbejdministeriet, November 24, 1976, in response to latter's letter of November 19, 1976.

[34] "Strike-break moves spark controversy," *Industrial Relations Europe*, Vol. IV (November 1976), p. 5.

propose rules to avoid future "misuse" of the rules governing the free movement of labor within the EC.[35]

The Danish government raised the question again at the December 1976 meeting of the EC social ministers. A report was requested on "problems" involving workers temporarily in an EC country other than their own. Also in December, Danish union representatives on the EC Advisory Committee on Free Movement again raised the issue. It was therefore suggested that the matter be referred to the EC working group on multinational enterprises.[36]

International and regional union groups also became involved. The HK is an affiliate of the International Federation of Commercial, Clerical, Professional and Technical Employees (FIET). On September 30, 1976, the day before the strike commenced, FIET General Secretary Heribert Maier sent a telegram from FIET's Geneva headquarters to the general manager of Hertz Denmark "on the behalf of 6 million members," announcing its support of the "effort of HK, our Danish affiliate to conclude collective agreement without delay," and promising that "FIET will intervene with European members of your company."[37] Hertz did not acknowledge the telegram nor did it experience any "intervention" in its other European operations.

EURO-FIET brought the matter before the European Trade Union Confederation (ETUC), which passed a strong resolution on December 10, 1976, deploring Hertz's alleged actions and then added these paragraphs:

> The ETUC points out that in case this example should spread to other multinational companies, it may have incalculable consequences for the situation of the employees within the EC. On this background, the ETUC invites the Council and the Commission to take appropriate action without delay to prevent a repetition of this clear violation of the intentions of the EC regulations on the free movement of labour. In particular the ETUC draws attention to the OECD declaration on the conduct of multinational companies. The example of Hertz proves that it is indispensable in the eyes of the ETUC that the directives of the OECD should become manadatory.
>
> The ETUC is of the opinion that the European Commission and EFTA should now take steps towards the drawing-up of actually binding rules in respect of multinational companies, so as to secure against such attacks on the employment, wages, and conditions of work of European employees.[38]

---

[35] "Labour Mobility Change," p. 1.
[36] Letter from J. Stenbejerre, Danish Employers' Federation, January 24, 1977.
[37] Copy in author's possession.
[38] ETUC resolution on the Hertz Case, December 10, 1976.

Submission to the OECD

The unions did not drop the matter there. TUAC of the OECD presented the Hertz case to the OECD as an example of the ineffectiveness of voluntary corporate guidelines for multinationals. The OECD declined to act on individual cases like this one, but the unions then turned to the ILO's "Tripartite Advisory Committee on the Relationship of Multinational Enterprises and Social Policy" which met in Geneva from April 4 through 7, 1977.

At this ILO committee meeting, the parties did adopt part of the OECD guidelines as a proposed ILO statement. The wording of the ILO Declaration of Principles bears a close relationship to that in the OECD guidelines, although the ILO text contains much more detailed provision over a wider social field. In these negotiations, the unions demanded in addition a paragraph that would have encouraged international union actions within multinational corporations. This was rejected, but the committee did agree to the following paragraph:

> Multinational enterprises, in the context of *bona fide* negotiations with the workers' representatives on conditions of employment, or while workers are exercising the right to organise, should not threaten to utilise a capacity to transfer the whole or part of an operating unit from the country concerned in order to infuence unfairly those negotiations or to hinder the exercise of the right to organise; nor should they transfer workers from affiliates in foreign countries with a view to undermining *bona fide* negotiations with the workers' representatives or the workers' exercise of their right to organise.[39]

It is quite clear from conversations with those present that this paragraph was a direct result of the Hertz incident and was not especially objected to by employer delegates, particularly those from European countries where such resistance to union strike action is relatively infrequent. Thus, although an attempt by Hertz, or any other company, to maintain its operation and to provide service to the public during a strike by using some of its employees from other EC countries is evidently violative of a proper code of conduct for multinational corporations, no such corollary conduct by unions has been condemned. European national unions, the secretariats, and European regional union bodies all advocate coordinated union action across national boundaries as indicated by FIET's threat to "intervene with European members of your

---

[39] "Tripartite Declaration of Principles Concerning Multinational Enterprises and Social Policy," (Geneva: International Labour Organization, 1977), par. 52. In 1978, this paragraph was incorporated into the OECD Code of Conduct also.

(Hertz) company." Perhaps the illogic is based upon the failure of the international unions to achieve such promises, but certainly the illogic and disparate treatment are rather obvious.

Indeed, Danish law further illustrates the illogic of limiting multinationals' freedom of response to strikes, for under certain circumstances Danish law sanctions sympathy strikes by Danish employees for primary strikes occurring in foreign countries:

> A common interest . . . possibly exists when the Danish wage earners in enterprises belonging to a multinational concern initiate sympathy action in support of a legal primary conflict by wage earners in enterprises belonging to the concern in foreign countries. When the basic conditions of legality and the actual initiation of the primary conflict are fulfilled, the question of legality of sympathy action depends upon whether the strength of the interest of Danish wage earners is sufficient to justify solidarity with the foreign wage earners. If this interest is sufficiently strong, the sympathy conflicts will be permissible in spite of the peace obligations of the collective agreements.[40]

The CIIME's Amendments to Paragraph 8

Article 48 of the Treaty of Rome enshrines the principle of free movement of labor within the EC. Despite the legality of the movement of labor across national boundaries within the EC, the CIIME, in its 1979 review of the guidelines, held that such movement was against the guidelines' spirit. Thus, if the intent is to influence negotiations unfairly, the transfer of employees from a foreign affiliate

> while not specifically mentioned in the Guidelines certainly would not be in conformity with the general spirit and approach underlying the drafting of the Employment and Industrial Relations chapter. Accordingly, it is recommended that enterprises should definitely avoid recourse to such practices in the future. The Committee, therefore, proposes that this recommendation, which does not employ a major change of the Guidelines, should be made explicit in the text of Paragraph Eight.[41]

The recommendation that enterprises should not "transfer employees from the enterprises' component entities in other countries" thus was included. The extent to which the inclusion was influenced by the similar recommendation of the ILO's Declaration of Principles is explicit in the identical wording of the two. It may be argued that the guidelines do *not* prohibit the transfer of employees across

---

[40] "Denmark," *International Encyclopaedia for Labour Law and Industrial Relations,* Vol. II, R. Blanpain, ed., (The Netherlands: Kluwer, 1979), p. 267.
[41] CIIME Report on "Unfair influence in bona fide negotiations with employees," in R. Blanpain, *The OECD Guidelines for Multinational Enterprises and Labour Relations, 1976–1979* (The Netherlands: Kluwer, 1979), p. 226.

national boundaries during a labor dispute if the intent is to ensure the firm's economic viability. It is likely, however, that such an action would, as in the Hertz case, be viewed as intolerable by a variety of interest groups at the national and international level.

CONCLUSION

Until the Hertz case and its repercussions had occurred, the wording of Paragraph 8 referred to "threats" seeking to "influence unfairly" good faith negotiations. The amendment to the guideline is more restrictive, as it now condemns not just the threat of transfer of employees, but their actual transfer across national boundaries. The intent of the amendment is clear: to prevent multinationals from unfairly influencing negotiations. In practice, however, the wording introduces an imbalance in management's and labor's respective arsenals of acceptable tactics in the course of a labor dispute.

It was noted that Danish law does not prohibit sympathy strikes whose origins stem from a primary strike outside the country. The imbalance inherent in Paragraph 8 may have been tolerable because of the ineffectiveness or rarity of international union solidarity action. As in Denmark, however, a commentator on French law also contemplates the acceptability of such activity under national legislation: "there are no examples so far of cases involving international sympathy strikes. In our view, they might be considered justified [under French law] as relating to professional and occupational matters or as directed against the same employer or group of employers."[42] Future developments may expose the illogic of legal or quasi-legal provisions, for it is clear that international sympathy strikes cannot be protected, on the one hand, while on the other, international management response is prohibited.

---

[42] "France," *International Encyclopaedia for Labour Law and Industrial Relations,* Vol. III, R. Blanpain, ed., (The Netherlands: Kluwer, 1979). p. 210.

CHAPTER XII

Paragraph 9

Enterprises should:

> enable authorized representatives of their employees to conduct negotiations on collective bargaining or labour management relations issues with representatives of management who are authorized to take decisions on the matters under negotiation.

The portent of the final paragraph of the OECD Guidelines on Employment and Industrial Relations differs significantly from those that precede, for it alludes, however implicitly, to a decision-making authority beyond the scope of both the national context and the local subsidiary. It is, of course, fundamental to the concept of collective bargaining that the parties to an eventual agreement be those empowered to conclude such an agreement, without which collective bargaining is devoid of substance. This is an obvious statement of fact, and one with which both labor and management would agree. Beneath such agreement, however, lie the true parameters of meaning embodied in Paragraph 9.

Corporate executives have consistently argued that in the area of industrial relations the locus of decision making is vested in the subsidiary; and there is general agreement that multinational industrial relations is characterized by a high degree of decentralization. The findings of one writer in the field are representative: "I have conducted seminars on this subject with over 2,500 managers representing over 300 multinational companies throughout Europe and the United States. I know of no company that has centralized its employee relations decision making or tactical planning at either corporate headquarters or a regional office."[1]

The reasons for such decentralization are compelling. Professor B. C. Roberts states the case for decentralization as follows:

---

[1] Jerome Rosow, "Industrial Relations and the Multinational Corporation: The Management Approach," *Bargaining Without Boundaries*, R. Flanagan and A. Weber, eds., (Chicago: University of Chicago Press, 1974), p. 153.

Multinationals are well aware that there are significant differences between countries in their industrial relations systems, that they must respect these differences to avoid serious conflicts and difficulties, and that they must employ indigenous managers who have local understanding and knowledge to be primarily responsible for the conduct of most industrial relations issues. The international employers' organization survey reported that in fields of personnel recruitment, dismissals, and vocational training, practically every company delegated all decisions to its subsidiaries. On such matters as wages, fringe benefits, and other conditions of work the same delegation generally existed, with the exception of company pensions, which were often subject to the control of headquarters.[2]

Another reason for decentralized industrial relations is the nature of the function itself. Unlike other corporate functions such as finance, for example, industrial relations decisions, once made, acquire a degree of rigidity or, indeed, practical irreversibility, and thus rely greatly on a broader understanding of the local situation.

One of the most obvious, but very important, reasons for decentralization is the fact that the employment contract is drawn up at the local level in accordance with local law. Nevertheless, one major concern of the international trade union movement and some governments is the issue of the locus of decision making in the multinational. In particular, the International Confederation of Free Trade Unions (ICFTU) and associated International Trade Secretariats (ITSs), the most vocal of which is the International Federation of Chemical, Energy and General Workers' Unions (ICEF), have argued the need for a union counterforce similarly multinational in scope. They claim "that local affiliates of multinational companies are often limited in their capacity to bargain collectively with respect to certain fundamental subjects because decisions in these matters can be taken only by headquarters managements. Where this is the case, the unions claim they should be able to bargain face-to-face with central management."[3]

Amid what appear to be contradictory assertions by labor on the one hand and by management on the other concerning the locus of decision making, there is clearly a host of other issues, one of which is a definition of those "certain fundamental subjects" alluded to above. If these subjects—"labor management relations issues" in

---

    [2] B. C. Roberts "Comment," in *Multinationals, Unions, and Labor Relations in Industrialized Countries,* R. F. Banks and J. Stieber, eds. (Ithaca: New York State School of Industrial & Labor Relations, Cornell University, 1977), pp. 50–51.

    [3] USA-BIAC Committee on International Investment and Multinational Enterprises, *A Review of the OECD Guidelines for Multinational Enterprises: Employment and Industrial Relations* (New York, 1978), p. 29.

the wording of Paragraph 9—include, as many trade unionists believe, the area of corporate investment and disinvestment decisions, this changes the locus of decision making in industrial relations by changing what most employers view as the scope of industrial relations. As one industrial relations specialist put it:

> Attempts by trade union bodies, mostly at the international level, to involve themselves in multinational firms' basic investment decisions, rather than in the consequences of those decisions for trade union members, generally have prompted management to deny these organizations a role in these general decisions, and thus have provoked most of the trade union criticism about the locus of decision making.[4]

The interest in access to decision makers, therefore, would appear more fundamentally allied with issues of such topical concern as information disclosure and worker participation. These interests relate specifically to decisions affecting job security and plant closures which are items of note in a climate of high unemployment. Concerns such as these, however, may well be the fuel rather than the engine of union interest in access to decision makers, the fundamental objective remaining an enhancement of bargaining power.

THE SHAPE OF MULTINATIONAL BARGAINING ATTEMPTS

Two approaches to transnational bargaining manifest themselves. The first encompasses attempts by a coalition of unions, often led by or with the backing of an ITS, to bargain with a multinational company at headquarters level. Arrangements that have fallen short of actual bargaining in this approach have occurred. For example:

> Between 1967 and 1972, the giant Dutch electrical manufacturer, Philips, had four meetings with an EMF (European Metalworkers' Federation) European union committee. Meetings ceased when the EMF demanded that they be transformed into collective bargaining sessions and that a representative of the IMF (International Metalworkers' Federation) be present. Philips refused the first because it felt that bargaining was properly conducted nationally and locally, and the second because it had agreed to consultation only within an

---

[4] Robert Copp, "Locus of Industrial Relations Decision-Making in Multinationals," in *Multinationals, Unions, and Labor Relations*, p. 44.

European context, and the IMF presence at least implied a wider geographic reference.[5]

Other multinationals, such as BSN Gervais Danone, have conducted informational meetings with multinational groups of unions, while excluding the involvement of regional or international secretariats.

A second approach to transnational bargaining has sought the facility of public law. This approach has garnered a certain amount of success within the European Community (EC) where transnational agreements, of varying strengths, on corporate behavior and responsibilities and on the harmonization of working conditions have been formulated by the European Commission, the European Parliament (EP), and their dependent organs. Major proponents of such legislative formulations have included the European Trade Union Confederation (ETUC) and its many regional constituent bodies, such as the European Metalworkers' Federation (EMF).

Both approaches have elicited the support of different segments of the international union movement. In a general sense, the first approach has been espoused by the ICFTU and associated International Trade Secretariats, such as the ICEF. Their approach, moreover, is ideologically distinct from that of another international union confederation, the World Federation of Trade Unions (WFTU), whose communist perspective places in doubt the efficacy of a multinational union as counterforce to the multinational company. Thus, with regard to the ICFTU's initiative to establish company councils, the WFTU's differences appear to be significant, if somewhat subtle. In his statement to the UN inquiry on multinationals in 1973, WFTU Secretary Albertino Masetti declared that they could not "agree to any limitation on trade union action at the national level through agreements between so-called 'multinational trade unions' and the multinational corporations."[6] Obstacles to transnational bargaining other than purely ideological ones are daunting.

---

[5] Herbert R. Northrup, "Why Multinational Bargaining Neither Exists nor is Desirable," *Labor Law Journal,* June 1978, p. 7. For a thorough documentation of multinational bargaining attempts see Herbert R. Northrup and Richard L. Rowan, *Multinational Collective Bargaining Attempts,* (Philadelphia: Industrial Research Unit, The Wharton School, University of Pennsylvania, 1979).

[6] Everett Kassalow, "Trade Union Ideologies and the Multinational Companies," in *Multinationals, Unions, and Labor Relations,* p. 171.

Obstacles to Transnational Bargaining

The ideological position of the WFTU is joined by a more practical obstacle to transnational bargaining: union reluctance. As Northrup and Rowan have noted:

> Many observers have assumed that the international trade secretariats would be the natural representative, or at least coordinator, of the union side multinational bargaining arrangements. Yet, although the secretariats have served as a forum for the exchange of information among national unions, they have not managed to extend their activities to the coordination of collective bargaining. Even the ... IMF, the strongest secretariat in financial support, leadership, and staff, has had little success in the few times that it has attempted to inject itself into collective bargaining establishments.[7]

A reason cited by the authors for this lack of success is the probability that the structure of union organization would preclude the willingness on the part of union officials at various levels in the hierarchy of organization to cede power: "From the individual union official's point of view, such transfer of power could reduce his importance in the eyes of his constituents and therefore reduce his opportunities for maintaining his position against intraunion challenges."[8]

To this political-structural obstacle must be added another: lack of employee interest. For one thing, the relative well being as reflected in wages and fringe benefits of employees of multinationals may erode any sentiment of crossborder solidarity. As an ILO study concluded:

> the great bulk of union officers surveyed in this report saw little hope or prospect for full-scale or very substantial transnational collective bargaining with multinational companies....The relatively good wages and benefits at most MNEs, moreover, left most of the unions surveyed feeling that there was no pressing need for anything like full-scale transnational bargaining.[9]

It would seem likely in general, and particularly in a recessionary climate, that whatever horizon of solidarity exists among unionized workers may stop at the national border: "the idea that workers of one country will enthusiastically, or even reluctantly, support the cause of their brothers and sisters in another country is a figment of the intelligentsia imagination that persists over the years without either occurring to or permeating the thoughts of those who are

---

[7] Northrup and Rowan, *Multinational Collective Bargaining Attempts*, p. 540.
[8] *Ibid.*, p. 542.
[9] International Labour Office, *Multinationals in Western Europe: The Industrial Relations Experience* (Geneva, 1976), p. 43.

expected to lose pay to make it come true."[10] Such a view suggests an almost unbridgeable gap between the goals of some trade union officials and those of the rank and file.

As has been evident throughout this book, national diversity in law and practice has consistently inhibited the formation of an international framework for industrial relations. Efforts in the area of transnational bargaining must also inevitably encounter obstacles stemming from different legal and practical settings: "in the Federal Republic of Germany, for example, where so large a part of labour conditions in a given plant is regulated by national law, it was viewed as impossible to foresee collective bargaining with multinational enterprises that would embrace German members and plants with others which operated in countries where laws and collective agreements were so different."[11] The prevalence of industrywide collective bargaining in Germany must also be seen as an obstacle to multinational bargaining.

The existence of bargaining at national, industry, company, and plant levels, and the presence or absence of works councils are factors that vary among countries and would constitute both procedural and substantial impediments to multinational bargaining. Moreover, not only do the subjects of bargaining vary depending upon the level of bargaining, but subjects differ depending upon the country as well. In some European countries, for example, bargaining over fringe benefits constitutes a high percentage of all wage bargaining. In other countries, fringe benefits and a substantial number of working conditions are legislated, rather than bargained for, a fact that would considerably complicate bargaining beyond the national level.

Even if such impediments were somehow overcome, to impose a bargaining structure on multinationals which transcends that ensconced in law and practice for a domestic company is likely to be viewed as patently unfair by multinational employers. The significance of the "chapeau clause" of the guidelines is clearly paramount in these employers' view: "a number of employer association spokesmen in Western Europe believe it would be impractical and unfair to impose on multinational companies special rules that went beyond the requirements for national companies."[12]

Management's resistance to the concept of transnational bargaining on grounds of practicality and potential costliness constitutes a final obstacle:

---

[10] Northrup and Rowan, *Multinational Collective Bargaining Attempts*, p. 544.
[11] ILO, *Multinationals in Western Europe*, p. 53.
[12] *Ibid.*

The varied and complex arrangements which would be required to establish collective bargaining on a multinational basis would seem to demand a three-level structure. This would involve multinational discussions followed by national ones and, in turn, by local bargaining. Companies, as well as unions, would have difficulties in assigning responsibilities and priorities for the three levels. If, however, that were accomplished, the company would face a strike risk at each level of bargaining. Moreover, it is not unlikely that the results of bargaining would be more costly, because each bargaining level would have constituents to satisfy.[13]

Part of this costliness, Northrup and Rowan write, would stem from the structure of modern industrial concerns themselves, which renders inefficient the bargaining over wages and working conditions at a multinational level:

A fundamental weakness of coordinated or coalition bargaining, whether national or international, is its tendency to force wages and conditions on an industry that cannot be borne. Today, most major companies operate in several rather than only one industry. Within one company, some of the products made are often capital intensive, others labor intensive. The wider the bargaining unit, the less it suits the needs of diversity and the more likely that it will result in costs to a segment that cannot bear them. Multinational bargaining by its very nature seems too broad to meet the needs of a varied product mix.[14]

A survey of fifteen multinational companies drew similar conclusions in 1978.

A brief glance at the obstacles facing transnational bargaining suggests that these impediments are considerable. This, however, in no way lessens the vitality with which the issue of transnational bargaining is and will continue to be pursued by its proponents, largely because the conditions and motives involved are several. Interestingly, one view holds that tendencies toward plant-level bargaining, seemingly in the opposite direction of transnational bargaining, may in fact encourage the latter:

There have been . . . increasing tendencies among workers and their organizations in large German auto plants and in many other large plants in Western Europe to take greater initiatives to influence both wages and working conditions at the plant level, over and beyond what is provided by regional or national agreements. This tendency towards a growing degree of plant and company bargaining "separatism" improves the opportunity for at least some transnational cooperation in Western Europe, between unionists at plants of the same company in different countries."[15]

---

[13] Northrup and Rowan, *Multinational Collective Bargaining Attempts*, p. 537.
[14] *Ibid.*, p. 538.
[15] ILO, *Multinationals in Western Europe*, p. 45.

Thus far, however, the link between such a tendency and a greater degree of multinational bargaining would seem only hypothetical, supported by some attempts but no successful multinational agreements.

Some Attempts at Transnational Industrial Relations

The tendency apparent from the above quotation, in that author's view, favors the development of multinational bargaining through a multinational union. Clearly, the IMF's World Automotive Councils constitute among the more established multinational union arrangements, an arrangement that nevertheless excludes bargaining with management. In the words of one IMF official: "Basically, the function of the councils is to provide communication channels, solidarity action, and periodic company council meetings, all of which can involve coordinated collective bargaining."[16]

The words, "coordinated collective bargaining," are judiciously chosen, and clearly are not synonymous with multinational collective bargaining. Rather, the expression would appear, in practice, to signify communication among international union personnel and also with management at corporate headquarters involving a subsidiary's labor problems. The example offered by the same spokesman above referred to a 1974 strike at the Cuernavaca, Mexico, subsidiary of the Japanese auto maker, Nissan. Information obtained from the Japanese auto union in Tokyo was apparently relayed first to the IMF headquarters in Geneva, and then, through the IMF, to Cuernavaca. As a result of this relay of information, the official claims, and after "eventual concessions on both sides, a final settlement was made 7 percent above the local management's original offer."[17] Upon closer examination, however, the IMF's "success" appears qualified by the fact that the local company had originally offered a 17 percent increase—against the union's demand for an 80 percent wage rise. Management, moreover, settled at 22 percent, 5 percent, not 7 percent, above its original offer. The involvement of the Confederation of Japan Automobile Workers' Unions appears to have been greater than that of the IMF. Still, even the role of the Japanese confederation appears to have been minimal.

> They were an information channel but certainly not part of a coordinated bargaining effort. There was no action or threat of action against Nissan plants in Japan or against those in any other part of

[16] Burton Bendiner, "World Automotive Councils: A Union Response to Transnational Bargaining," in *Multinationals, Unions, and Labor Relations*, p. 187.
[17] *Ibid.*, pp. 187–88.

the world. The dispute settlement, although very high, was in line with previously agreed upon bargains by Ford, Volkswagen and other companies in the Mexican automobile industry.[18]

The IMF's claim outstrips its actual performance in the matter for, at the very least, the link between the cause and the effect of the IMF's involvement in the situation seems dubious.

Solidarity action, another function of the auto councils, has similarly offered few manifestations beyond national boundaries. In some cases, it has taken the form of a refusal of one subsidiary's employees to work overtime in an effort to frustrate the efforts of a subsidiary in another country to transfer production as the result of a strike.[19] The enhancement of unions' economic weapons has been sought through the demand for common contract expiration dates. The latter has been resisted by management but, upon occasion, also by the national unions themselves. An ILO report summarizes the experience of a 1973 Chrysler World Automotive Council meeting at which common contract expiration was discussed:

> One group of delegates at this meeting proposed that the council adopt the goal of working for a common expiration date for all collective agreements covering Chrysler plants regardless of country. Such a tactic it was contended would improve the unions' bargaining strength vis-a-vis this company. Several British delegates at this meeting opposed this suggestion and argued that common expiration dates could put tremendous financial pressure on the unions, if a strike occurred at the point of a common expiration date.[20]

Here, as elsewhere, the difficulty of exacting too great a sacrifice from local and national union officials would appear to inhibit multinational bargaining efforts.

The IMF has reassessed its earlier attempts at multinational collective bargaining which for a variety of reasons have yielded hollow results. In a speech made in November 1981, Herman Rebhan, general secretary of the IMF, imbued his remarks with a new realism:

> The idea was to achieve common trade union objectives, common conditions of service—similar holidays, the same age for retirement and so on—and a common start date for the contract or agreements in different countries. Well, it was a noble idea and the councils that

---

[18] Northrup and Rowan, *Multinational Collective Bargaining Attempts*, p. 42.

[19] The tactic would appear anything but widespread: "A very large majority of trade unionists expressed their ... willingness to refuse work on any 'struck' production ... In a few instances in the Netherlands and the Federal Republic of Germany some trade union leaders were uncertain as to the legal restraints which might block their rendering such solidarity assistance." ILO, *Multinationals in Western Europe*, p. 51.

[20] *Ibid.*, p. 46.

were set up then are still doing important work. We have set up similar world union councils to cover employers like ITT, IBM and Philips. But the vision of the future of 20 years ago, that saw global collective bargaining with a supranational trade union body meeting the top managers of the big MNCs to draw up a collective agreement that would cover workers from Detroit to Dagenham, from Turin to Tokyo, has not turned into reality.[21]

Such, according to Rebhan, were the goals established by "an earlier generation of international trade union leaders,"[22] goals that ultimately confronted a vast array of national differences, each constituting its own barrier to supranational solidarity. "In other words, and here I am being perfectly frank, it may not be possible to produce a united trade union side that has a detailed claim for negotiations to cover workers in several countries."[23]

Other examples of the multinational union approach to multinational bargaining nevertheless do exist. Some MNEs have exchanged information with international labor groups, some have undertaken discussions with these groups or with groups of national unions on a regular but informal basis. An exception to this informality is the agreement between the French multinational, BSN Gervais Danone and unions from several countries. In 1975, the company signed an agreement with union representatives from five countries, Austria, Belgium, France, Germany, and the Netherlands.[24] The agreement "provides for a Permanent Employment Commission composed of representatives of the general management of Glaverbel-Mecaniver and of each of its three operational entities—Benelit, which includes operations in Belgium and Holland; Boussois, the French operations; and Flachglas, Delog-Detag, covering those in Germany and Austria—and of one delegate from each union in a country, with a minimum of two delegates per country."[25] Northrup and Rowan further note:

> The agreement emphasizes that national companies and unions will continue to handle basic social affairs as they have in the past, that the commission will not cause superior conditions in any country to be reduced and that it will not diminish the significance of negotiations between management and labor in each country. The primary job of the commission is to examine technical, social, and economic matters in a quest to maintain employment. Its agenda in so doing includes "information and discussion" on the problems of invest-

---

[21] H. Rebhan, "Multinational Bargaining: The Union Point of View," speech given in Brussels, November 1981, pp. 5–6.
[22] *Ibid.*
[23] *Ibid.*, p. 15.
[24] Northrup and Rowan, *Multinational Collective Bargaining Attempts*, p. 176.
[25] *Ibid.*

ment, disinvestment, and other activities of the company, with emphasis on maintaining an equilibrium among the countries in which BSN operates. Before meetings of the commission, which are to be held twice per year, an agenda is to be established by a representative of the general management and a designated union correspondent. Pertinent documents are to be made available to participants two weeks before each scheduled meeting. At the February 1976 meeting, for example, the company reported on the employment effects of the closing of a number of plants that occurred without incident and on plans to install new equipment. As management representatives pointed out to the authors, this was an agreement on procedure and information and was confined to the subject of employment or matters affecting employment. Moreover, the commission was given no power to alter decisions once made and thus has no collective bargaining function.[26]

As a labor-management arrangement on an international scale, the BSN Permanent Employment Commission was the most highly evolved example of the first approach to multinational bargaining, the multinational union. It was not to last, however. On September 15, 1979, BSN announced the sale of its flat glass operations in Germany, Austria, Belgium, and the Netherlands; although the actual sale did not take place for several years. The transfer of ownership put an end to the unique, labor-management relationship that had been created by BSN and the unions.[27]

Through the second approach, law and regulations transcending national boundaries which pertain to industrial relations, momentum would appear to be gaining. A variety of international fora—the UN, the ILO, and the OECD, for example—have lent considerable support to the concept of supranational accountability for multinational firms. The present discussion of the relation of the OECD guidelines to the international union movement is an obvious case in point.

In the opinion of many, however, the most vital center of activity in this area is the European Community (EC). Backed by the interests and efforts of the European Trade Union Confederation (ETUC) and some regional industry union groups, the most active of which is the European Metalworkers' Federation (EMF), the European Commission and dependent committees are actively formulating a broad range of social legislation affecting industrial relations. Jack Peel, the former director of industrial relations of the European Commission, envisages the development of "Euro-bargaining," which "concerns bargaining at industry level, as distinct from one

---

[26] *Ibid.*, pp. 176–77.
[27] *Ibid.*, p. 184.

firm bargaining multinationally . . . and would be particularly suitable for laying down minimum standards of wages and working conditions for a specific industry across Europe.''[28] In Peel's view, the
rationale for Euro-bargaining

> is a logical consequence of the existence of the European Community,
> which in basic terms is concerned with developing resources of its
> member states for the eventual benefit of everyone. The industrial
> implications of this policy include the customs union and the gradual
> coordination of company law systems, both measures being designed
> to facilitate the freer flow of trade throughout the Community and to
> maximize its wealth-producing potential. A whole new code of labour
> legislation being constructed at board level is also well advanced.[29]

Transnational Initiatives on the National Level

Specific countries in the EC have been more active than others in
promoting industrial relations initiatives at the international, or at
least the European, level. These countries, Belgium, the Netherlands, and Luxembourg, for example, tend to be those where not
only is the presence of foreign subsidiaries particularly great, but
where the bureaucratic machinery of the EC and the European trade
union movement is located, as well. As Northrup and Rowan have
observed:

> More direct union leadership support of multinational bargaining
> emanates from union officials of small countries who already play a
> key role in European regional unions. Thus, the general secretaries of
> the ETUC and the EMF are from Luxembourg and Belgium, respec-
> tively, and the president of the ETUC, from the Netherlands.
> Undoubtedly, international and regional unions offer a much greater
> role for small country union leaders than is possible within the nar-
> row confines of their now very limited territories.[30]

To a greater degree than other countries, moreover, the Benelux
countries are less prone to one of the obstacles to multinational bargaining, differences in national legislation. Rather, the countries
evince a high degree of economic, as well as institutional integration, a factor that may lessen the barrier of the national boundary.

National legislation and practice in some countries, moreover,
appears to endow efforts at multinational bargaining, in theory at
least, with the institutional rudiments to claim greater involvement
by the parent company in the industrial relations affairs of its sub-

---

[28] Jack Peel, *The Real Power Game: A Guide to European Industrial Relations*
(Maidenhead, UK: McGraw Hill, UK, 1979), p. 99.
[29] *Ibid.*, p. 95.
[30] Northrup and Rowan, *Multinational Collective Bargaining Attempts*, p. 548.

sidiary. Codetermination in the German iron, steel, and coal industries, for example, allows for the presence of international union personnel, from outside the particular company, to sit on the supervisory board, and thus provides these union officials with considerable say in corporate decision making. Table XII-1 lists such

TABLE XII-1

International Union Officials on German Supervisory Boards

Name	Principal Position	Company Board
Herman Rebhan[a]	General Secretary, International Metalworkers' Federation	Ford of Germany
Werner Thönnessen[b]	Assistant General Secretary, International Metalworkers' Federation	Standard Elektrik Lorenz (ITT)
Charles Levinson[c]	Secretary General, International Federation of Chemical, Energy and General Workers' Unions	DuPont of Germany
Heribert Maier[d]	General Secretary, International Federation of Commercial, Clerical and Technical Employees	"bilka" Kaufhaus GmbH
Günter Köpke[b]	Managing Director, European Trade Union Institute; formerly General Secretary, European Metalworkers' Federation	Philips of Germany

Source: Herbert R. Northrup and Richard L. Rowan, *Multinational Collective Bargaining Attempts: The Record, the Cases, and the Prospects* (Philadelphia: Industrial Research Unit, The Wharton School, University of Pennsylvania, 1979), p. 550.

[a] American citizen, born in Germany

[b] German citizen

[c] Levinson, a Canadian citizen, was replaced on the DuPont board in early 1983 by Heinrich Selzer, a minor union official from the German Industrial Union of Chemical, Paper and Ceramic Workers (Industriegewerkschaft Chemie, Papier, Keramik— IG Chemie).

[d] Canadian citizen

[e] Austrian citizen

officials and the dual positions they hold.

Worker participation through codetermination is unusually broad in the German formulation. Still, in several European countries, the works council appears to be the vehicle through which national legislation has created a platform for multinational bargaining efforts. The platform is founded on the dual planks of greater information disclosure and broader consultation/negotiation rights. Thus a draft directive on collective dismissals, integrated by 1977 into individual countries' laws, provides for prior information on the causes of such dismissals and consultation on their effects to be channeled through works councils or other organs of employee representation in all EC member states.

Prior consultation with employee representatives over collective dismissals amounts to consultation over a firm's investment (or in this case disinvestment) decisions. It is not all that distant from the scope of consultations accorded unions in the BSN Gervais Danone agreement, for example, or, for that matter, from consultations over the employment effects of any investment decision. In this light, then, the bond between collective dismissals' legislation and the broadening scope of employee consultation rights is a fluid one. As Northrup and Rowan observe:

> Plant closures in Europe result in tremendously adverse publicity for multinational corporations. Often, managements fail to explain completely the needs for such actions, thus compounding the difficulties. A rush of such closures could well trigger support for multinational union action, although, to date, unions have tended to seek national settlements despite international agitation.[31]

As subsequent discussion of specific "cases" will show, the employment effects of corporate investment decisions provide what has become the most exploited basis for multinational bargaining attempts. This is so because legislation in several countries—the Netherlands, Sweden, Finland, and Germany among them— requires that consultation with employee representatives precede certain investment decisions. The attempts are multinational, for as has been observed elsewhere, investment decisions most often remain the province of corporate headquarters. It is, again, the subject of decision making, rather than its locus, that has been challenged, and the attempt is to include corporate investment within the scope of the "labour management relations issues" referred to in Paragraph 9.

Information, Participation, and National Legislation

Clearly, part of the reason that Paragraphs 6 and 9 are especially critical in this study is that both refer, however implicitly, to the expanding role of labor in the management of the firm. The direction of this expansion verges ultimately on the firm's ability to allocate

---

[31] *Ibid.*, p. 552.

its resources through investment and disinvestment decisions. Were one to probe the origins of this interest, one could arguably find both "reactive" and "assertive" motives. The reaction origin has already been mentioned: the paramount concern over job security, a reflection of the high unemployment and slow or negative growth of recent years, provides the link between greater information disclosure, greater "transparency" of the MNE, and employment. Such concern has manifested itself, as was noted in the discussion of Paragraph 6, in the provision of "reasonable notice" and consultation rights over plant closure decisions. At the EC level, interest in broader information disclosure finds expression in the "Vredeling proposal."

A more assertive motive is the interest in workers' participation in the management of the firm related, as it is, to a host of concepts embodied in the expression "industrial democracy." Here again, the interest has been formulated at the EC level, first, in a proposed, voluntary statute that would create a "European company" complete with a Europeanwide works council.[32] Second, and much more likely to be considered seriously, is the proposed Fifth Directive on Company Law, which owes much to the German model of codetermination and, if passed, would become compulsorily integrated into the national law of EC member states.

It is obvious that broad differences on the national level impose formidable obstacles to the concept of worker participation. In the United Kingdom, for example, "the Bullock report on industrial democracy was certainly a bold plan to put workers on the boards of large companies, but it was destined for an early pigeonhole . . . . The plain fact is that an effective system of worker participation cannot be legislated into existence."[33] This would seem especially true in a country such as the United Kingdom, where the adversary nature of the industrial relations system is greater and where unions or employee representatives are not equipped with the structural organ of worker participation, the works council. Put simply, in the United Kingdom as in the United States, "you cannot sit on a com-

---

[32] "The European Commission has proposed legislation which covers this controversial point, in the form of a European Companies' Statute. This will constitute the directly applicable Community law under which enterprises . . . will be able if they wish, to form a European Company to influence the decision-making of the company in a number of ways. First, a European works council is to be formed . . . which is to be responsible for representing the interests of all the employees of the company on matters which concern the company as a whole or concern several establishments." Peel, *The Real Power Game,* p. 93.

[33] *Ibid.,* p. 132.

pany board and be part of management and still retain the unbridled luxury of criticizing it."[34]

As with international union attempts at multinational collective bargaining, ideological differences among societies, as reflected in their industrial relations structures and patterns, also erode the meaningfulness of worker participation. Even a proponent of worker participation must acknowledge that

> it is worth remembering that the idea of worker directors is completely at variance with the private enterprise philosophy of many industrialized countries—Japan, Australia, Canada and the USA, for instance. In other countries where there are powerful trade union organizations with a Marxist philosophy, the concept of worker directors has received little support, as such a move is seen as being incompatible with the outright rejection of capitalism which these trade unions favor. France, Italy, and to a lesser degree Belgium, fall into this category . . . .[35]

Even in countries of social democratic tradition—Norway, Sweden, Germany, Denmark, and the Netherlands—where works councils have provided a rudimentary form of participation, it is not clear that rights already acquired are transitory and merely betoken more extensive rights to come. One reason for this is that worker participation means different things to different people: "At one end of the ragbag of ideas there are the socialist aspirations for workers' control, and at the other end of the spectrum a limited reform which offers consultation whilst preserving the management's right to take a final decision."[36]

In Sweden, the Meidner plan of eventual employee ownership (and union control) of companies through proposed wage-earner funds would, if enacted, provide an example of the first end of the spectrum.[37] Of the other end, consultation with employee representatives where management is reserved the final decision, more will be said in the remaining pages of this chapter. The relationship between the concept of worker participation and Paragraph 9 of the guidelines gains immediacy in a climate of high unemployment by the reactive motive for greater labor influence in decision making. The critical link remains the employment effects of investment decisions, a link that unions have interpreted as well within the labor-management relations issues inscribed in Paragraph 9.

[34] *Ibid.*, p. 138.
[35] *Ibid.*, p. 134.
[36] *Ibid.*, p. 133.
[37] Geoffrey W. Latta, *Profit Sharing, Employee Stock Ownership, Savings, and Asset Formation Plans in the Western World* (Philadelphia: Industrial Research Unit, The Wharton School, University of Pennsylvania, 1979), p. 104.

The discussion now turns to an analysis of three of the "cases" submitted to the OECD's Committee on International Investment and Multinational Enterprises (CIIME). In all three, the locus of decision making is an explicit subject of the unions' claims. Upon closer examination, however, it is the unions' claim for participation in decision making that becomes the most dynamic focus of debate. In the first two discussions, BOCI-Viggo and Philips Finland, it is clear that the claim for the right to participate in decision making is closely allied to the legal status of the works councils in Sweden and Finland. A recent ILO symposium highlighted the growing significance of the works council in the field of worker participation in decision making:

> Among the different forms of joint participation machinery, *works councils* are undeniably the first in importance. It is an importance they have regained since at the Oslo meeting in 1974 there were signs that their influence was waning, and experts, including those in the ILO, are generally agreed that one of the major changes in recent years has been the renewal of the influence works councils can have. The reasons for this comeback are almost certainly the considerably *strengthened rights and powers* they have been given, which has meant that they occupy in a number of countries a key position in the labour relations system. This has been particularly marked in countries where collective agreements are usually concluded other than at the plant level and has not been without causing conflicts at times over questions of competence within the collective bargaining structure.[38]

The third case discussion, KSSU/ATLAS, joins the unions' interest in collective bargaining structure with the definition of a multinational enterprise.

BOCI-Viggo

Viggo AB (Viggo) is a Swedish manufacturer of disposable intravenous therapy products, located in Helsingborg, Sweden. In 1973, the company was acquired by Medishield Corporation Limited (Medishield), itself a subsidiary of the London-based British Oxygen Corporation International (BOCI). Since BOCI's acquisition of Viggo, "sales have risen by some 30 percent p.a. compound, taking full advantage of the marketing facilities of the group, and Viggo now holds a dominant position in the European market for its prime products, 85 percent of output being exported from Sweden.

---

[38] "Current developments in the field of workers' participation in decisions within undertakings," *IOE Information Bulletin* Supplement (August 1981), p. 1.

Employment at Helsingborg has risen from 160 at the date of acquisition to over 600 now."[39] In mid-1978, Viggo announced its plans to
invest abroad rather than to expand production in Sweden. No layoffs at Viggo were contemplated to result from this decision.

In accordance with the Swedish Codetermination at Work Act,
Viggo's management discussed its investment plans with the Swedish labor federations. The unions attempted to convince Viggo to
expand its plant in Helsingborg, rather than to invest overseas. The
consultation ended with Viggo management's refusal to alter its
investment plans, citing high labor costs in Sweden as a deterrent to
expansion there and high tariffs abroad as rendering efforts to
expand exports impractical.

Not content with the Viggo management's decision, the labor federations attempted to talk directly with BOCI. In December 1978,
the unions wrote to BOCI to request that the parent company negotiate with them over Viggo's investment decisions. The unions
claimed that, under Paragraph 9 of the guidelines, they were entitled to "negotiate with representatives of management who are
authorized to take decisions on the matters under negotiation."
BOCI declined to negotiate with the Swedish unions. With support
from the Confederation of British Industry (CBI) and the Swedish
Employers' Federation (SAF), BOCI recommended that if any consultations were to be held, they should be between the unions and
Viggo. BOCI argued that Swedish law was not pertinent outside
Sweden and that, in any event, the requirements of Swedish law had
been fulfilled by Viggo management.

Unable to draw BOCI into the dispute, the unions then appealed
to the Swedish government. On September 27, 1979, a meeting
chaired by Sten Niklasson was convened by the Swedish government to discuss the BOCI-Viggo case. Niklasson, the deputy under
secretary of industry, has served as the deputy chairman of the
CIIME and as chairman of the UN working group for the preparation of the Code of Conduct for Transnational Corporations. He took
the view that the "labor management relations issues" cited in Paragraph 9 should be defined by the Swedish Codetermination at
Work Act, which includes decisions relating to capital investment.
Moreover, he held that the decision as to whether BOCI's or Viggo's
management must negotiate with the Swedish unions would depend
on where the decision-making authority for capital investment was
located.

---

[39] "Sweden: Test case on Multinational bargaining," *European Industrial Relations Review*, No. 74 (March 1980), p. 8.

Niklasson proposed that the unions and Viggo's management, including a director of BOCI, should meet to establish the condition of Viggo's future development. Again, BOCI declined the proposition and was supported by the SAF. The proposition, they argued, would have involved a non-Swedish parent company in a national issue—bargaining with national unions. The Swedish unions then asked the Swedish government to take the matter up with the British government. On December 4, 1979, Niklasson went to London to discuss the matter "informally" with the appropriate British officials and left them with what they understood to be a confidential, nonofficial document. Upon returning to Stockholm, Niklasson distributed this document to union and other officials. The Niklasson document supported the position of the Swedish unions in regard to the meaning of the guidelines and the duty of BOCI's headquarters, as the locus of decision-making authority, to negotiate with them about investment decisions.

Following the discussions with Niklasson, the United Kingdom's Department of Industry concluded that BOCI and Viggo had acted in accordance both with the guidelines and the Swedish Codetermination at Work Act. The Swedish officials had argued that "the minutes of the 22 September 1979 meeting appeared to show that BOCI controlled the 'strategic and substantive decisions regarding the development, production and marketing of products manufactured by the subsidiary.' Consistent with the Swedish law and practice these matters are subject to negotiations between the employees and the management of the Swedish subsidiary."[40]

The position of the British government was conveyed to the Swedish ministry of industry in the form of a brief outlining the relevant facts in the case. The brief observed that Viggo had held negotiations on the question of new investments and had thus fulfilled its obligation under Swedish law. The British government emphasized that even if one were to accept the unions' interpretation of the guidelines, the facts of the case indicate that Viggo was indeed competent to negotiate the investment issue.

In February 1980, the Swedish Confederation of Trade Unions (Landsorganisationen i Sverige—LO) sent a letter to TUAC in which it adopted the unions' charges and alleged that BOCI was in violation of Paragraph 9. The LO then requested that TUAC present the case before the CIIME for a clarification of Paragraph 9.

---

[40] "Report on developments in the Viggo Case in Sweden since the presentation at OECD (CIIME) on March 6, 1980," report of the Working Group on the Guidelines for Multinational Enterprises, presumably June 1980, p. 2.

Relevance of the Swedish Codetermination at Work Act

Presented too late for the March 1980 meeting of the CIIME with the advisory committees, and in too ill-focused a form, the case was not discussed at the March meeting. Instead, the Working Group for the Guidelines for MNEs (the Lévy Group) was charged with the task of discussing the issues involved in the Viggo case during its June 1980 meeting. To this end, the view of the Swedish minister of industry was elicited in a written response to questions posed by the Lévy Group. The minister wrote: "It is the Swedish Government's opinion that it would be desirable that meaningful negotiations should be carried out with a foreign company in Sweden, even if the final decisions on the matters which are the subject of the negotiations are taken overseas."[41]

The British and Swedish governments differ in their opinions as to whether such meaningful negotiations were in fact carried out. It is thus useful to summarize the passages of Swedish law that pertain to the rights of employee representatives to consult on investment decisions. Table XII-2 contains these passages.

TABLE XII-2
*Passages from the Swedish Codetermination at
Work Act Relating to BOCI-Viggo*

Passage	Content
Paragraph 10	A trade union shall have the right to negotiate with an employer on matters which concern the relations between the employer and members of the union who are or have been employees of that employer. An employer has the same right to negotiate with a trade union. A trade union has the right to negotiate under section one also, with an organization to which the employer belongs, and likewise the employers' organization with the trade union.
Paragraph 11	Before an employer decides concerning an important change of his activity, he shall on his own initiative summon to negotiations and negotiate with the trade union to which he is bound by a collective agreement. The same stipulation shall apply before the employer decides on any important change of the working or employment conditions for employees belonging to the trade union. Should there be extraordinary reasons at hand against a postponement of the decision, the employer may take the decision and put it in effect before he has fulfilled his obligation to negotiate under the provisions of the first paragraph.
Paragraph 12	When a trade union as mentioned in clause 11 calls for it, the employer shall also in cases other than those covered by clause 11 negotiate with the trade union before he issues or applies a decision

---
[41] *Ibid.*

TABLE XII–2 (continued)

Passage	Content
	which affects members of the union. The employer is, however, not obliged to wait until such obligation to negotiate has been fully discharged before making or applying the decision if there are special reasons against such delay.
Paragraph 16	The negotiations shall be carried on without delay. If requested by either party, minutes shall be kept of the negotiations to be signed by both parties. Unless otherwise agreed upon negotiations shall be considered finished when a party who has fulfilled his duty to negotiate has given the owner side notice in writing that he withdraws from the negotiation.

From Table XII-2, it is first of all apparent that Swedish law (Paragraphs 10 and 11) may allow a broad meaning of the phrase "labor management relations issues." The meaning would arguably extend to investment decisions and their impact upon the work force. As was earlier noted, however, although such decisions require negotiations under Swedish law, the locus of these negotiations continues to remain a matter of dispute between the British and Swedish governments, the latter contending that Viggo's investment decisions were made at corporate headquarters in London, whereas the former stated that the decisions were made at the local management level of Viggo. We shall return to a discussion of the British position below. As Table XII-2 indicates, Swedish law would appear to establish two essential points. Firstly, unions have the right to negotiate with the employer "on matters which concern the relations between the employer and members of the union," (Paragraph 10). Secondly, these negotiations must occur at the employer's initiative "before an employer decides concerning an important change of activity," (Paragraph 11). A relevant issue thus emerges in the event that the parties to the negotiation do not agree. This issue is related to the meaning of negotiation in the context of Swedish law. The Swedish Employers' Federation has observed that: "the term 'negotiation' in codetermination matters in the new Swedish Act has the same sense as 'consultation before decision.' If no concensus is reached, the employer has the right, according to Swedish law, to take his decision unilaterally."[42] The ultimate decision-making authority of the employer is implied in Paragraph 12 of the act.

---

[42] J. Coates, "OECD Guidelines—Employment and Industrial Relations: Note for BIAC Working Party," (Paris: Business and Industry Advisory Committee to the OECD, 1980), p. 3.

It must be recalled that the unions differed not only with the employer's decision, but charged that the decision had in fact been made at a level above that of the locus of negotiations. As for the latter point, under Swedish law "there is no obligation for an employer to be represented at the negotiations by representatives authorized to take decisions in the matters under negotiation."[43] A crucial point, however, is that the unions do not appear to have exhausted all the avenues open to them under Swedish law. Specifically, the unions had the right to claim damages through Swedish courts if they were not satisfied, as they were not, that Viggo had fulfilled its obligation to negotiate.

That the unions did not do this weakens their position, as it would appear to underscore discontent with the actual decision, rather than with the manner in which it was made. Dissatisfaction with the decision would be difficult to justify in light of the fact that since its takeover of Viggo, BOCI had invested 10 million pounds in the subsidiary, had increased its work force from 160 to 600 people, and had affirmed Viggo's promise that the new investment plans would not result in any layoffs.[44]

The Substance of Viggo's Investment Plans

It was not the threat of immediate layoffs resulting from Viggo's decision that concerned the unions. Rather, it was the long-term impact of the company's plans. The details of these plans were provided to the CIIME and advisory bodies in a "factual note" submitted by the UK delegation to the CIIME and prepared by the UK department of industry. The brief began:

> Two quite separate instances are involved in the TUAC document and in order to have a correct understanding of the events described it is necessary to deal with them separately. The first concerns the establishment by Medishield of the subsidiary company Pioneer Viggo Inc. in the United States, and in particular the development, manufacture and marketing of a product named Vasculon; and the second, the company's assessment and choice of location for further expansion.[45]

With regard to the first issue, since 1969, at least, Viggo had been attempting to penetrate the U.S. market with a product named Venflon. After the acquisition, Medishield and Viggo managements

---

[43] *Ibid.*

[44] "Follow-up to the consultations between the Committee and the advisory bodies held on 6 March 1980," note by the United Kingdom Delegation, Committee on International Investment and Multinational Enterprises, 22 May 1980, p. 2.

[45] *Ibid.*

jointly examined the reasons for their lack of marketing success. They concluded that the product design was not tailored to the specifications of the U.S. market and, moreover, that an 18 percent import tariff into the United States in addition to transport costs rendered the product uncompetitively priced.

In 1976, Medishield hired an American expert who developed the new product, Vasculon, which was better suited to the American market. The American developed the product at Viggo in Helsingborg and went on to become president of a newly established U.S. subsidiary, Pioneer Viggo Inc. The subsidiary was created to facilitate entry into the American market with the new product Vasculon. "From the beginning of the development of Vasculon, however, it was intended that, if test marketing proved successful, full scale production would be carried out by Pioneer in the United States for the North American market"[46] for reasons cited earlier. It was furthermore made clear that if the new product were subsequently marketed in Europe, "first consideration for manufacturing for that market would be Helsingborg."[47]

Plans for the development and marketing of Vasculon were formulated by the managing director of Viggo, the president of Pioneer Viggo, and Mr. Rostron, the director of Medishield and member of the board of Viggo. Additional plans involved another product group produced by Viggo, infusion stopcocks. Again, the company's attempts to penetrate the U.S. market with this product line had been frustrated by the product's price and performance. One model of the stopcock, however, that represented one percent of the product group's total production at Viggo was thought to have potential for the U.S. market. "This model, however, sold in only very small quantities in Europe, and the tooling was such that costs were high. At the same time total moulding capacity at Viggo was fully committed and a large back-order existed on all models of stopcocks."[48]

The plan called for Viggo's mold for this one stopcock to be lent to Pioneer Viggo, where the product would be manufactured and test-marketed in the U.S. At a point following this step, Viggo would have the option of either taking back its mold for manufacture of the product in the European market, or of purchasing the American product directly from Pioneer Viggo. Negotiations in Sweden were concluded over these plans as well, as stipulated under the Swedish Codetermination at Work Act. Plans for marketing and manufactur-

---

[46] *Ibid.*, p. 4.
[47] *Ibid.*
[48] *Ibid.*

ing the Viggo stopcock in the United States, however, were subsequently scrapped when further analysis concluded that the product did not meet market demand.

The British government brief observed that the September 1978 negotiations between Viggo and the unions were over the subject of decisions relating to Vasculon and infusion stopcocks. "Two extracts from the protocol," the brief noted, "appear to have attracted particular attention among the trade unions:

> Up till now Viggo AB has been the only firm within the group to market infusion Stopcocks and this has been mainly on the European market and as a separate product. The development of the market has led to a demand for infusion Stopcocks in the USA, primarily as a component in a composite product. As a result of the present marketing policy within the group, infusion Stopcocks for the USA are to be sold by Pioneer Viggo Inc. which was why the group decided that Pioneer Viggo Inc. should also manufacture this product partly because of the lower production cost and partly because of the fact that at least in the short term Viggo AB does not have the production capacity . . . . It was noted that the decision regarding infusion Stopcocks was taken by the group management and the decision on Vasculon is dependent on the product's further development on the market.[49]

The British government brief notes further: "The 'group management' referred to consisted of the managing director of Viggo AB, the president of Pioneer, and Mr. Rostron as described above. The company knows of no document signed by the management of Viggo AB stating that Viggo's management 'could not negotiate on the question of transfer of production because these decisions are made in London,'" as the TUAC document had claimed.[50]

The unions' interest in the future vitality of product development efforts relates to the second issue referred to by the UK Department of Industry, the future investment of the Viggo subsidiary itself. Viggo's management had itself investigated the issue and concluded that expansion at the Helsingborg site was, for the present, infeasible. "Lack of space, relative lack of labour, high costs for labour intensive products and the need to manufacture in major export markets"[51] were cited as the principal factors informing management's decision.

Together with the unions, Viggo's management undertook a study of possible sites for investment during 1978–1979:

---

[49] *Ibid.*, p. 5.
[50] *Ibid.*
[51] *Ibid.*, p. 6.

> The Viggo management has now reached a conclusion on the pre-
> ferred location for the new investment—the chosen site is in the UK—
> although the representatives of the workforce have registered their
> disagreement with the proposal to invest abroad. The Viggo manage-
> ment is expected to submit its proposals to the Medishield Board for
> approval in the near future. This is required because, under the terms
> of Viggo's delegated authority from Medishield and in line with the
> practice in all Medishield subsidiaries, all substantial investments
> calling on group funds have to be submitted to Medishield's Board
> for approval. This arrangement, under which the authorization for
> major projects is reserved to the parent company, is no different from
> the normal practice of most multinational groups.[52]

The passage above is highly significant, serving, as its does, to high-
light the hierarchy of decision making in this investment decision.
The location of the future investment was the subject of study by
Viggo management—that is, the decision itself was a decentralized
one; only the funding for the decision requiring central approval.
Negotiations with the unions occurred at the appropriate level, that
of the subsidiary, where no agreement was reached. One could quite
plausibly argue from the available evidence that the unions' efforts
to negotiate with corporate headquarters constitute more an
attempt to overrule a decision in which they did not concur than the
result of not having had access to the decision makers. The decision
itself was objectionable, although the manner in which it was made,
conventional in law and practice.

Negotiations between Viggo and the unions ended in disagreement in December 1979. It is the view of Viggo's management that
the investment decision does not entail a lessening in importance of
the Swedish subsidiary's research and development. "It will in fact
provide the opportunity for Viggo to increase R&D activity and, in
due course, employment as part of an even bigger operation."[53] This
conclusion addresses the heart of the unions' concern, for although
the plan called for no reduction of Viggo's work force, the unions
had feared that the expansion across national borders would bring
in its wake the subordination in importance of Viggo.

To summarize, then, the two major issues involved in Viggo's
investment decisions, the British brief upheld the company's view-
point that: 1) the authority of the decision was vested in Viggo's
management; and 2) negotiations with the unions were concluded at
this level although no agreement was reached. With regard to the
product manufacturing and marketing decision, group management

---

[52] *Ibid.*
[53] *Ibid.*

214 MNEs and the OECD Guidelines

consisted of the director of Medishield, the managing director of Viggo, and the president of Pioneer Viggo. As the director of Medishield, Rostron is also a member of Viggo's board of directors. Viggo management asserts that "access" to the decision makers was thus assured at the local level, both because the decision in question was a joint decision (not a *fait accompli* received by local management) and by the presence of Rostron on the board. With regard to the location of the new plant, both studies and the decision were made at the level of Viggo management.

Activity at the OECD Level

The March 6, 1980, meeting of the CIIME and advisory bodies produced a recommendation that the Lévy Group (the working group on the guidelines for multinationals chaired by the Swiss delegate to the OECD, Philippe Lévy) entertain reports from the two national contact points with respect to the Viggo case, in accordance with procedure recommended in the 1979 review report. At a subsequent meeting of the Lévy Group held on June 9 and 10, 1980, the conclusions of both contact points held that "the procedures on the questions under dispute had been concluded under relevant Swedish law."[54] There remained, however, issues related to the meaning of Paragraph 9 which the group sought to isolate for discussion.

Recalling that it is not the business of the CIIME to comment upon specific situations involving individual companies, the Lévy Group presented three statements of broad agreement among the parties to the meeting:

—The company concerned is a subsidiary of a parent company located abroad. Within the corporate structure of the Group major decisions about investment plans are taken at the group-level or, at least, are subject to approval by the board of the parent company.

—Swedish legislation requires negotiations on "any matter relating to the relationship between the employer and any member of the organisation who is or has been employed by that employer" and in particular on "important changes of (the employer's) activity" to take place. Final decisions on these matters are left to management.

—The management of the subsidiary has held several meetings with employee representatives during which the investment plans of

---

[54] "Consideration of certain issues arising from materials presented by TUAC at the consultations with the Committee on 6 March 1980," Note by the Secretariat, Committee on International Investment and Multinational Enterprises, September 19, 1980, p. 1.

the company were discussed. These contacts were terminated by management without agreement being reached, and the company proceeded to execute its plans.[55]

On the basis of these facts, the group formula · the central issue introduced by the Viggo matter: "If national legislation provides for negotiations on future plans of the enterprise including investment and the final decisions on these matters are taken by the parent company, what are the implications of Paragraph 9?"[56] The implications, in the group's view, were threefold: the relationship between future investment plans and the wording of Paragraph 9 pertaining to "collective bargaining or labour management relations"; the meaning of the term "negotiations" in Paragraph 9; and the methods by which managements may comply with the duty to negotiate embodied in Paragraph 9. Table XII-3 summarizes the major views

TABLE XII-3

Excerpts from the Lévy Group's Discussion
of the Issues Involved in the Viggo Case

Issue	Major Statements
Coverage of the Terms "Collective Bargaining or Labour Management Relations"	There is still no internationally agreed standard of the scope of 'collective bargaining' or 'labour management relations' which would give guidance in interpreting the meaning of these parts of paragraph 9. National practices in this area have continued to evolve however and the diversity found today is probably greater than when the Guidelines were drafted. There are countries...where a trend can be observed towards including information and consultations on the economic and financial management of the enterprise, encompassing also future production and investment plans...The terms 'collective bargaining' and 'labour management relations' thus appear to be sufficiently broad...(and)...their specific meaning can be determined by the reference to national laws, regulations, prevailing labour relations and employment practices in the (chapeau clause).
Meaning of the term "negotiation"	As a general rule, the concept of negotiations implies an effort to reach agreement by the parties concerned. In several national systems, the term negotiation, as distinct from consultations, means that if in case of disagreement a party takes a unilateral decision the other party is justified in having recourse to industrial action or to

[55] *Ibid.,* pp. 2–3.
[56] *Ibid.,* p. 4.

TABLE XII-3 (continued)

Issue	Major Statements
	external decision making procedures...In these countries 'consultations' seem to assume a management right to make and to carry out the decision it thinks best, given all the circumstances and having listened to the views of employee representatives. In other countries negotiations are understood to imply an effort to reach agreement although the final decision-making power of management remains unaffected and in such an instance the distinction between 'negotiations' and 'consultations' is in practice difficult to draw...The Working Group...supposes that negotiations are being conducted in the framework of national laws and practices...It is therefore natural that the precise sense of the word negotiation used...in paragraph 9 should be defined by these laws and practices.
Management methods to enable negotiations to take place with those "authorized to take decisions on the matters under consideration."	Management of the MNE as a whole would seem to have a number of options among which no a priori preference would be assigned: —To delegate decision-making authority in the matters under negotiation to the management of the subsidiary in the country where the negotiations are to take place; —To delegate one or more representatives of the decision-making centre...to the negotiating team of the subsidiary, with power to negotiate...; —To engage directly in negotiations.

Source: Note by the Secretariat, OECD, Committee on International Investment and Multinational Enterprises, September 19, 1980, pp. 4–7.

of the group on each issue.

The Lévy Group's discussion of the issues formed the basis for the subsequent clarification of Paragraph 9, undertaken by the CIIME. Like the group's findings, the CIIME's pronouncement included no easy formulas for interpreting Paragraph 9. Consistent with its mission, the CIIME's clarification was neither intended, nor could easily be viewed, as a judgment of right or wrong in the Viggo matter, a fact that elicited the criticism of the unions.

> The unions ... understand the clarification as meaning that whenever an MNC has a "centralized" decision-making system, they have an automatic right to direct negotiations at headquarters level .... The CIIME rejected this interpretation: if a company states that a particular negotiating team is empowered to make significant decisions, it will be up to the nations to show that it is not, before they

can claim that the proper forum for discussion is group head-quarters.[57]

As the statements in Table XII-3 illustrate, the thrust of the Lévy Group remarks, particularly with regard to the first two issues, would appear squarely aimed at the "chapeau clause" of the guidelines and thus a national structure of industrial relations.

Consensus would appear to have been reached by the group on the two fundamental aspects of the Viggo matter. Negotiations with the unions on the investment decisions did in fact occur in accordance with Swedish law, and under the law, management has the right to make its decision unilaterally in the event of disagreement between the parties to negotiation. With respect to the third issue, the methods by which management might enable meaningful negotiations to occur, it has been throughout the company's view, supported by those of the Swedish and British employers' groups and the British government, that the decision-making authority was in fact at the level of Viggo management. Approval of the decision for funding purposes only would subsequently involve a higher level of authority.

PHILIPS FINLAND

Issues similar to those involved in the Viggo affair, yet with some important differences, surfaced anew in the announcement of a plant closure at Oy Philips Ab, a subsidiary of the Dutch multinational, N.V. Philips. On March 3, 1980, the Helsinki plant's consultation committee was informed that, owing to a change in market demand for the audio products that Oy Philips manufactures, management's view was that the plant should close down by May 1981. Oy Philips management claimed that the manner in which the employee representatives on the consultation committee were informed was perfectly consistent with Finnish legislation in this area. Supporting management's view was the fact that the end of a one-and-a-half-hour meeting held with the consultation committee on March 3, 1980, produced unanimous agreement. This agreement included the signatures of the parties of the minutes of the meeting which stated: "that 'notification procedure and the negotiation requirement had been observed in accordance with the law in con-

---

[57] "OECD clarifies consultation code," *Business Europe*, Vol. 21, No. 16 (April 17, 1981), p. 121.

nection with the closure decision.' These minutes excluded the possibility of the Union to undertake juridical action."[58]

The closure decision would potentially affect 248 blue-collar workers represented by the Helsinki Radio Workers' Union, itself affiliated with the Finnish Metalworkers' Union (FMU). The closure
decision prompted an immediate response from the latter group:

> The Finnish Metalworkers' Union has taken up the matter officially
> with the following instances: the Executive Committee of the Euro-
> pean Metalworkers' Federation (4 March); the meeting of the Philips
> working group of the Nordic Metalworkers' Secretariat (18 March);
> the EMF Philips working group (19 March); the national contact
> point of the Finnish Government (letter of 2 April); EMF (23 April);
> IMF (23 April); the Ministry of Social Affairs and Health (15 May);
> and the Finnish Government (15 September).[59]

It is significant to note that the FMU's activity on behalf of its
affiliate "went international" almost immediately following the
March 3 meeting. A plausible cause for this direction would appear
to be the fact that the employee representatives on the plant's consultation committee had signed the minutes of the meeting, signal-
ling their compliance with the manner in which negotiations had
been handled and precluding any recourse to the Finnish courts.
This left the international level as the one having greatest potential
for channeling dissatisfaction.

The International Metalworkers' Federation (IMF) and the European Metalworkers' Federation (EMF) jointly brought the matter to
the attention of TUAC and, through this group, to the CIIME.
Table XII-4 summarizes TUAC's submission of the company's

TABLE XII-4

*Oy Philips' Alleged Infractions of the OECD Guidelines Submitted
by the Finnish Metalworkers' Union to the International
Metalworkers' Federation*

Paragraph	Comment
Paragraph 5, General	Philips has violated Article 5 in the General Policies since its plant in Finland has not been allowed to freely develop its activities in Finland. In the information handed to the employees it was stated that one of the reasons for the closure was considerable underloading in the European plants of the Philips Group manufacturing consumer goods. It was further stated that "for

---

[58] "Follow-up to the review of the declaration and decisions on international investment and multinational enterprises," Communication by TUAC, (Committee on
International Investment and Multinational Enterprises, October 13, 1980), p. 5.
[59] *Ibid.*, p. 4.

TABLE XII–4 (continued)

Paragraph	Comment
	this reason we have not been given an opportunity to continue the production of our present products." This means that the decision to close down the plant was based on the situation in other entities of the group but the Finnish one.
Paragraph 3, Employment and Industrial Relations	Oy Philips Ab has consistently given its employees a picture of its business prospects that has proven to be false…the employees have been assured that even though reductions in the production would take place, jobs would not be threatened. This has given the employees an idea of steady jobs.
Paragraph 6, Employment and Industrial Relations	Philips has not followed Article 6 in the chapter on Employment and Industrial Relations, since they have not, for instance, had talks with the appropriate authorities in order to mitigate the adverse effects caused by the closure.
Paragraph 9, Employment and Industrial Relations	Philips has violated Article 9…since no real negotiations have been conducted, and especially not with representatives of management who are authorized to make decisions. We refer to our arguments in connection with Article 5 of the General Policies.
Paragraph 1, Science and Technology	Philips has violated Article 1… since it has not contributed to 'the establishment in the host country of the capacity to innovate.'

Source: "Closure of Oy Philips Ab's plant in Finland," letter from the Finnish Metalworkers' Union to the International Metalworkers' Federation, April 23, 1980.

alleged infractions of five paragraphs of the guidelines.

The panoply of charges in Table XII–4 suggests what was noted earlier in this chapter: the issue of plant closure, particularly when it involves a multinational's subsidiary, can form the basis of a wide range of claims against the MNE, culminating in the demand for multinational bargaining. With regard to the closure decision itself, therefore, the FMU's claims center on the timing of the decision, (Paragraphs 3 and 6, Employment and Industrial Relations), the manner in which the decision was made, (Paragraph 9, Employment and Industrial Relations), and the wisdom of the decision itself, (Paragraph 5, General Policies, Paragraph 9, Employment and Industrial Relations, and Paragraph 1, Science and Technology). The breadth of these charges recalls the Dutch union federation's involvement in another case, as well as the problems surrounding Ford Nederland's recent closure of its Amsterdam subsidiary.[60]

[60] In both cases, the unions challenged not only management's right to make disinvestment decisions, but the economic basis of the decisions themselves. Discussion of these incidents is contained in the chapter on Paragraph 6.

As in the two latter instances, the allegations against Oy Philips would appear to contain an implicit hierarchy of interests, ranging from the employment effects of the decision to employee representatives' involvement in it, and finally to the validity of the decision itself. The first two stages, the effects of the decision, would seem to act as a spring board for the third, the demand for multinational bargaining as a means of participating in and influencing corporate investment and disinvestment decisions.

This is not to suggest that, had the timing of the decision and negotiations been over a longer period, union dissatisfaction with the decision would necessarily have been mitigated. To the union, however, timing was a problem and ultimately undermined, from the union's point of view, local management's role in the decision: "In the view of TUAC notice of the decision was made in a manner and time-frame which did not allow for any meaningful negotiations as laid out in the OECD Guidelines for Multinational Enterprises. In fact the employees were presented with a 'fait accompli' which they saw no way to avoid."[61] Implied in the criticism was that local management was equally powerless to avoid the decision as it had been made at corporate headquarters' level. The perception was bolstered by the union's claim that, some weeks prior to the closure decision, "local management had given works councillors the clear impression that employment prospects were good."[62] Subsequently, however, in February 1980, Oy Philips' management had stated to the employee representatives that the subsidiary was facing some difficulties and that management would be in a better position to inform representatives of the extent of these difficulties upon management's return from a meeting at corporate headquarters.

However sensitive the decision, there is really no mystery surrounding the locus of authority in the decision to close a subsidiary, and no one would contend that authority is normally vested at a level below headquarters. Thus, despite considerable union and political pressure against the decisions, the Dutch courts ultimately acknowledged Ford's disinvestment decision as legally and economically sound. As will be seen with respect to Oy Philips, the evidence suggests that local management's foreknowledge of the decision to close was brief—although brevity implies neither capriciousness nor the intent to deceive.

As BIAC communicated to the CIIME concerning issues arising under Paragraph 9: "Requiring management to hold long informa-

---

[61] "Follow-up to the review," p. 3.
[62] "OECD Code Test Case," *European Industrial Relations Review,* No. 83 (December 1980), p. 2.

tion and consultation sessions with employee representatives before making any important decisions unduly encumbers the decision-making process. Any weakening of the decision-making process which is central to effective corporate management in a competitive market is ill-advised and counter-productive."[63] Particularly when the subject of the decision is unpopular, the relevant questions to pose are, again, whether the company's conduct has contravened Finnish law and practice and whether Finnish law provides for negotiations between labor and management to occur at headquarters level. With regard to the former question, the Finnish contact point addressed the FMU's allegations in the contact point's submission to the CIIME.

The Remarks of the Finnish Contact Point

In reply to a letter by the FMU, the Finnish contact point detailed its comments on the Oy Philips case which were subsequently submitted to the CIIME through the Finnish Delegation. In so doing, the contact group recalled that: "The Code guidelines recommend ...that matters under dispute be discussed and that efforts be made to solve them at the national level, if possible."[64] Contained in TUAC's document to the CIIME, the FMU concluded that the Finnish contact point had evinced a view generally favorable to the union's claims. The text of the letter does not necessarily support this conclusion. For example, the FMU had alleged a violation of Paragraph 5, General Policies, which states that multinationals should allow their subsidiaries "to develop their activities and to exploit their competitive advantage in domestic and foreign markets. . . ." The contact group replied that

> multinational enterprises should also take into account the general policy objectives of their host countries as well as their aims and priorities. The Guidelines do not, however, call for the freezing of the structures of multinational enterprises. Enterprises have the right to dissolve the investments they have made, in accordance with the regulations of national legislation and contracts concluded.[65]

The comment would appear to uphold the principles of flexibility as it concerns headquarters' decisions over investments, and focuses rather on whether the decision accords with national law.

---

[63] Coates, "OECD Guidelines—Employment and Industrial Relations,: Note for BIAC Working Party," p. 8.

[64] "Issues arising under the Guidelines with respect to a plant closure in Finland," note by the Finnish Delegation, Committee on International Investment and Multinational Enterprises, January 22, 1981, p. 3.

[65] *Ibid.*

Continuing its remarks, the contact group found that "regulations contained in the general policies chapter have special relevance
in cases where a subsidiary is closed down. In such cases, the enterprise concerned would be well advised to seek clarification in
advance with the government of the host country."[66] Clearly, the
question of clarification in advance of precisely what—the decision
or the decision's effects—is central. The company notified the relevant Finnish authorities of its decision on March 10, 1980. The
FMU, however, contended that "Philips has not proceeded on these
lines" and thus that the contact group "has to this extent endorsed
the Union's complaint on the issue."[67] Such an endorsement is belied
by the contact group's letter:

> the Contact Group notes that the notice concerning the closedown of
> the factory was given well in advance of the closure of the entity and
> that the enterprise, in conjunction with the manpower authorities,
> has taken steps to mitigate the adverse effects caused by the closure.
> According to a notification received dismissals will not be carried out
> during the current year.[68]

The FMU's allegation of an infraction of Paragraph 6, Employment and Industrial Relations, elicited some criticism from the contact group. In its view, the company did not go far enough in providing reasonable notice of the decision to close to its employees so that
meaningful negotiations on the decision could take place. Rather,
the contact group concluded that "the decision on closure had factually been taken prior to the stage of notification."[69] The contact
group thus concluded that the last opportunity to influence the closure decision must have occurred prior to March 3, 1980, the date of
notification. Obviously, the issue is central to the FMU's charges,
and the discussion will return to this question in the section to follow. As has been noted, the question of when the decision was made,
in the FMU's view, is rather closely related to where it was made.
As will be seen, Finnish law addresses the former concern, Paragraph 9 of the guidelines, the latter.

To the contact group, other claims made by the FMU appeared
more readily soluble. Thus, with regard to the union's allegation
that the company had consistently provided information that
proved to be false, the contact group's view dissented from the
union's:

---

[66] *Ibid.*

[67] "Follow-up to the review of the declaration and decision on international investment and multinational enterprises," p. 7.

[68] "Issues arising under the Guidelines with respect to plant closure in Finland,"
p. 5.

[69] *Ibid.*, p. 4.

> There is a difference in views between the parties concerned as to whether or not the employees have been provided with such information as would have enabled them, before the factual decision on closure was taken, to obtain a true and fair view of the performance of the entity concerned. The opinion of the Contact Group is that Philips Finland has endeavored to communicate information according to the OECD guidelines.[70]

Despite the contact group's view, moreover, that the decision had been taken prior to the March 9, 1980, meeting of the consultation committee, the group nevertheless noted that the matter "was discussed in accordance with the Act on Co-operation in Enterprises by the Consultative Committee provided by the Act."[71] In view of the FMU's charge of an infraction of Paragraph 9 of the guidelines, it is useful to discuss the legality of the company's comportment under Finnish law.

The Relevance of Finnish Law

It has been noted that the contact group held that the plant-closure decision "had factually been taken prior to the stage of notification," and that the FMU charged that the decision appeared to have emanated from a level higher than that of local management in Finland. Thus, the union held, "the last formal opportunity to influence things was in the negotiations between Oy Philips Ab and Philips central management in Eindhoven the previous week."[72] Finnish law, however, would appear to imply otherwise.

Similar to Swedish law, the act on employee participation in companies in Finland imposes stringent requirements on the employer both to provide information on and to negotiate the decision to close a plant. The FMU summarized the relevant passages of the act:

> The paragraphs 3, 4, 5, 7, 8, 9 and 11 of the Act on employee participation deal with negotiation procedure. Paragraph 7 of the Act provides for compulsory negotiations by the employer. This entails the employer's calling for and arranging negotiations *before* any decisions on matters mentioned in the Act can be made. According to paragraph 11, prior to negotiations information shall be provided on the background causes for the changes to be discussed in negotiations. The preamble to the Act also emphasizes the need for information on financial matters whenever this is relevant to the subject under negotiation. The Act prescribes a penalty for any employer who fails to provide such information and arrange negotiations.[73]

---

[70] *Ibid.*

[71] *Ibid.*

[72] "Follow-up to the review of the declaration and decisions on international investment and multinational enterprises," p. 9.

[73] *Ibid.*, p. 5.

Two issues are of particular importance. Firstly, it is significant that no mention is made in Finnish law that decisions in matters of plant closures need be jointly made. Rather, as in Sweden, the ultimate decision-making authority rests with management. The second issue concerns the negotiations themselves. If, indeed, the employee representatives were in effect presented with a *fait accompli,* the remedy under Finnish law would presumably be the penalty mentioned in the quotation above. The employee representatives therefore could have commenced legal proceedings at the national level beginning with a refusal to sign the minutes of the meeting. Before this legal step, a refusal to sign could conceivably have been accompanied by a demand for further information, a delay in the proceedings, or ultimately by bringing charges against the company through the national courts.

That none of these avenues was chosen is peculiar. Why, for example, had the negotiating union signed the minutes of the March 3 meeting, thus signaling its assent? The FMU contends that "the distressed condition of the workers accounts for the fact that they signed the minutes."[74] As was noted earlier, by signing the minutes of the meeting, the negotiating union forfeited other remedies, including recourse to Finnish courts, to stay or otherwise influence the decision. The FMU's depiction of the employee representatives as victims powerless to influence the closure decision hinges closely on the FMU's portrayal of the employees representatives as distressed. Even if the ultimate decision-making authority resides with management, the power of the employee representatives to influence such decisions would, under Finnish law, appear to have been broader than is implied in the FMU's statement. Finally, it would seem an effort to recoup on the international level what was not legally possible on the national level.[75]

In the contact group's view, the company had endeavored to provide information in accordance with the OECD guidelines and had negotiated the closure decision in accordance with Finnish law. It is not an insignificant point that the duty to negotiate with employee representatives before a decision is made would appear safeguarded by remedies up to and including recourse to the courts. Management may well have formulated its decision on the plant closure before the negotiations occurred. Indeed, it is unreasonable to assume that management would approach the negotiations with

---

[74] *Ibid.*

[75] Arguably, many of the "cases" to have come before the CIIME would seem inspired by the same effort.

employee representatives on such a weighty matter as a plant closure in a state of indecision! The crucial point would seem that, however formulated, the decision was final only with the signatures to an agreement. Legal action was not pursued on the national level. Moreover, the FMU's attempt to involve the Finnish government in the matter was not successful although the union had sought to procure the government's complaint against the company's comportment as a violation of the ILO Declaration of Principles: "Individual cases are at present not considered by the ILO, but governments can include the conduct of multinational enterprises in their country reports to the ILO. However, this was not done despite the recommendation of the Finnish Metalworkers' Union to the Finnish government."[76] The CIIME's clarification of Paragraph 9 appears to have been the vehicle for comment at the international level.

Activity at the OECD Level

As was noted in the discussion of the Viggo case, three options were suggested to facilitate compliance with Paragraph 9, ranging from total reliance on subsidiary management to direct negotiations with corporate headquarters. As both the Viggo and Oy Philips examples illustrate, the interest in multinational bargaining is primarily aimed at investment and disinvestment decisions. As such, the international union movement's efforts to attain multinational bargaining are reflective not only of the concern for the locus of decision-making in industrial relations, but with the scope of industrial relations as well.

Commenting on the CIIME's clarification, BIAC stated the following

> BIAC is appreciative of the efforts which the CIIME Committee has made to provide clarification of the issues which have been raised by the application of Paragraph 9 of the Employment and Industrial Relations Guidelines to investment matters. However, it must be emphasized that BIAC has undertaken to commend the Guidelines as originally negotiated to the enterprises and Member Federations which it represents, and the introduction of new elements or new interpretations of the existing wording risks further misunderstanding and possibly the weakening of commitments previously made in good faith. The original wording of the Guidelines was accepted as being broad enough to cover the varying situations which exist in the real world in which businesses operate. . . .[77]

---

[76] "Follow-up to the review of the declaration and decisions on international investment and multinational enterprises," p. 6.

[77] OECD Committee on International Investment and Multinational Enterprises, "Comments on Document . . . dealing with the Application of Paragraph 9 of the Employment and Industrial Relations Guidelines to Investment Matters (Note by BIAC), March 1981, p. 1.

A second major reservation concerns the implication, which seems to run through Paragraphs 7, 8 and 9 of the document, that in most multinational enterprises there is a single "decision making centre" with monolithic authority. In practice the management process is much more complex and will generally involve many levels of management. All decisions affecting a subsidiary will, however, need the support of local management, subject also to the legal requirements laid on directors of companies. Matters which are generally understood to fall within the scope of collective bargaining or labour relations must be handled locally by authorised representatives of management. It is for these reasons that BIAC has always opposed the concept of international collective bargaining which would entirely disrupt the national framework of law and practice by which industrial relations are governed. . . .[78]

In *Paragraph 9* we must disagree with the emphasis which is placed upon the "management of the enterprise as a whole" in regard to labour relations questions, and believe that we are being realistic in arguing that the conduct of negotiations should be the responsibility of the management of each entity or each national management as may be the case, representing the views of the management of the enterprise as a whole.[79]

BIAC's remarks seem directed at TUAC's attempt to render legitimate the concept of multinational bargaining through discussion of these cases at the international level. Clearly, such an attempt at legitimacy would be furthered if the recourse to remedies at the national level proved powerless to cope with the issues arising from the cases presented to the CIIME. In the Oy Philips case, TUAC's efforts to illustrate the powerlessness of activity on the national level are belied not only by the legality of the company's comportment as found by the contact group, but by the signed agreement that was reached with the consultative committee. Compliance with national law notwithstanding (and also notwithstanding the considerable negotiating rights with which the Finnish consultation committee, for example, is endowed), the union interest would appear to be that, in every case, it have the right of information on the decision-making structure of the multinational enterprise.

Following a meeting with the CIIME on March 12, 1981, and in view of TUAC's complaint that the CIIME's clarification of Paragraph 9 had been unclear, TUAC formulated its own interpretation of corporate obligations. The CIIME, at this meeting, had stated that it "cannot at this stage agree to a broader obligation on companies to give information of their decision-making structure in general, unless the request comes up in a specific negotiating situation;

[78] *Ibid.*
[79] *Ibid.*, p. 2.

for such a broader obligation a new Guideline would be needed."[80]
The CIIME's view of corporate obligation in this area remained,
therefore, at the very least, the delegation of decision-making
authority such that meaningful negotiations could occur. TUAC's
view transcends this:

> The TUAC conclusion is that even if the OECD has not agreed to a
> general obligation to give information on the decision-making struc-
> ture of the multinational enterprise, every time unions commence
> negotiations with a multinational enterprise, they have the right to
> request and receive information on the decision-making structure of
> the enterprise in order to ensure that they are negotiating with real
> decision makers.[81]

In the context of the CIIME's clarification, TUAC's assertion
appears too strong—perhaps deliberately so, as the language that
has been used to discuss the issue of multinational bargaining has
often been subtly inclined toward the future, as exemplified by the
CIIME's view that it could not "at this stage" agree to a broader
corporate obligation. As one report held: "If a company states that
a particular negotiating team is empowered to make significant
decisions, it will be up to the unions to show that it is not, before
they can claim that the proper forum for discussion is group headquarters."[82] Perhaps especially because Swedish and Finnish laws
endow the employee representatives with such broad negotiating
rights, the proper fora for discussion and negotiation even of investment matters would appear to have remained the local level in both
the Viggo and Oy Philips cases.

KSSU/ATLAS

The issues surrounding the attempts of an international trade secretariat, the International Transport Workers' Federation (ITF) to
negotiate directly with groupings of European airlines, KSSU (composed of KLM, Swissair, SAS, and UTA) and ATLAS (composed of
Alitalia, Lufthansa, Air France, and Sabena), differ significantly
from those of the previous case discussions. Not only are the companies in question state-owned, but the ITF's demand for negotiations
at "headquarters" level poses the initial problem of whether these

[80] "OECD Guidelines: TUAC Makes Formal Statement following talks with
CIIME," *Multinational Service Fortnightly,* No. 106 (April 24, 1981), p. 2.
[81] *Ibid.*
[82] "OECD Clarifies Consultation Code," *Business Europe,* Vol. 21, No. 16 (April 17,
1981), p. 121.

airline groupings constitute multinational companies either in behavior or in fact.

Brief History of the Airline Groupings

KLM, Swissair, SAS, and UTA (a French airline joining in June 1969) formed the KSSU group in May 1968. Their objectives were to standardize the layout, equipment, and facility requirements of the Boeing 747s that the airlines were to purchase. Subsequent KSSU agreements determined that KLM would handle airframe maintenance, SAS would perform engine overhauls, and crew training would be conducted on a KLM simulator. After the French airline, UTA, joined the group, the agreement was extended to accommodate its fleet of McDonnell-Douglas DC-10s.

Air France, Alitalia, Lufthansa, and Sabena (the main proponents of earlier attempts to form an agreement in the late 1950s and early 1960s) joined to form the ATLAS group in 1969. This agreement, like the KSSU one, was based upon purchasing Boeing 747 aircrafts with identical technical specifications. In ATLAS' case, Air France would take care of the airframe overhaul on the combined fleet, while Lufthansa would overhaul the Pratt & Whitney JT 9D engines. Alitalia and Sabena provided for the overhaul of components.

The First Issue: Is an Airline Grouping a Multinational?

The ITF has attempted to meet directly with the airline groupings at intervals ever since the airline groups were formed. In its efforts, the ITF has consistently argued that

> decisions taken at group level are, in fact, implemented within the individual airlines, and the unions have little or no possibility of influencing them at that level. They therefore believe that their existing rights of negotiations with the individual airlines must be supplemented by the right to be consulted and to state their views at group level also. Harmonization of working conditions within the grouping is made unnecessarily difficult in the present situation, and there is also the fear that individual negotiating positions and the capacity to take effective industrial action in dispute situations could be immensely weakened by airline group cooperation.[83]

Spokesmen for the airline groupings themselves have with equal consistency denied requests by the ITF for labor-management meet-

---

[83] "ITF submission to the TUAC and to the OECD Committee on International Investment and Multinational Enterprises in the case of European airline groupings," April 20, 1978, pp. 2–3.

ings at the group level. Both KSSU and ATLAS contend that each airline in the group is an autonomous entity with its own, different strategic objectives. In the context of such autonomy, unions have frequently been consulted at the national airline level, as is appropriate, the airlines argue, for companies that do not have multinational dimension. The airlines contend finally that cooperation among them is of a purely technical nature and thus outside the bounds of normal labor-management issues. International meetings would thus serve no useful purpose.

At the first quarterly meeting of the CIIME with BIAC and TUAC in April 1978, the ITF registered its disagreement with the airlines' view by submitting, through TUAC, a request for comment on whether the OECD guidelines do in fact apply to these airline groupings. The submission made reference to Paragraph 8 of the Introduction to the Guidelines, the relevant section of which reads:

> A precise legal definition of multinational enterprise is not required for the purposes of the Guidelines. These usually comprise companies or other entities whose ownership is private, state or mixed, established in different countries and so linked that one or more of them may be able to exercise a significant influence over the activities of others, and in particular, to share knowledge and resources with the others.[84]

Does this definition, the submission asked, apply to the airline groupings?

The ITF clearly believed it should, for as it detailed in its 1978 submission, the areas of cooperation undertaken by both KSSU and ATLAS involve, directly and indirectly, areas that have been traditionally negotiated on a national level by the individual airline unions. The areas of cooperation isolated by the ITF are four in number: marketing, operations, specifications for the aircraft design, and technical, such as joint overhaul agreements. As the ITF asserted:

> The unions have a strong interest in a number of these items and have been accustomed to negotiate on them nationally—e.g. the implications of joint handling at airports; interchange (of personnel); flight deck design and other specification; crew training and joint overhaul facilities. The division of maintenance work indicated both here and in APL 75 obviously affects ground maintenance workers interalia, in their future job prospects and from the standpoint of training and retraining. In such a situation, the ability to negotiate nationally may not mean very much and needs to be supplemented by an international system of consultation and negotiation.[85]

---

[84] *Ibid.,* p. 1.
[85] *Ibid.,* p. 3.

In subsequent discussions at the OECD level, informal consultations between TUAC and the Lévy group focused on the ITF's complaint against the airline groupings.

Follow-up to the 1978 Submission

The Lévy Group noted that the results of these discussions had found some resolution in the 1979 review of the guidelines where, in Paragraphs 39 and 40, the issue of what constitutes a multinational is addressed. In TUAC's summary, Paragraph 39 "underlined that equity participation is not necessary for the purpose of establishing whether or not separate entities, viewed collectively, constitute an MNE within the meaning of the guidelines. Stress was also laid, in Paragraph 40 of the report, on the fact that the guidelines, wherever relevant, 'reflect good practice for all.'"[86] The ITF viewed both paragraphs as an implicit reference to their specific charges and further felt vindicated by the wording of the paragraphs.

The issue of what constitutes a multinational remained, however, and in a meeting with the Lévy Group in September 1979, TUAC "pressed for the IME Committee to come to an early final conclusion on the case."[87] In preparation for further consultations on the matter, the Lévy Group requested that TUAC cite "a concrete example . . . of consultation problems."[88] Such an example was forthcoming in the form of a complaint voiced by the KLM Flight Engineers' Association (affiliated with the ITF) in a letter to the ITF which requested that the matter be brought before the CIIME.

The 1980 Round

The complaint centered on the decision by KLM to purchase the Airbus A310 aircraft which, unlike other large, commercial aircraft, requires a cockpit crew of only two people rather than three. Presented by the union as a staffing decision over which the union had ostensibly had no opportunity to negotiate, the root of the problem is in fact an investment decision—the purchase of new equipment. The ITF detailed the union's position for the Lévy Group's consultations with TUAC in February 1980:

> In essence, the problem is that the airlines concerned have clearly reached a joint decision on ordering the Airbus A310 aircraft designed in accordance with what is known as the Forward Facing

---

[86] "TUAC submission on the European Airline groupings KSSU and Atlas," p. 1.

[87] "Current situations regarding cases submitted on 6 March 1980," TUAC Working Group on Multinational Enterprises, September 29–30, 1980, p. 3.

[88] *Ibid.*

Cockpit Concept (FFCC), and intended for two-man operation, as opposed to the three-man crew (usually two pilots plus a flight engineer) which is the existing norm—in favour of which all flight crew organizations have firm and well-established policies.

Without going into too much technical detail, it should be explained that existing cockpit layouts include a sidefacing instrumentation panel for the use of the third crew member carrying out the flight engineering function, with the two pilots seated up front in a forward-facing position. The FFCC would omit the flight engineer's panel. The switches and instruments from this would be installed on the pilots' overhead panel. However, since the space allocated to such instrumentation is approximately one-third of that available on the existing side panel and since the overhead panel was already occupied by many switches and instruments, their number has had to be drastically reduced and the remaining ones miniaturized.

In the unanimous view of both the pilots' and flight engineers' organizations, this has strongly adverse effects on both air safety and flight deck work-load. As one leading pilot representative put it at the Frankfurt meeting: "If the third crew member is taken away or is given an unfavorable working position, then the pilots are faced with a more difficult task and a higher workload, and therefore a lower level of safety."[89]

According to the ITF, the unions were given no opportunity to consult with either the national airlines or the airline groupings regarding this decision. KLM, claimed the ITF, "could not consider the views of its pilots and flight engineers because of the prior Swissair decision"[90] to purchase the A310. Meanwhile, the European regional affiliate of the International Federation of Airline Pilots' Associations (IFALPA), Europilote, wrote to the individual airlines as well as to the airline groupings requesting a meeting to discuss the issue. The request was denied by the groupings, which claimed that they had no executive authority in the decision.

The Status of Airline Groupings: The Lévy Group's Report

On March 6, 1980, TUAC presented the new findings concerning the flight deck configuration of the A310 to the CIIME and claimed that neither flight engineer nor pilot organizations had been "adequately consulted as these organizations did not have access to the decision making process at the level of the grouping."[91] At the CIIME's request and in accordance with the procedure outlined in

---

[89] "Background Notes by the International Transport Workers' Federation," TUAC Working Group on Multinational Enterprises, February 21, 1980, p. 1-2.

[90] *Ibid.*, p. 3.

[91] "Issues raised under the guidelines with respect to airline groupings," Committee on International Investment and Multinational Enterprises, December 17, 1980, p. 1.

Paragraphs 79 and 83 of the 1979 review, further input into the discussion was sought from the various national contact points. At two subsequent meetings of the Lévy Group in June and November 1980, reports from individual contact points were received and discussed. The Lévy Group summarized elements regarding the structure and decision-making process of the airline groupings which, the group noted, were common to the reports received and consistent with the group's earlier findings:

—The airline groupings ATLAS and KSSU are instruments for cooperation between independent national airline companies, most of which are state-owned. This co-operation includes evaluation of future flight equipment, aircraft specifications such as cockpit equipment and flight deck configuration, maintenance and overhaul facilities and the coordination of certain activities such as planning, data processing and the purchase and storage of spare parts.

—The groupings are not constituted as legal entities and have neither management nor staff of their own. Their functions are carried out by management committees and working groups composed of representatives of the participating airlines. In KSSU one of the most important committees is responsible for the practical details of the maintenance and overhaul arrangements.

—Agreements reached within the groupings are subsequently carried out on a contractual basis by the airlines concerned. On such matters each airline keeps its ultimate decision-making power.

—Contacts and consultation between management and employee representatives take place at the level of the individual airlines where they are governed by national law, collective agreements and practices. These contacts include matters being coordinated within the grouping.

—With respect to the introduction of a new flight deck configuration for A310 aircraft, the so-called forward facing crew concept (FFCC), KLM, Swissair, Air France, Sabena and Lufthansa have engaged in consultations with national employee organizations representing the interests of pilots and flight engineers. SAS and Alitalia do not at present envisage the purchase of the A310 and therefore are not directly concerned by the matter under dispute.[92]

The findings of the Lévy Group would appear to vindicate the position of the airline groupings themselves through this dispute. Of particular significance are three observations: the locus of decision making ("each airline keeps its ultimate decision-making power"); access to decision makers ("contacts and consultation between management and employee representatives take place at the level of the individual airlines . . . and . . . include matters being

---

[92] *Ibid.,* p. 2.

coordinated within the grouping"); and, finally, whether consultations actually occurred ("KLM . . . [has] engaged in consultations with national employee organizations . . .").

The locus of decision making and access to the decision makers are provided for through channels at the national level, even when the decisions in question relate to joint arrangements within the airline groupings. As has been noted through this chapter, it is not only the locus of decision making, but the subject of the decision itself that would appear to motivate the concern of the international union movement. While the essential decentralization of industrial relations is upheld by the Lévy Group's conclusions, the more pertinent, if veiled, issue would again appear to be the investment decisions of the airlines. As we have seen, national law and practice define employee representatives' involvement in investment decisions in varied ways. As the Lévy Group noted, consultations with regard to investment decisions "in the Netherlands . . . are required by Act 25 of the Works Council Act; in Germany and Switzerland they take place within the framework of collective agreements. In the case of Switzerland the relevant collective agreements do not provide co-determination of employee representatives with respect to decision on flight equipment."[93] The Swiss case, in this example, would thus appear to confirm the fears embodied in BIAC's comment on the CIIME's clarification of Paragraph 9—statements, however general, tending to favor broader negotiating rights for employee representatives will encounter national situations, such as in Switzerland, where negotiating rights are not as broad.

Recommendations of the Lévy Group

In view of its findings, the Lévy Group concluded that "the factual elements (of the case) do not appear to raise new issues calling for clarification of the Guidelines."[94] One reason for this, the group concluded, is that there is really no need to determine whether the airline groupings conform to a particular definition of a multinational enterprise. A far more salient point, in the group's view, is the fact that the guidelines describe good practice for multinationals and domestic firms alike.

The group recalled that the fundamental purpose of Paragraph 9 is:

---

[93] "Issues raised under the guidelines with respect to airline groupings," Committee on International Investment and Multinational Enterprises (Note by the Secretariat), November 3, 1980, pp. 2–3.

[94] *Ibid.*, p. 3.

to ensure that negotiations conducted under national practices take place in a meaningful manner involving those representatives of management mandated by decision-making bodies for the matters under consideration and prepared to negotiate in an effort to reach an agreement. Where under relevant national law and practices negotiations have taken place prior to final decisions being reached they should provide employee representatives an opportunity to conduct negotiations with authorized management representatives before major elements of the decision are pre-determined through coordination and/or contractual arrangements between the enterprises concerned.[95]

The Lévy Group did not foresee the need for negotiations at the level of the airline groupings, finding that the ultimate decision-making authority resided at the national level. Access to decision makers at this level precluded the need for multinational bargaining. Lastly, it is interesting to note once again that had the group decided otherwise—that bargaining at the level of the airline groupings had merit—the effect may well have been to endow some employee representatives (those of Swissair, for example) with broader negotiating rights than exist within their national contexts. Such a recommendation, had it been produced, would have set two precedents, the first relating to the level of bargaining, and the second, to the scope of bargaining. That such was not recommended reinforces the meaning of the "chapeau clause" of the guidelines, a recognition of national diversity in industrial relations.

---

[95] "Issues raised under the guidelines," pp. 3–4.

CHAPTER XIII

Conclusion

The original aim of the 1976 OECD declaration was to facilitate the positive contributions of multinationals in the member states. This aim is reinforced in the Committee on International Investment and Multinational Enterprises' (CIIME) 1982 mid-term report on the guidelines:

> In the Declaration, the governments of OECD Member countries stated, inter alia, "that international investment has assumed increased importance in the world economy and has considerably contributed to the development of their countries"; "that multinational enterprises play an important role in this investment process"; and "that cooperation by Member countries can improve the foreign investment climate, encourage the positive contribution which multinational enterprises can make to economic and social progress, and minimise and resolve difficulties which may arise from their various operations." These considerations are as valid now as when they were first issued.[1]

As OECD member states experience high rates of unemployment and lagging investment rates, national malaise fuels the desire by some for national and international control over multinational companies even though their positive contributions are clearly recognized. Perceptions of the role of multinational companies in the solution to economic problems appear to be polarized. From the standpoint of labor-management relations, and the industrial relations guidelines that address them, the opposing perspectives seem to pit support for voluntary guidelines against demands for legislated controls. As this is written, debates are in progress at the European level on the Vredeling directive—a proposed directive on information and consultation in companies with complex structures that would greatly expand the rights of employee representatives to information and consultation with multinational parent companies. Mindful of the central role that private investment plays in the solution of economic and social problems, multinational corporations strongly prefer voluntary guidelines, such as those developed by the

---

[1] Organization for Economic Cooperation and Development, *Mid-term Report on the 1976 Declaration and Decisions*, (Paris: 1982), p. 8.

OECD, to political or legal directives presently being discussed at the European Community (EC) level.

THE CONCEPT OF VOLUNTARY GUIDELINES

Compliance with the OECD Guidelines on Employment and Industrial Relations is voluntary, a fact that was carefully specified and generally accepted by all parties when the guidelines were developed and issued in 1976. The "voluntariness," however, is, conditional on how they are viewed by the parties whom they address, whether government, industry, or labor. As the 1982 mid-term report on the guidelines comments:

> The Guidelines are voluntary and not legally enforceable; but they do carry the weight of a joint Recommendation by OECD governments addressed to all MNEs which represents a firm expectation of MNE behavior. They have served as a frame of reference for governments, business and labour organisations ... It is not to suggest that the acceptance of the Guidelines would lead to legal or quasi-legal obligation for the enterprise.[2]

Although voluntary, compliance with the Guidelines is expected. This expectation, moreover, has extended beyond the mere moral suasion implied by the weight of OECD governments. The strongest challenge to the voluntary status of the guidelines has come from the Trade Union Advisory Committee (TUAC) and its affiliates. The preceding chapters indicate that the unions have sometimes used the guidelines as a frame of reference through which to channel their demands at the international level.

TUAC has questioned the continued efficacy of voluntary guidelines in a climate of "changing economic circumstances."[3] Expressing disappointment that the guidelines have not been integrated into national legislation, the unions continue to press for their implementation in more compulsory ways. In effect, the issuing of clarifications on the meaning of the guidelines by the CIIME has constituted one way of enhancing their effectiveness from the unions' point of view. The originally non-prescriptive wording of Paragraph 9, for example, became clarified as three specific means of implementing the paragraph's provisions. Similarly, the more restrictive wording of Paragraph 8, resulting from the 1979 review of the guidelines, was clearly influenced by TUAC's submission of a specific "case" before the CIIME. The end result was a more restric-

---

[2] OECD *Mid-term Report*, (1982), p. 57.
[3] "Trade Union Group to Put More Teeth into OECD Guidelines on MNCs," *Business International,* April 23, 1982, p. 131.

tive frame of reference regarding the provisions of that paragraph. Employers have resisted these "clarifications" and have issued formal reservations in regard to them.

Despite their voluntary status, the existence of the guidelines as a frame of reference at the national level has also been apparent. European unions, for example, have sought the explicit inclusion of the guidelines in collective bargaining agreements.[4] TUAC, as well, has recently attempted to devise a stronger role for the national contact point in the implementation of the guidelines.[5] Labor organizations, however, have not been the only groups to have adopted the guidelines as a frame of reference in the evaluation of labor-management disputes. One significant instance, for example, was noted in which a Dutch court appeared to support its decision against the closure of a multinational subsidiary through reference to a company's stated adherence to the OECD guidelines.[6]

THE INDUSTRIAL RELATIONS FUNCTION

Regardless of the OECD member country, the industrial relations function is considered by management to be one that should be practiced at the local and/or national level. It is argued that decisions affecting people's livelihood are best taken at the point where their problems are best understood. Conditions of employment are determined by private parties at the local level where management interfaces directly with labor. Decisions pertaining to wages, hours, and conditions of employment are clearly viewed as requiring local agreement. Corporate decisions affecting job security through extensive layoffs and plant closures have raised local union interests to the international level. Recognizing that they may not be able to avoid job losses through plant closures, local union leaders have attempted to involve the international trade union movement with the hopes that they can arrange meetings with corporate management to discuss decisions to close.

There has been a lack of understanding pertaining to plant closure decisions and the industrial relations function. Usually, a decision to close a subsidiary plant of a multinational firm has involved discussions with local plant management and top company executives. It is highly unlikely that a plant would be closed without participation in the decision on the part of local management. Management, however, considers the decision to close as an investment decision and

---

[4] *Ibid.*
[5] See Chapter IX, p. 151.
[6] *Ibid.*

not an industrial relations problem per se that requires union participation. The *effects* of the investment decision to close a plant, of course, legitimately fall within the industrial relations function, and the guidelines specify that management should attempt to mitigate the adverse effects stemming from such decisions. Cases presented in this monograph indicate that management has fulfilled its voluntary obligations under the guidelines with respect to the mitigation of adverse effects. Emphasis on national law and practice in the field of industrial relations is stated in the "chapeau clause" in the guidelines.

THE MEANING OF THE "CHAPEAU CLAUSE"

As recently as 1980, an experienced negotiator of international codes of conduct for the U.S. government observed with respect to the OECD's industrial relations guidelines that:

> The guidelines dealing with employment and industrial relations boil down to compliance with local law, tempered by the observance of standards "not less favorable than those observed by comparable employers in the host country . . . ." Since it is clear the guidelines do not override national laws, they provide no new rights or obligations either for enterprises or employees.[7]

This interpretation appears to flow from the wording of the "chapeau clause" which commends the behavior of multinationals to the "framework of law, regulations and prevailing labor relations and employment practices, in each of the countries in which they operate." The preceding chapters have shown, however, that, far from "boiling down to compliance with local law," several of the issues raised under the guidelines have extended beyond the national framework. How has this extension occurred?

It is clear that the foundation of corporate adherence to the industrial relations guidelines resides in the explicit meaning of the "chapeau clause" that refers the behavior of the subsidiary to the context of national law and practice. The clarity of this meaning, however, is not shared by all those involved in the discussion and use of the guidelines. Indeed, the CIIME's 1982 mid-term report, in recalling the intent of the guidelines, observes that the area of employment and industrial relations is one "where long-established national procedure, sanctioned by law or by practice, exists and the introduction to this chapter of the guidelines underlines the impor-

---

[7] Raymond J. Waldmann, *Regulating International Business through Codes of Conduct,* (Washington: American Enterprise Institute for Public Policy Research, 1980), p. 39.

tance of the framework of national law, but where the Guidelines, where relevant, can serve as a valuable supplement."[8] It is the CIIME's view, furthermore, that "the Guidelines as clarified by the Committee in response to requests from Member governments, BIAC and TUAC, and after consultation with them, should continue to provide a useful supplement to national laws and practices . . . ."[9] The ambiguity surrounding the meaning of the "chapeau clause" would thus seem inherent in the mid-term report, for the industrial relations guidelines cannot at one and the same time "boil down to compliance with local law" while constituting a "useful supplement" to those laws.

It is not surprising that this ambiguity is most apparent in those paragraphs of the industrial relations guidelines that have elicited the most controversy. Specifically, Paragraphs 3, 6, and 9 have been variously referred to by the unions as either directly or indirectly related to the responsibilities of the parent company, as well as those of subsidiaries, whereas the majority of the remaining paragraphs regard industrial relations issues more explicitly within the domain of local law and practice. Thus, while these latter have posed few problems with respect to the meaning of the "chapeau clause," the same is not true for the former.

Elsewhere in this study, it has been noted that several of TUAC's submissions to the CIIME allude at least implicitly to the unions' perception of the inadequacy of the national level in the resolution of certain issues. It was also noted that these issues tend to be those in the forefront of union demands at various political and industrial levels—broader disclosure of information, and enhanced worker participation in decision making. Although the study has discussed several aspects of these demands in their relationship to the unions' use of the guidelines, it is clearly the most recent TUAC submission to the CIIME that most explicitly addresses the perceived inadequacy of the national context. There, it is mooted that a company can still be in violation of the OECD guidelines, even if the company's conduct has conformed to national law and practice.[10]

It would seem, therefore, that the terrain of discourse on the guidelines has evolved, through the voice of some at least, from compliance with national law and practice to a consideration of "useful" supplements to those laws. In its mid-term report, the CIIME refers to the evolution of labor-management relations, noting that:

---

[8] OECD, *Mid-term Report*, (1982), Par. 8, p. 10.

[9] *Ibid.*, Par. 10, p. 11.

[10] See Chapter IX, p. 150.

Discussions of the Committee and its Working Party on the Guidelines have also been influenced by the evolution of national practices
where collective bargaining and labour management relations were
concerned. The national laws and/or practices of some Member Countries now deal with the provision of general information and consultation on the economic and financial management of the enterprise,
extending, in some of these countries, to negotiations encompassing
future production and investment plans.[11]

It is true that labor-management relations have evolved during the
six years of the guidelines' existence; that they have evolved in all or
even in the majority of OECD countries to the extent cited above,
however, is not the case. The continued use of the guidelines both as
a frame of reference and as a supplement to national law would seem
contrary to the interpretation of many persons of both the voluntary status of the guidelines and the meaning of the "chapeau
clause."

This is so because the unions' tendency has been for the national
context meaning of the "chapeau clause" to be extended to the supplement to national law interpretation in the areas of greatest controversy. As was noted, the clarification procedure would seem to
accommodate the expansion of meaning. For example, the 1982 mid-
term report notes the importance of Paragraph 6:

> The present economic situation inevitably poses difficult problems
> when adaptation and restructuring of company activities are envis-
> aged.[12]

The report then recalls the language of Paragraph 6, but adds a
significant change, that the notice to employees of the type of
changes contemplated in Paragraph 6 "has to be sufficiently timely
for the purpose of mitigating action to be prepared and put into
effect, and it would be appropriate, in the light of the specific circumstances of each case, if management were able to provide such
notice prior to the final decision being taken."[13]

In a few member states, this latter recommendation should pose
little problem to companies, for it is consistent with national law. In
others, however, including the United States, the provision of notice
prior to a decision's having been taken regarding plant closure is
clearly not the norm. Because such disparities among countries
exist, it is clear that what boils down to compliance with local law in
some member countries constitutes a very distinct supplement to
national law in others. BIAC has argued that emphasis must be

---

[11] OECD, *Mid-term Report*, (1982), p. 15.
[12] *Ibid.*, p. 10.
[13] *Ibid.*, p. 11.

placed on the specific circumstances of each case and that it would be for management to decide whether it is possible to provide prior notice.

While the effectiveness of the guidelines is, in part, contingent upon their ability to evolve, international codes of conduct must derive from the great diversity at the national level, rather than attempt to supercede that diversity. Otherwise, the conditions under which many multinationals, as well as governments and labor organizations, have extended their voluntary support of the guidelines are in constant flux. The 1982 mid-term report notes that "efforts have been made to promote greater awareness of the nature and content of the Guidelines and their role as a common point of reference for good business practice."[14] Evolution of the content of the guidelines, if such evolution is away from the diversity of the national contexts of industrial relations, would seem inimical both to promoting an awareness of the guidelines as well as to their use as a voluntary point of reference for good business practice.

---

[14] *Ibid.,* p. 9.

Appendix A

DECLARATION
ON INTERNATIONAL INVESTMENT
AND MULTINATIONAL ENTERPRISES
(21st June 1976)
(Revised 1979)

THE GOVERNMENT OF OECD
MEMBER COUNTRIES

CONSIDERING

that international investment has assumed increased importance in the world economy and has considerably contributed to the development of their countries;

that multinational enterprises play an important role in this investment process;

that co-operation by Member countries can improve the foreign investment climate, encourage the positive contribution which multinational enterprises can make to economic and social progress, and minimise and resolve difficulties which may arise from their various operations;

that, while continuing endeavours within the OECD may lead to further international arrangements and agreements in this field, it seems appropriate at this stage to intensify their co-operation and consultation on issues relating to international investment and multinational enterprises through interrelated instruments each of which deals with a different aspect of the matter and together constitute a framework within which the OECD will consider these issues:

DECLARE:

Guidelines for Multinational Enterprises	I. that they jointly recommend to multinational enterprises operating in their territories the observance of the Guidelines as

set forth in the Annex hereto having regard to the considerations and understandings which introduce the Guidelines and are an integral part of them;

National Treatment

II. 1. that Member countries should, consistent with their needs to maintain public order, to protect their essential security interests and to fulfill commitments relating to international peace and security, accord to enterprises operating in their territories and owned or controlled directly or indirectly by nationals of another Member country (hereinafter referred to as "Foreign-Controlled Enterprises") treatment under their laws, regulations and administrative practices, consistent with international law and no less favourable than that accorded in like situations to domestic enterprises (hereinafter referred to as "National Treatment");

2. that Member countries will consider applying "National Treatment" in respect of countries other than Member countries;

3. that Member countries will endeavour to ensure that their territorial subdivisions apply "National Treatment";

4. that this Declaration does not deal with the right of Member countries to regulate the entry of foreign investment or the conditions of establishment of foreign enterprises;

International Investment Incentives and Disincentives

III. 1. that they recognise the need to strengthen their co-operation in the field of international direct investment;

2. that they thus recognise the need to give due weight to the interests of Member countries affected by specific laws, regulations and administrative

practices in this field (hereinafter called "measures") providing official incentives and disincentives to international direct investment;

3. that Member countries will endeavour to make such measures as transparent as possible, so that their importance and purpose can be ascertained and that information on them can be readily available;

Consultation Procedures

IV. that they are prepared to consult one another on the above matters in conformity with the Decisions of the Council relating to Inter-Governmental Consultation Procedures on the Guidelines for Multinational Enterprise, on National Treatment and on International Investment Incentives and Disincentives;

Review

V. that they will review the above matters within three years* with a view to improving the effectiveness of international economic co-operation among Member countries on issues relating to international investment and multinational enterprises.

Annex to the Declaration of 21st June, 1976 by Governments of OECD Member Countries on International Investment and Multinational Enterprises

GUIDELINES FOR MULTINATIONAL ENTERPRISES

1. Multinational enterprises now play an important part in the economies of Member countries and in international economic relations, which is of increasing interest to governments. Through international direct investment, such enterprises can bring substantial benefits to home and host countries by contributing to the efficient

---

Note: The Turkish Government did not participate in the Declaration and abstained from the Decisions; however, Turkey adhered to the Declaration and the Decisions in March 1981.

* The review took place in the OECD Council meeting at Ministerial level on 13th and 14th June, 1979. It was decided to review the Declaration again at the latest in five years.

utilisation of capital, technology and human resources between countries and can thus fulfil an important role in the promotion of economic and social welfare. But the advances made by multinational enterprises in organising their operations beyond the national framework may lead to abuse of concentrations of economic power and to conflicts with national policy objectives. In addition, the complexity of these multinational enterprises and the difficulty to clearly perceiving their diverse structures, operations and policies sometimes give rise to concern.

2. The common aim of the Member countries is to encourage the positive contributions which multinational enterprises can make to economic and social progress and to minimise and resolve the difficulties to which their various operations may give rise. In view of the transnational structure of such enterprises, this aim will be furthered by co-operation among the OECD countries where the headquarters of most of the multinational enterprises are established and which are the location of a substantial part of their operations. The guidelines set out hereafter are designed to assist in the achievement of this common aim and to contribute to improving the foreign investment climate.

3. Since the operations of multinational enterprises extend throughout the world, including countries that are not Members of the Organisation, international co-operation in this field should extend to all States. Member countries will give their full support to efforts undertaken in co-operation with non-member countries, and in particular with developing countries, with a view to improving the welfare and living standards of all people both by encouraging the positive contributions which multinational enterprises can make and by minimising and resolving the problems which may arise in connection with their activities.

4. Within the Organization, the programme of co-operation to attain these ends will be a continuing, pragmatic and balanced one. It comes within the general aims of the Convention on the Organisation for Economic Co-operation and Development (OECD) and makes full use of the various specialised bodies of the Organisation, whose terms of reference already cover many aspects of the role of multinational enterprises, notably in matters of international trade and payments, competition, taxation, manpower, industrial development, science and technology. In these bodies, work is being carried out on the identifiction of issues, the improvement of relevant qualitative and statistical information and the elaboration of proposals for action designed to strengthen inter-governmental co-operation. In some of these areas procedures already exist through which issues related to the operations of multinational enterprises

can be taken up. This work could result in the conclusion of further and complementary agreements and arrangements between governments.

5. The initial phase of the co-operation programme is composed of a Declaration and three Decisions promulgated simultaneously as they are complementary and inter-connected, in respect of guidelines for multinational enterprises, national treatment for foreign-controlled enterprises and international investment incentives and disincentives.

6. The guidelines set out below are recommendations jointly addressed by Member countries to multinational enterprises operating in their territories. These guidelines, which take into account the problems which can arise because of the international structure of these enterprises, lay down standards for the activities of these enterprises in the different Member countries. Observance of the guidelines is voluntary and not legally enforceable. However, they should help to ensure that the operations of these enterprises are in harmony with national policies of the countries where they operate and to strengthen the basis of mutual confidence between enterprises and States.

7. Every State has the right to prescribe the conditions under which multinational enterprises operate within its national jurisdiction, subject to international law and to the international agreements to which it has subscribed. The entities of a multinational enterprise located in various countries are subject to the laws of these countries.

8. A precise legal definition of multinational enterprises is not required for the purposes of the guidelines. These usually comprise companies or other entities whose ownership is private, state or mixed, established in different countries and so linked that one or more of them may be able to exercise a significant influence over the activities of others and, in particular, to share knowledge and resources with the others. The degree of autonomy of each entity in relation to the others varies widely from one multinational enterprise to another, depending on the nature of the links between such entities and the fields of activity concerned. For these reasons, the guidelines are addressed to the various entities within the multinational enterprise (parent companies and/or local entities) according to the actual distribution of responsibilities among them on the understanding that they will co-operate and provide assistance to one another as necessary to facilitate observance of the guidelines. The word "enterprise" as used in these guidelines refers to these various entities in accordance with their responsibilities.

9. The guidelines are not aimed at introducing differences of treat-

ment between multinational and domestic enterprises; wherever relevant they reflect good practice for all. Accordingly, multinational and domestic enterprises are subject to the same expectations in respect of their conduct wherever the guidelines are relevant to both.

10. The use of appropriate international dispute settlement mechanisms, including arbitration, should be encouraged as a means of facilitating the resolution of problems arising between enterprises and Member countries.

11. Member countries have agreed to establish appropriate review and consultation procedures concerning issues arising in respect of the guidelines. When multinational enterprises are made subject to conflicting requirements by Member countries, the governments concerned will co-operate in good faith with a view to resolving such problems either within the Committee on International Investment and Multinational Enterprises established by the OECD Council on 21st January, 1975 or through other mutually acceptable arrangements.

Having regard to the foregoing considerations, the Member countries set forth the following guidelines for multinational enterprises with the understanding that Member countries will fulfil their responsibilities to treat enterprises equitably and in accordance with international law and international agreements, as well as contractual obligations to which they have subscribed:

GENERAL POLICIES

Enterprises should
1. take fully into account established general policy objectives of the Member countries in which they operate;
2. in particular, give due consideration to those countries' aims and priorities with regard to economic and social progress, including industrial and regional development, the protection of the environment, the creation of employment opportunities, the promotion of innovation and the transfer of technology;
3. while observing their legal obligations concerning information, supply their entities with supplementary information the latter may need in order to meet requests by the authorities of the countries in which those entities are located for information relevant to the activities of those entities, taking into account legitimate requirements of business confidentiality;
4. favour close co-operation with the local community and business interests;

5. allow their component entities freedom to develop their activities and to exploit their competitive advantage in domestic and foreign markets, consistent with the need for specialisation and sound commercial practice;
6. when filling responsible posts in each country of operation, take due account of individual qualifications without discrimination as to nationality, subject to particular national requirements in this respect;
7. not render—and they should not be solicited or expected to render—any bribe or other improper benefit, direct or indirect, to any public servant or holder of public office;
8. unless legally permissible, not make contributions to candidates for public office or to political parties or other political organisations;
9. abstain from any improper involvement in local political activities.

DISCLOSURE OF INFORMATION

Enterprises should, having due regard to their nature and relative size in the economic context of their operations and to requirements of business confidentiality and to cost, publish in a form suited to improve public understanding a sufficient body of factual information on the structure, activities and policies of the enterprise as a whole, as a supplement, in so far as necessary for this purpose, to information to be disclosed under the national law of the individual countries in which they operate. To this end, they should publish within reasonable time limits, on a regular basis, but at least annually, financial statements and other pertinent information relating to the enterprise as a whole, comprising in particular:

 i) the structure of the enterprise, showing the name and location of the parent company, its main affiliates, its percentage ownership, direct and indirect, in these affiliates, including shareholdings between them;

 ii) the geographical areas* where operations are carried out

---

* For the purposes of the guideline on disclosure of information the term "geographical area" means groups of countries or individual countries as each enterprise determines is appropriate in its particular circumstances. While no single method of grouping is appropriate for all enterprises or for all purposes, the factors to be considered by an enterprise would include the significance of operations carried out in individual countries or areas as well as the effects on its competitiveness, geographic proximity, economic affinity, similarities in business environments and the nature, scale and degree of interrelationship of the enterprises' operations in the various countries.

and the principal activities carried on therein by the parent company and the main affiliates;

  iii) the operating results and sales by geographical area and the sales in the major lines of business for the enterprise as a whole;

  iv) significant new capital investment by geographical area and, as far as practicable, by major lines of business for the enterprise as a whole;

  v) a statement of the sources and uses of funds by the enterprise as a whole;

  vi) the average number of employees in each geographical area;

  vii) research and development expenditure for the enterprise as a whole;

  viii) the policies followed in respect of intra-group pricing;

  ix) the accounting policies, including those on consolidation, observed in compiling the published information.

COMPETITION

Enterprises should, while conforming to official competition rules and established policies of the countries in which they operate,

  1. refrain from actions which would adversely affect competition in the relevant market by abusing a dominant position of market power, by means of, for example,

     a) anti-competitive acquisitions,

     b) predatory behaviour toward competitors,

     c) unreasonable refusal to deal,

     d) anti-competitive abuse of industrial property rights,

     e) discriminatory (i.e. unreasonably differentiated) pricing and using such pricing transactions between affiliated enterprises as a means of affecting adversely competition outside these enterprises;

  2. allow purchasers, distributors and licensees freedom to resell, export, purchase and develop their operations consistent with law, trade conditions, the need for specialisation and sound commercial practice;

  3. refrain from participating in or otherwise purposely strengthening the restrictive effects of international or domestic cartels or restrictive agreements which adversely affect or eliminate competition and which are not generally or specifically accepted under applicable national or international legislation;

  4. be ready to consult and co-operate, including the provision of

information, with competent authorities of countries whose interests are directly affected in regard to competition issues or investigations. Provision of information should be in accordance with safeguards normally applicable in this field.

FINANCING

Enterprises should, in managing the financial and commercial operations of their activities, and especially their liquid foreign assets and liabilities, take into consideration the established objectives of the countries in which they operate regarding balance of payments and credit policies.

TAXATION

Enterprises should
1. upon request of the taxation authorities of the countries in which they operate, provide, in accordance with the safeguards and relevant procedures of the national laws of these countries, the information necessary to determine correctly the taxes to be assessed in connection with their operations, including relevant information concerning their operations in other countries;
2. refrain from making use of the particular facilities available to them, such as transfer pricing which does not conform to an arm's length standard, for modifying in ways contrary to national laws the tax base on which members of the group are assessed.

EMPLOYMENT AND INDUSTRIAL RELATIONS

Enterprises should, within the framework of law, regulations and prevailing labour relations and employment practices, in each of the countries in which they operate,
1. respect the right of their employees to be represented by trade unions and other bona fide organisations of employees, and engage in constructive negotiations, either individually or through employers' associations, with such employee organisations with a view to reaching agreements on employment conditions, which should include provisions for dealing with disputes arising over the interpretation of such agreements, and for ensuring mutually respected rights and responsibilities;
2. *a)* provide such facilities to representatives of the employees as may be necessary to assist in the development of effective collective agreements.,

b) provide to representatives of employees information which is needed for meaningful negotiations on conditions of employment;

3. provide to representatives of employees where this accords with local law and practice, information which enables them to obtain a true and fair view of the performance of the entity or, where appropriate, the enterprise as a whole;

4. observe standards of employment and industrial relations not less favourable than those observed by comparable employers in the host country;

5. in their operations, to the greatest extent practicable, utilise, train and prepare for upgrading members of the local labour force in co-operation with representatives of their employees and, where appropriate, the relevant governmental authorities;

6. in considering changes in their operations which would have major effects upon the livelihood of their employees, in particular in the case of the closure of an entity envolving collective lay-offs or dismissals, providing reasonable notice of such changes to representatives of their employees, and where appropriate to the relevant governmental authorities, and co-operate with the employee representatives and appropriate governmental authorities so as to mitigate to the maximum extent practicable adverse effects;

7. implement their employment policies including hiring, discharge, pay, promotion and training without discrimination unless selectivity in respect of employee characteristics is in furtherance of established governmental policies which specifically promote greater equality of employment opportunity;

8. in the context of bona fide negotiations* with representatives of employees on conditions of employment, or while employees are exercising a right to organise, not threaten to utilise a capacity to transfer the whole or part of an operating unit from the country concerned nor transfer employees from the enterprises' component entities in other countries in order to influence unfairly those negotiations or to hinder the exercise of a right to organise**;

---

* Bona fide negotiations may include labour disputes as part of the process of negotiation. Whether or not labour disputes are so included will be determined by the law and prevailing employment practices of particular countries.

** Note: This paragraph includes the additional provision adopted by OECD Governments at the meeting of the OECD Council at Ministerial level on 13th and 14th June, 1979.

9. enable authorised representatives of their employees to conduct negotiations on collective bargaining or labour management relations issues with representatives of management who are authorised to take decisions on the matters under negotiation.

SCIENCE AND TECHNOLOGY

Enterprises should

1. endeavour to ensure that their activities fit satisfactorily into the scientific and technological policies and plans of the countries in which they operate, and contribute to the development of national scientific and technological capacities, including as far as appropriate the establishment and improvement in host countries of their capacity to innovate;
2. to the fullest extent practicable, adopt in the course of their business activities practices which permit the rapid diffusion of technologies with due regard to the protection of industrial and intellectual property rights;
3. when granting licences for the use of industrial property rights or when otherwise transferring technology do so on reasonable terms and conditions.

Appendix B

ILO TRIPARTITE DECLARATION OF PRINCIPLES CONCERNING MULTINATIONAL ENTERPRISES AND SOCIAL POLICY

1. Multinational enterprises play an important part in the economies of most countries and in international economic relations. This is of increasing interest to governments as well as to employers and workers and their respective organisations. Through international direct investment and other means, such enterprises can bring substantial benefits to home and host countries by contributing to the more efficient utilisation of capital, technology and labour. Within the framework of development policies established by governments, they can also make an important contribution to the promotion of economic and social welfare; to the improvement of living standards and the satisfaction of basic needs; to the creation of employment opportunities, both directly and indirectly; and to the enjoyment of basic human rights, including freedom of association, throughout the world. On the other hand, the advances made by multinational enterprises in organising their operations beyond the national framework may lead to abuse of concentrations of economic power and to conflicts with national policy objectives and with the interest of the workers. In addition, the complexity of multinational enterprises and the difficulty of clearly perceiving their diverse structures, operations and policies sometimes give rise to concern either in the home or in the host countries or in both.

2. The aim of this Tripartite Declaration of Principles is to encourage the positive contribution which multinational enterprises can make to economic and social progress and to minimise and resolve the difficulties to which their various operations may give rise, taking into account the United Nations resolutions advocating the Establishment of a New International Economic Order.

3. This aim will be furthered by appropriate laws and policies, measures and actions adopted by the governments and by cooperation among the governments and the employers' organisations of all countries.

4. The principles set out in this Declaration are commended to the governments, the employers' and workers' organisations of home and host countries and to the multinational enterprises themselves.

5. These principles are intended to guide the governments, the employers' and workers' organisations and the multinational enterprises in taking such measures and actions and adopting such social policies including those based on the principles laid down in the Constitution and the relevant Conventions and Recommendations of the ILO, as would further social progress.

6. To serve its purpose this Declaration does not require a precise legal definition of multinational enterprises.* Multin. enterprises include enterprises, whether they are of public, mixed or private ownership, which own or control production, distribution, services or other facilities outside the country in which they are based. The degree of autonomy of entities within multinational enterprises in relation to each other varies widely from one such enterprise to another, depending on the nature of the links between such entities and their fields of activity and having regard to the great diversity in the form of ownership, in the size, in the nature and location of the operations of the enterprises concerned. Unless otherwise specified, the term "multinational enterprise" is used in this Declaration to designate the various entities (parent companies or local entities or both or the organisation as a whole) according to the distribution of responsibilities among them, in the expectation that they will co-operate and provide assistance to one another as necessary to facilitate observance of the principles laid down in this Declaration.

7. This Declaration sets out principles in the fields of employment, training, conditions of work and life and industrial relations which governments, employers' and workers' organisations and multinational enterprises are recommended to observe on a voluntary basis; its provisions shall not limit or otherwise affect obligations arising out of ratification of any ILO Convention.

GENERAL POLICIES

8. All the parties concerned by this Declaration should respect the sovereign rights of States, obey the national laws and regulations, give due consideration to local practices and respect relevant international standards. They should respect the Universal Declaration of Human Rights and the corresponding International Covenants adopted by the General Assembly of the United Nations as well as the Constitution of the International Labour Organisation and its principles according to which freedom of expression and association are essential to sustained progress. They should also

---

* This paragraph is designed to facilitate understanding of the Declaration, and not to provide such a definition.

honour commitments which they have freely entered into, in conformity with the national law and accepted international obligations.

9. Governments which have not yet ratified Conventions Nos. 87, 98, 111 and 122 are urged to do so and in any event to apply, to the greatest extent possible, through their national policies, the principles embodied therein and in Recommendations Nos. 111, 119 and 122.[1] Without prejudice to the obligation of governments to ensure compliance with Conventions they have ratified, in countries in which the Conventions and Recommendations cited in this paragraph are not complied with all parties should refer to them for guidance in their social policy.

10. Multinational enterprises should take fully into account established general policy objectives of the countries in which they operate. Their activities should be in harmony with the development priorities and social aims and structure of the country in which they operate. To this effect, consultations should be held between multinational enterprises, the government and, wherever appropriate, the national employers' and workers' organisations concerned.

11. The principles laid down in this Declaration do not aim at introducing or maintaining inequalities of treatment between multinational and national enterprises. They reflect good practice for all. Multinational and national enterprises, wherever the principles of this Declaration are relevant to both, should be subject to the same expectations in respect of their conduct in general and their social practices in particular.

12. Governments of home countries should promote good social practice in accordance with this Declaration of Principles, having regard to the social and labour law, regulations and practices in host countries as well as to relevant international standards. Both host and home country governments should be prepared to have consultations with each other, whenever the need arises, on the initiative of either.

---

[1] Convention (No. 87) concerning Freedom of Association and Protection of the Right to Organise;

Convention (No. 98) concerning the Application of the Principles of the Right to Organise and to Bargain Collectively;

Convention (No. 111) concerning Discrimination in Respect of Employment and Occupation;

Convention (No. 122) concerning Employment Policy;

Recommendation (No. 111) concerning Discrimination in Respect of Employment and Occupation;

Recommendation (No. 119) concerning Termination of Employment at the Initiative of the Employer;

Recommendation (No. 122) concerning Employment Policy.

EMPLOYMENT

Employment Promotion

13. With a view to stimulating economic growth and development, raising living standards, meeting manpower requirements and overcoming unemployment and under-employment, governments should declare and pursue, as a major goal, an active policy designed to promote full, productive and freely-chosen employment.[2]

14. This is particularly important in the case of host country governments in developing areas of the world where the problems of unemployment and under-employment are at their most serious. In this connection, the general conclusions adopted by the Tripartite World Conference on Employment, Income Distribution and Social Progress and the International Division of Labour (Geneva, June 1976) should be kept in mind.[3]

15. Paragraphs 13 and 14 above establish the framework within which due attention should be paid, in both home and host countries, to the employment impact of multinational enterprises.

16. Multinational enterprises, particularly when operating in developing countries, should endeavour to increase employment opportunities and standards, taking into account the employment policies and objectives of the governments, as well as security of employment and the long-term development of the enterprise.

17. Before starting operations, multinational enterprises should, wherever appropriate, consult the competent authorities and the national employers' and workers' organisations in order to keep their manpower plans, as far as practicable, in harmony with national social development policies. Such consultation, as in the case of national enterprises, should continue between the multinational enterprises and all parties concerned, including the workers' organisations.

18. Multinational enterprises should give priority to the employment, occupational development, promotion and advancement of nationals of the host country at all levels, in co-operation as appropriate, with representatives of the workers employed by them or of the organisations of these workers and governmental authorities.

19. Multinational enterprises, when investing in developing countries, should have regard to the importance of using technologies

---

[2] Convention (No. 122) and Recommendation (No. 122) concerning Employment Policy.
[3] ILO, World Employment Conference, Geneva, 4–17 June 1976.

which generate employment, both directly and indirectly. To the extent permitted by the nature of the process and the conditions prevailing in the economic sector concerned, they should adapt technologies to the needs and characteristics of the host countries. They should also, where possible, take part in the development of appropriate technology in host countries.

20. To promote employment in developing countries in the context of an expanding world economy, multinational enterprises, wherever practicable, should give consideration to the conclusion of contracts with national enterprises for the manufacture of parts and equipment, to the use of local raw materials and to the progressive promotion of the local processing of raw materials. Such arrangements should not be used by multinational enterprises to avoid the responsibilities embodied in the principles of this Declaration.

Equality of Opportunity and Treatment

21. All governments should pursue policies designed to promote equality of opportunity and treatment in employment, with a view to eliminating any discrimination based on race, colour, sex, religion, political opinion, national extraction or social origin.[4]

22. Multinational enterprises should be guided by this general principle throughout their operations without prejudice to the measures envisaged in paragraph 18 or to government policies designed to correct historical patterns of discrimination and thereby to extend equality of opportunity and treatment in employment. Multinational enterprises should accordingly make qualifications, skill and experience the basis for the recruitment, placement, training and advancement of their staff at all levels.

23. Governments should never require or encourage multinational enterprises to discriminate on any of the grounds mentioned in paragraph 21, and continuing guidance from governments, where appropriate, on the avoidance of such discrimination in employment is encouraged.

Security of Employment

24. Governments should carefully study the impact of multinational enterprises on employment in different industrial sectors. Governments, as well as multinational enterprises themselves, in all

---

[4] Convention (No. 111) and Recommendation (No. 111) concerning Discrimination in Respect of Employment and Occupation; Convention (No. 100) and Recommendation (No. 90) concerning Equal Remuneration for Men and Women Workers for Work of Equal Value.

countries should take suitable measures to deal with the employment and labour market impacts of the operations of multinational enterprises.

25. Multinational enterprises equally with national enterprises, through active manpower planning should endeavour to provide stable employment for their employees and should observe freely-negotiated obligations concerning employment stability and social security. In view of the flexibility which multinational enterprises may have, they should strive to assume a leading role in promoting security of employment, particularly in countries where the discontinuation of operations is likely to accentuate longterm unemployment.

26. In considering changes in operations (including those resulting from mergers, take-overs or transfers of production) which would have major employment effects, multinational enterprises should provide reasonable notice of such changes to the appropriate government authorities and representatives of the workers in their employment and their organisations so that the implications may be examined jointly in order to mitigate adverse effects to the greatest possible extent. This is particularly important in the case of the closure of an entity involving collective lay-offs or dismissals.

27. Arbitrary dismissal procedures should be avoided.[5]

28. Governments in co-operation with multinational as well as national enterprises should provide some form of income protection for workers whose employment has been terminated.[6]

TRAINING

29. Governments in co-operation with all the parties concerned, should develop national policies for vocational training and guidance, closely linked with employment.[7] This is the framework within which multinational enterprises should pursue their training policies.

30. In their operations, multinational enterprises should ensure that relevant training is provided for all levels of their employees in the host country, as appropriate to meet the needs of the enterprise as well as the development policies of the country. Such training should, to the extent possible, develop generally useful skills and promote career opportunities. This responsibility should be carried

---

[5] Recommendation (No. 119) concerning Termination of Employment at the Initiative of the Employer.

[6] Ibid.

[7] Convention (No. 142) and Recommendation (No. 150) concerning Vocational Guidance and Vocational Training in the Development of Human Resources.

out, where appropriate, in co-operation with the authorities of the country, the organisations of employers and workers and the competent local, national or international institutions.

31. Multinational enterprises operating in developing countries should participate, along with national enterprises, in programmes, including special funds, encouraged by host governments and supported by employers' and workers' organisations. These programmes should have the aim of encouraging skill formation and development as well as providing vocational guidance and should be jointly administered by the parties which support them. Wherever practicable, multinational enterprises should make the services of skilled resource personnel available to help in training programmes organised by governments, as part of a contribution to national development.

32. Multinational enterprises, with the co-operation of governments and to the extent consistent with the efficient operation of the enterprise, should afford opportunities within the enterprise as a whole to broaden the experience of local management in suitable fields such as industrial relations.

CONDITIONS OF WORK AND LIFE

Wages, Benefits and Conditions of Work

33. Wages, benefits and conditions of work offered by multinational enterprises should be not less favourable to the workers than those offered by comparable employers in the country concerned.

34. When multinational enterprises operate in developing countries, where comparable employers may not exist, they should provide the best possible wages, benefits and conditions of work, within the framework of government policies.[8] These should be related to the economic position of the enterprise, but should be at least adequate to satisfy basic needs of the workers and their families. Where they provide workers with basic amenities such as housing, medical care or food, these amenities should be of a good standard.[9]

35. Governments, especially in developing countries, should endeavour to adopt suitable measures to ensure that lower income groups and less-developed areas benefit as much as possible from the activities of multinational enterprises.

---

[8] Recommendation (No. 116) concerning Reduction of Hours of Work.

[9] Convention (No. 110) and Recommendation (No. 110) concerning Conditions of Employment of Plantations Workers. Recommendation (No. 115) concerning Workers' Housing; Recommendation (No. 69) concerning Medical Care; Convention (No. 130) and Recommendation (No. 134) concerning Medical Care and Sickness.

Safety and Health

36. Governments should ensure that both multinational and national enterprises provide adequate safety and health standards for their employees. Those governments which have not yet ratified the ILO Conventions on Guarding of Machinery (No. 119), Ionising Radiation (No. 115), Benzene (No. 136) and Occupational Cancer (No. 139) are urged nevertheless to apply to the greatest extent possible the principles embodied in these Conventions and in their related Recommendations (Nos. 118, 114, 144, and 147). The Codes of Practice and Guides in the current list of ILO publications on Occupational Safety and Health should also be taken into account.[10]

37. Multinational enterprises should maintain the highest standards of safety and health, in conformity with national requirements, bearing in mind their relevant experience within the enterprise as a whole, including any knowledge of special hazards. They should also make available to the representatives of the workers in the enterprise, and upon request, to the competent authorities and the workers' and employers' organisations in all countries in which they operate, information on the safety and health standards relevant to their local operations, which they observe in other countries. In particular, they should make known to those concerned any special hazards and related protective measures associated with new products and processes. They, like comparable domestic enterprises, should be expected to play a leading role in the examination of causes of industrial safety and health hazards and in the application of resulting improvements within the enterprise as a whole.

38. Multinational enterprises should co-operate in the work of international organisations concerned with the preparation and adoption of international safety and health standards.

39. In accordance with national practice, multinational enterprises should co-operate fully with the competent safety and health authorities, the representatives of the workers and their organisations, and established safety and health organisations. Where appropriate, matters relating to safety and health should be incorporated in agreements with the representatives of the workers and their organisations.

---

[10] The ILO Conventions and Recommendations referred to are listed in: "Publications on Occupational Safety and Health," ILO, Geneva, 1976, pp. 1–3.

INDUSTRIAL RELATIONS

40. Multinational enterprises should observe standards of industrial relations not less favourable than those observed by comparable employers in the country concerned.

Freedom of Association and the Right to Organise

41. Workers employed by multinational enterprises as well as those employed by national enterprises should, without distinction whatsoever, have the right to establish and, subject only to the rules of the organisation concerned, to join organisations of their own choosing without previous authorisations.[11] They should also enjoy adequate protection against acts of anti-union discrimination in respect of their employment.[12]

42. Organisations representing multinational enterprises or the workers in their employment should enjoy adequate protection against any acts of interference by each other or each other's agents or members in their establishment, functioning or administration.[13]

43. Where appropriate in the local circumstances, multinational enterprises should support representative employers' organisations.

44. Governments, where they do not already do so, are urged to apply the principles of Convention No. 87, Article 5, in view of the importance, in relation to multinational enterprises, of permitting organisations representing such enterprises or the workers in their employment to affiliate with international organisations of employers and workers of their own choosing.

45. Where governments of host countries offer special incentives to attract foreign investment, these incentives should not include any limitation of the workers' freedom of association or the right to organise and bargain collectively.

46. Representatives of the workers in multinational enterprises should not be hindered from meeting for consultation and exchange of views among themselves, provided that the functioning of the operations of the enterprise and the normal procedures which govern relationships with representatives of the workers and their organisations are not thereby prejudiced.

47. Governments should not restrict the entry of representatives of employers' and workers' organisations, who come from other countries at the invitation of the local or national organisations con-

---

[11] Convention No. 87, Article 2.
[12] Convention No. 98, Article 1(1).
[13] Convention No. 98, Article 2(1).

cerned for the purpose of consultation on matters of mutual concern, solely on the grounds that they seek entry in that capacity.

Collective Bargaining

48. Workers employed by multinational enterprises should have the right, in accordance with national law and practice, to have representative organisations of their own choosing recognised for the purpose of collective bargaining.

49. Measures appropriate to national conditions should be taken, where necessary, to encourage the full development and utilisation of machinery for voluntary negotiation between employers or employers' organisations and workers' organisations, with a view to the regulation of terms and conditions of employment by means of collective agreements.[14]

50. Multinational enterprises, like national enterprises, should provide workers' representatives with such facilities as may be necessary to assist in the development of effective collective agreements.[15]

51. Multinational enterprises should enable duly authorised representatives of the workers in their employment in each of the countries in which they operate to conduct negotiations with representatives of management who are authorised to take decisions on the matters under negotiations.

52. Multinational enterprises, in the context of bona fide negotiations with the workers' representatives on conditions of employment, or while workers are exercising the right to organise, should not threaten to utilise a capacity to transfer the whole or part of an operating unit from the country concerned in order to influence unfairly those negotiations or to hinder the exercise of the right to organise; nor should they transfer workers from affiliates in foreign countries with a view to undermining bona fide negotiations with the workers' representatives or the workers' exercise of their right to organise.

53. Collective agreements should include provisions for the settlement of disputes arising over their interpretation and application and for ensuring mutually respected rights and responsibilities.

54. Multinational enterprises should provide workers' representatives with information required for meaningful negotiations with the entity involved, and where this accords with local law and prac-

---

[14] Convention No. 98, Article 4.
[15] Convention (No. 135) concerning protection and facilities to be afforded to workers' representatives in the undertaking.

tices, should also provide information to enable them to obtain a true and fair view of the performance of the entity or, where appropriate, of the enterprise as a whole.[16]

55. Governments should supply to the representatives of workers' organisations on request, where law and practice so permit, information on the industries in which the enterprise operates, which would help in laying down objective criteria in the collective bargaining process. In this context, multinational as well as national enterprises should respond constructively to requests by governments for relevant information on their operations.

Consultation

56. In multinational as well as in national enterprises, systems devised by mutual agreement between employers and workers and their representatives should provide, in accordance with national law and practice, for regular consultation on matters of mutual concern. Such consultation should not be a substitute for collective bargaining.[17]

Examination of Grievances

57. Multinational as well as national enterprises should respect the right of the workers whom they employ to have all their grievances processed in a manner consistent with the following provisions: any worker who, acting individually or jointly with other workers, considers that he has grounds for a grievance should have the right to submit such grievance without suffering any prejudice whatsoever as a result, and to have such grievance examined pursuant to an appropriate procedure.[18] This is particularly important whenever the multinational enterprises operate in countries which do not abide by the principles of ILO Conventions pertaining to freedom of association, to the right to organise and bargain collectively and to forced labour.[19]

---

[16] Recommendation (No. 129) concerning Communications between Management and Workers within Undertakings.

[17] Recommendation (No. 94) concerning Consultation and Co-operation between Employers and Workers at the Level of the Undertaking. Recommendation (No. 129) concerning Communications within the Undertaking.

[18] Recommendation (No. 130) concerning the Examination of Grievances within the Undertaking with a View to their Settlement.

[19] Convention (No. 29) concerning Forced or Compulsory Labour; Convention (No. 105) concerning the Abolition of Forced Labour; Recommendation (No. 35) concerning Indirect Compulsion to Labour.

Settlement of industrial disputes

58. Multinational as well as national enterprises jointly with the representatives and organisations of the workers whom they employ should seek to establish voluntary conciliation machinery, appropriate to national conditions, which may include provisions for voluntary arbitration, to assist in the prevention and settlement of industrial disputes between employers and workers. The voluntary conciliation machinery should include equal representation of employers and workers.[20]

---

[20] Recommendation (No. 92) concerning Voluntary Conciliation and Arbitration.

Appendix C

AKZO-ENKA: THE TEN YEAR HISTORY
OF A PLANT CLOSURE

Akzo N.V. is a multinational enterprise headquartered in Arnhem, the Netherlands. With operations in more than fifty countries, the corporate group had sales of Hfl 14.5 billion and a worldwide employment level of approximately 78,000 at the end of 1981. The corporation's major products include man-made fibers, commodity and specialty chemicals, pharmaceuticals, coatings, salt, electronic, consumer, and miscellaneous industrial products. The group's major divisions are Enka, Akzo Zout Chemie, Akzo Chemie, Akzo Coatings, Akzo Pharma, and Akzo Consumenten Produkten, which operate worldwide. Akzona is Akzo's North American subsidiary.[1]

AKZO'S RETRENCHMENT PLAN

Akzo was formed by a merger of two Dutch concerns that were already industrial combinations: Algemene Kunstzijde Unie NV (AKU) and Koninkijke Zout-Organon NV (KZO). In 1975, 1976, and 1977, Akzo suffered severe losses.[2] Akzo's economic troubles have centered in the European synthetic fibers business of its largest subsidiary, Enka Glanzstoff.[3]

---

[1] Annual Report for 1981, (Akzo N.V. Arnhem, the Netherlands), p. 1. Most of the discussion to follow has been previously published in Herbert R. Northrup and Richard L. Rowan, *Multinational Collective Bargaining Attempts,* (Philadelphia: Industrial Research Unit, The Wharton School, University of Pennsylvania, 1979), Chapter VII, pp. 187–203.

[2] *Fortune,* Vol. 100 (August 13, 1979), p. 195; Akzo's annual reports for 1975, 1976, and 1977.

[3] The basic information for this section is based on extensive field interviews in the Netherlands in July 1973 and 1974 by Professors Herbert R. Northrup and Richard L. Rowan, plus two books written in Dutch—Aad Van Cortenberghe and Jeroen Terlingen, *Enka Dossier; Handboek Voor Bezetters* (Utrecht and Antwerpen: A. W. Bruna & Zoon, 1972); and Albert Benschop and Ton Kee, *De bedrijfsbezetting van de Enka-Breda* (Nijmegan: Socialistiese Uitgeverij Nijmegen, 1974)—on a number of documents by Akzo management; and on field interviews in Europe, summer 1973. The books, both written by socialist union adherents from a union point of view, give vivid accounts of the action. Other sources are Ernst Piehl, *Multinationale Konzerne und internationale Gewerkschaftsbewegung* (Frankfurt am Main: Europäische Verlagsanstalt, 1974). Dr. Piehl was on the research staff of the Deutsche Gewerkschaftsbund (DGB), the German Confederation of Labor, and has been appointed senior policy official for the European Trade Union Confederation; and Pierre Hoff-

The slump in the fibers market in the early 1970s prompted Akzo management to study the situation. The conclusion was that "measures for a further concentration [of manufacturing facilities] are of vital importance to the Group's survival."[4] Accordingly, on April 6, 1972, plans were announced to close facilities in Breda and Emmercompascum, the Netherlands; one in Fabelta, Belgium; another in Wuppertal-Barmen, Germany; and one in Feldmühle, Switzerland. An estimated 5,000 to 6,000 employees were affected by the announcement. In 1972, Akzo's worldwide employment was 101,000, 83,700 of whom were employed in Western Europe.[5]

The company's press release announcing the closings emphasized that the plants would be phased out over a period of time, *e.g.*, one year in the case of Breda. It promised displaced workers employment, where possible, in other Akzo plants and offered to help those not placed to find employment elsewhere. Akzo further indicated that the Emmercompascum employees would be absorbed by the nearby Emmen plant and that it was negotiating to sell a part of the Wuppertal-Barmen facility to "a well-known European producer," which would mean the "possibility of continued employment" for a "large number" of the 3,000 employees. For anyone in any of the closed plants not continued in Akzo employment, "a release arrangement" (severance pay) was promised. Finally, Akzo pledged to inform unions of closings in all affected countries and to seek advice from various local and central works councils.[6]

Reaction to Plant Closing Plan

The Akzo announcement created an uproar in all the countries involved as the works councils and the unions appealed to the national authorities and to the bureaucrats of the European Community (EC) to save their jobs. Pressure was especially strong on the Netherlands' government to intervene. In light of these developments, an agreement was reached among the Dutch government, the company, the Dutch and German trade unions, and the Central Employees' (Works) Council[7] of Enka-Netherlands to appoint a

---

mann and Albert Langwieler, *Noch sind wir dal* (Reinbek bei Hamburg: Rowohlt, 1974).

[4] "The Situation in the Chemical Fibre Industry," duplicated document, March 30, 1972. English version provided by Akzo management.

[5] Enka Glanzstoff Press Release, April 6, 1972 (English version provided by Akzo management); and Akzo, *1972 Annual Report* (Arnhem, the Netherlands, 1973), p. 9. All Akzo annual reports referred to are the English versions.

[6] Enka Glanzstoff Press Release, April 6, 1972.

[7] John P. Windmuller points out that, in the Netherlands "at the level of individual industries, labor's influence is of a somewhat lesser order [than at the level of

"Committee of Outside Experts" (COE) to examine the company plans and to report to its principals its "Views on the Restructuring Plan."[8]

The sharp reaction to its "restructuring plan" obviously surprised the Akzo management. The chairman of the Akzo Supervisory Board stated at the general meeting of the shareholders on May 10, 1972, that "it is alarming to find that clear and practical arguments meet with so little response in present-day society."[9] In answer to the criticism that unions and works councils had not been notified prior to the announcement, the chairman pointed out that so many such bodies were involved that it "would have been asking too much to demand from them secrecy for a longer period." Since, however, a gradual, not an abrupt, closedown was involved, he declared "there is now every opportunity for codetermination and consultation." But he assured the shareholders that he expected that "the investigation by independent experts" would "confirm his view" of the economic situation and the necessity of the proposed actions.[10]

The Committee of Outside Experts did confirm in its August 18, 1972, report that Akzo management could not be blamed for the excess capacity in the synthetic fiber business, and it agreed that "drastic measures" were required. The committee also found that the reduction of capacity plans was based on proper data and "realistic assumptions." It found, therefore, that, "in terms of business economics, the plan is well-thought out . . . and has been drawn up with care." But the committee declared, "This does not settle the question. Where such drastic closedowns are concerned, as the ones envisaged for Breda and Barmen, social, technological and economic factors should be weighed with extra care." It recommended that a cutback in all production facilities, instead of closing some, be con-

---

national, social, and economic decisions]. . . . Below the industry level . . . the influence of unions declines rapidly . . . the contribution of unions to the personnel policies of individual enterprises is either remote and derivative or nonexistent . . . most unions have no shop-level or worksite structure through which they could attempt to exert direct influence on working conditions. Work-place representation belongs by long tradition, reinforced in 1950 by law, to an independent institution, the works council. . . . It is in no sense a part of the union structure. In this regard, . . . the Netherlands shares a common heritage with other Western European countries. It also shares to a large extent a set of common problems growing out of the divided structure of employee representation." *Labor Relations in the Netherlands* (Ithaca: Cornell University Press, 1969), pp. 399–400.

[8] Press Release and Report Issued by Committee of Outside Experts, August 18, 1972, p. 2.

[9] Speech made by J. R. M. van den Brink at the general meeting of shareholders of Akzo NV, held in Amsterdam on May 10, 1972. Akzo Press Release, p. 1.

[10] *Ibid.*, pp. 1–2.

sidered and that governments or industry, acting as a cartel, allocate production.[11]

The Enka Glanzstoff Board of Management agreed to study carefully the COE report, but it pointed out that the COE proposals had already been the subject of much analysis and discussion with Akzo management both before April 6 and thereafter. It concluded: "This did not result in the discovery of fresh possibilities for the reorganization and rationalization of Enka Glanzstoff by other means."[12] It warned that failure to proceed could jeopardize the entire company. Meanwhile, the nylon textile filament plant in Switzerland was closed,[13] and the Enka-Netherlands Central Works Council appeared to be leaning toward the company proposals.[14]

Sit-in and Closing Cancellation

On September 18, 1972, the Breda plant employees, who were the largest, most directly affected group, occupied the plant. Short strikes, including a sit-in, also occurred at Wuppertal, Germany, but the agitation was led by members of the Netherlands Catholic Trade Union Federation (NKV). Other groups, including those affiliated with the socialist National Federation of Trade Unions (NVV) and the Protestant National Trade Union Federation (CNV) were also involved. Since Breda is a Catholic area, the NKV has the largest membership there, although it is smaller than the NVV in the Netherlands as a whole.[15]

The sit-in lasted one week. As a result, Akzo abandoned its plans to close the Breda plant and therefore could close none except for

---

[11] Press Release and Report Issued by Committee of Outside Experts, p. 1.

[12] Provisional comments of the Enka Glanzstoff Board of Management on the Report of the Committee of Outside Experts (COE), August 17, 1972.

[13] Letter from B. Klaverstijn, head, Public Relations Department, Akzo NV, to Professors Herbert R. Northrup and Richard L. Rowan, October 25, 1973.

[14] Benschop and Kee, who provide a day-by-day account of the events, report protests by the NKV Breda group against rumors that union officials or works council members were agreeing with the need for plant closings. *De bedrijfsbezetting*, pp. 28, 123.

[15] According to Professor Windmuller's excellent study, "Dutch workers remained devoutly loyal to Calvinist Protestantism in the north and to Roman Catholicism in the south. This devotion a few decades later became the basis for the creation of confessional trade unions whose viability and power of attraction would far exceed that of Christian labor movements in most western European countries." *Labor Relations in the Netherlands*, p. 5. In 1972, the socialist NVV had 39.4 percent of the 1,583,000 union members in the Netherlands; the Catholic NKV, 25.3 percent; the Protestant CNV, 15.1 percent; and other trade unions, 20.2 percent. Data from *Statistical Yearbook of the Netherlands*, 1972, reproduced in *Industrial Relations-Europe Newsletter*, Vol. 1, No. 9 (September 1973), supplement, p. 2. In 1975, the NVV and the NKV agreed to a merger to form the FNV. The CNV decided not to join the FNV (Federation of Netherlands Unions).

the already shut facility in Switzerland, since it is bound by provisions of its merger rules, insisted upon by various countries, to treat equally Belgian and German plant groups with Dutch ones. Instead, the company adopted the proposals for cutbacks in each facility. Employment in the chemical fibers section of Akzo actually decreased by 6,800 in 1972,[16] but, except for Switzerland, plant closures were avoided.

Aftermath

In retrospect, it is quite clear that Akzo management underestimated the impact and emotional reaction to what it regarded as a sensible business decision. In a later evaluation, management observed: "Perhaps one can conclude that, after the long period of expansion, the employees were mentally unprepared to accept the unprecedented restructuring measures, despite the economic need for them."[17] To the Dutch worker, as to his European counterpart, however, job security is the most significant issue; and a plant closure, the most direct, flagrant attack on job security. As Professor Roberts has noted: "Where jobs are at stake, there has been a positive and militant response."[18] In reflecting on what happened, the Akzo management reported that it called off the restructuring plan because

> forced implementation would have caused Akzo more damage—both immediately and in the longer run—than the so-called linear curtailment of production that has now been accepted. It should be noted that the extensive and repeated talks with consultative bodies, such as works councils and groups of personnel within and outside the chemical fibres sector, and with the trade unions, failed to win support for our plan. In these talks, the strategy designed to safeguard the long-term interests of our company and our employees was overridden by—in themselves quite understandable—short-term considerations. Moreover, these talks took so long that a well-nigh unbearable and much-deplored strain was placed on the employees involved. The events have taught us that we should allow even more scope in our policy and decision making to the shifting opinions in society.[19]

The Akzo *1972 Annual Report* notes that the financial consequences will be "more unfavorable" because it did not close the plants and that it will be necessary "to actively continue the ration-

---

[16] Akzo, *1972 Annual Report,* p. 9.

[17] "Übersicht über die Anpassungsmassnahmen bei Enka-Europa indenjahren 1972–1982, sowir die dabei befolgte Informations-und Konsultantionsprouis," Enka document in author's possession, p. 8. (Author's translation.)

[18] Roberts, "Multinational Collective-Bargaining," p. 10.

[19] Akzo, *1972 Annual Report,* p. 9.

alization measures in our Western European chemical fibre companies."[20] It also indicates that business was improving. In September 1973, Akzo announced that it was doubling the texturizing capacity for polyester filament fibers at the Breda plant.[21] According to a company spokesman: "The number of spinning machines will not be increased; the process, however, is going to be adapted to a new technology which yields a substantially higher output."[22] Between the announcement of the abortive restructuring plan (April 8, 1972) and the beginning of the sit-in (September 18, 1972), about four hundred employees voluntarily terminated at the Breda plant. This created a shortage of labor for certain production jobs at Breda and caused Akzo, with the consent of the works council and unions, to request Dutch government approval to import fifty to one hundred Spanish workers. By November 1973, the government had approved the first fifty.[23] This turn of events, however logical or explained, naturally confirmed in the minds of those who were opposed to closedowns that their position was correct. The upturn, nevertheless, proved to be of short duration.

NEGOTIATING A NEW STRUCTURE, 1975-77

The recovery of the chemical fibers business lasted until mid-1974, then gave way to a sharp recession. In Akzo's *1973 Annual Report,* it is stated that the company's "objective to maintain [its] leading position in chemical fibres in Western Europe calls for investments to raise capacity, notably for products exhibiting continued strong growth. . . . Outside Western Europe, investments for expansion [continue] to be predominant."[24] One year later, however, Akzo's annual report states that the second half of 1974 was featured by "sales problems that led to cut-backs in production with attendant losses due to undercapacity operation."[25] The following year saw no relief. With a general recession, the fibers losses could not be offset. Akzo incurred a general deficit and paid no dividends to shareholders. In early 1975, it had 23,000 employees—about one-third of its Western European work force—on short time.[26] Enka also cut its

---

[20] *Ibid.,* p. 6.

[21] *Times* (London), September 1, 1973, p. 21.

[22] Letter from B. Klaverstijn to the authors, October 25, 1973.

[23] *Ibid.*

[24] Akzo, *1973 Annual Report* (Arnhem, the Netherlands, 1974), p. 7.

[25] Akzo, *1974 Annual Report* (Arnhem, the Netherlands, 1975), p. 10.

[26] *Ibid.,* p. 11. Short time, or reduced workweeks, are used instead of layoffs in many countries. Usually in such cases, government social insurance makes up much of the wages lost by employees on reduced workweeks. The cost of dividing the work to the

work force by 4,200 persons in 1975, largely by attrition.[27] Heavy layoffs were likewise effectuated by its United Kingdom subsidiary,[28] British Enkalon, and by American Enka, which also closed a North Carolina plant. Meanwhile, Akzo sought a permanent solution for its overcapacity problem that could not be thwarted by union and/or political action. It employed the management consulting firm McKinsey & Company to make a study of Enka's markets and to recommend appropriate action.

The Effectiveness of Union Action

Beginning with the sit-in at Breda in September 1972, union opposition to the company's restructuring plans met with considerable success in postponing the plans' implementation. The very success appeared to attract the more ambitious interests of the International Federation of Chemical, Energy and General Workers' Unions (ICEF) which, claiming credit for the postponement of the closures, viewed the issue as a convenient platform for furthering the demand for bargaining at the multinational level.[29] Upon closer examination, however, the ICEF's claims appear inflated and their involvement in the matter, minimal.[30]

Professors Herbert R. Northrup and Richard L. Rowan note, rather, that the effectiveness of union pressure on the company centered on the local level, and particularly on one union, the NKV: "Most of the credit . . . appears to belong to the Catholic NKV members and leadership in Breda. They led the direct action, despite a more cautious approach by the NKV national organization, and pushed the plant occupation as a means of saving their plant when

---

company is, however, substantial. For a general discussion of this point, see Gordon F. Bloom and Herbert R. Northrup, *Economics of Labor Relations,* 9th ed. (Homewood, Illinois: Richard D. Irwin, Inc., 1981), pp. 551–571.

[27] Akzo, *1975 Annual Report* (Arnhem, the Netherlands, 1976), p. 9.

[28] Rhys David, "Heavy staff redundancies feared at British Enkalon," *Financial Times,* September 11, 1975, p. 8.

[29] Northrup and Rowan note that the ICEF (then, the ICF) claimed influential involvement against activities of a number of multinationals, all of which claims proved, upon closer examination, unsubstantiated in fact. For a detailed account of the claims versus the facts in these events, see Chapters VI-XI, *Multinational Collective Bargaining Attempts,* pp. 155–358.

[30] *Ibid.,* p. 195. ". . . The ICEF secretary general claims to have had informal meetings 'with the top officers of a certain number of companies,' including Akzo. But in response to the written question 'Did the company or its representatives ever meet with Levinson?' Akzo's official spokesman stated, 'No'. The same company answer was given to the question 'During the discussions [of the proposed closedowns] did the company or its representatives ever meet with a committee of trade unionists with [ICEF secretary general, Charles] Levinson present, or sponsored by ICF?'

the Enka Central Works Council appeared about to agree to a modified company plan for its closure."[31]

This is not to say, however, that multinational union pressure played no role in influencing the company's plans. Following the 1972 developments, the company did meet twice with multinational union groups, once with Dutch and German union representatives, and a second time with Dutch, German, and Belgian union officials. Neither of these meetings had included representatives of the ICEF or any other international secretariat.[32] In 1975, meanwhile, the company, "expressing interest in international company-union discussion," agreed to meet with the ICEF's Akzo World Council, a body established soon after the 1972 developments, but which had not met officially before 1975.[33] Management's first meeting with the council was to be its last, however, as the council demanded that it be designated as the employees' representative. Management refused, citing that such a designation would exclude unions not members of the ICEF, among which were the NKV and CNV of the Netherlands, and the Christian CSC of Belgium, and other unions representing the company's salaried personnel.[34]

On August 29, 1975, Enka's management did meet with employee representatives of the unions and works councils of all the plants affected in the restructuring plan to discuss the McKinsey report. The report had seen "little or no prospect for improvement in several of Enka's fibers businesses, especially in the nylon filament and rayon lines. The unions asked, and later received, additional information both from Enka and from McKinsey, and the latter's report was thoroughly examined in a nine-hour session."[35] A second meeting was held on September 12, 1975, at which the unions, having reviewed all the information obtained, rejected the company's plan to gradually close facilities in the Netherlands, Belgium, and Germany, and to rely on attrition to handle as many as possible of the 6,000 redundant workers who would have to be laid off.[36] A third meeting had been scheduled for October, but was cancelled as pointless by management in view of the unions' refusal to accept the company's plan.

Since Akzo readily confirmed . . . that it did meet once with representatives of Dutch and German unions and once with Dutch, German and Belgian unionists, it seems logical to credit its version."
[31] *Ibid.,* p. 196.
[32] *Ibid.,* p. 195.
[33] *Ibid.,* p. 198.
[34] *Ibid.,* pp. 198–199.
[35] *Ibid.,* p. 199.
[36] *Ibid.*

Union Divisions

Despite threats by the ICEF of international union action if Akzo did not return to international consultations,[37] no such actions occurred, and further, the unions soon split wide apart. The Central Works Council of Enka-Netherlands approved the company's restructuring program by a vote of fourteen to twelve, "despite heavy union lobbying for a confrontation."[38] The Catholic (NKV) and Protestant (CNV) unions entered into direct national negotiations, and IG Chemie did likewise, being so required pursuant to the German Shop Constitution Law. Isolated, despite support from the then Dutch prime minister for international consultation,[39] Industriebond-NVV retreated from its confrontation position and began national talks but later demanded that a tripartite tribunal be appointed to supervise Akzo operations.[40]

In Belgium, the government acted to save the jobs in Akzo's Fabelta subsidiary by pursuing a majority interest therein.[41] This effectively eliminated any Belgian union interest in international action. By late October 1975, the ICEF was talking about the experience as a learning one and "an important step forward."[42] Previously, the ICEF secretary general was quoted as believing that, "if

---

[37] "Charles Levinson, general secretary of the ICEF, claims that the international group has the support of workers as far away as Brazil and the International Brotherhood of Teamsters in the U.S. where Akzo controls American Enka Co.... But a German union official at the talks (with Akzo) says no international support has been asked for and that multinational strikes or boycotts are not under discussion." "Multinationals, Bargaining on an international scale," p. 40.

[38] "Akzo: Divided we fall," *Economist*, November 1, 1975, p. 85.

[39] Prime Minister Den Uyl made a nationwide speech supporting the Industriebond-NVV position in November 1975. He was sharply rebuked by Akzo officials in a counterrelease.

[40] Michael Van Os, "Enka reduces union opposition," *Financial Times*, November 7, 1975, p. 20; "Dutch labor ranks split," *Chemical Week*, November 26, 1975, p. 22; and Paul Kemezis, "Unions: Setback Abroad," *New York Times*, February 1, 1976, sec. 3, p. 12. A bill was introduced in the Dutch Parliament by NVV supporters which in effect would put Akzo into receivership under a tripartite board. No action occurred.

[41] The Belgian government took a 60 percent interest in Fabelta by investing $7.5 million and assuming $11 million worth of debts. Akzo retained a 40 percent interest. The Belgian company now markets Enka products, mainly carpet yarn and tire cord in Belgium, and Enka sells Fabelta's output of nylon and acrylic fibers outside of Belgium. The agreement calls for technical information exchanges and joint research. See "Belgium buys into fibers," *Chemical Week*, February 18, 1976, p. 19. Discussion at the time that this deal was consummated indicated that the interest of the Belgian government was increased because the Fabelta plant scheduled for closing was in the Flemish sector of Belgium, and Akzo was simultaneously expanding a non-fiber chemical plant in the Walloon sector. Fear not only of unemployment but also of disturbing the delicate balance between these groups was involved.

[42] Kemezis, "Unions: Setback Abroad," p. 12.

the unions can force formal negotiations with Akzo, it would set a work precedent and increase pressure on other multinationals."[43]

No other union agreements were reached on the company program during 1976, but no union action occurred to prevent Akzo from making forced reductions. Total Akzo employment declined in 1975 and 1976 by 14,300. Of this decrease, 3,800 was attributable to the deconsolidations of businesses, particularly in Fabelta (Belgium). The fibers sector of Akzo accounted for 9,300 of the remaining 10,500 lost jobs.[44] Akzo's *1976 Annual Report* confirms its withdrawal from the polymide (nylon) hosiery business.[45]

In 1976, Akzo again failed to make a profit (although it reduced its losses) and paid no dividends. Faced with economic realities, the Dutch unions and works councils, negotiating separately, came to final agreement in April 1977 with the company, which compromised on a planned reduction of 400 instead of 600 persons. This included 110 to be laid off at Breda and the closing of the Emmercompascum plant by August 1, 1977, which involved 300 employees, who would be eligible for transfer elsewhere. In addition, the headquarters of the Enka division was consolidated in Wuppertal, Germany, thus eliminating some jobs at Arnhem.[46] Except for some exchange of information, the Dutch and German unions have apparently made no further attempt to act in concert. The economic situation in fibers worldwide has remained severely depressed into 1979.

The Persistence of Economic Difficulties

By 1980, it had become clear that further measures were required to trim Enka's losses of Hfl 150 million in 1979, and Hfl 200 million in 1980.[47] Additional market analysis undertaken by the company revealed three major causes of Enka's continuing problems:

- —Weakness of the European textile and carpet industries through declining demand and import competition;
- —The "second oil crisis" with further price increases in energy and raw materials;
- —A worsening competitive position of the European fiber producers

---

[43] Kemezis, "A Multinational vs. United Nations," pp. 1, 6.

[44] Akzo, *1976 Annual Report* (Arnhem, the Netherlands, 1977), p. 12.

[45] *Ibid.,* p. 4.

[46] Rhys David, "Akzo attacks fibre losses," *Financial Times,* May 11, 1977, p. 26; and "Afsluitend Overleg Met Vakbonden Over Aanvallende Maatregelen," Enka Glanzstoff Press Release, April 7, 1977.

[47] "Übersicht über die Anpassungsmassnahmen bei Enka-Europa in den jahren 1972–1982, sowie die dabei befolgte Informations-und Konsultantionspraxis," Enka company document in the author's possession, p. 13.

in the face of foreign (U.S.) competition and the artificial preservation of unprofitable overcapacity through subsidies.[48]

Enka's management formulated plans based upon these new circumstances which were announced to the unions and works councils in January 1981. The proposals included the following measures:

—The discontinuation of production in Breda (Netherlands), Kassel (Germany), and Antrim (Northern Ireland);
—Gradual reduction of steel cord production (Oberbruch);
—Concentration of adjusted capacity for synthetic fibers;
—Rationalization of the workforce in the central divisions and in research and development.[49]

The company's plans would affect an additional 4,000 employees in the Netherlands, Germany, and Northern Ireland.

Pursuant to German and Dutch law, plant management at the Kassel and Breda sites entered into negotiations with the respective unions and works councils. Enka management observed that: "Local management had been fully instructed on the European dimension and background of the restructuring measures so that this information would also be at the disposal of the employee representatives in order that they might fully evaluate the consequences of their own situation."[50]

Still, the works councils and unions at both sites were not at all quiescent in the face of a prospective shutdown of the plants. Breda's works council rejected management's plan to close the plant, prompting management to observe later that

In Breda's case, the unions and works council . . . obtained all the information they requested. This did nevertheless not prevent them from exhausting different legal means to deny Enka the right of withdrawing earlier promises to preserve at least a part of their activities in Breda.[51]

The unions involved at Breda took the company to court under a Dutch law which allows employee representatives to challenge management decisions that affect employment.[52] In October 1981, the Dutch court ruled that: "Enka may not shut its polyester filament yarn factory in Breda (in November 1981). In rejecting the advice of the factory works council, Enka took insufficient account of all the interests involved."[53]

---

[48] *Ibid.* (Author's translation).
[49] *Ibid.* (Author's translation).
[50] *Ibid.*, p. 14 (Author's translation).
[51] *Ibid.*, p. 15 (Author's translation).
[52] For a discussion of this legislation and its implications, see Chapter IX, pp. 141–52.
[53] Charles Batchelar, "Court bar on Enka factory closure," *Financial Times,* October 27, 1981, p. 15.

The second attempt in nearly ten years to close down the Breda facility had thus been forestalled, despite management's claim that the court's decision "would endanger jobs in the entire group and mean there was no money for new projects."[54] The decision compelled Enka's management to reenter negotiations with the works council over the overcapacity problem.

Enka's management intensified its efforts to find buyers for the Breda site and succeeded after an exhaustive attempt to interest four companies in setting up operations in Breda.[55] From the largest of these, an Amsterdam-based chocolate company, Enka bought its Amsterdam property, which it would try to resell, in return for the chocolate company's relocation in Breda.[56] The new business in Breda would create 1,000 job opportunities, well compensating for the 600 that Enka would eliminate with the closing of the Breda plant. Finally, then, the company's efforts won the agreement of the works council. Enka's Breda plant, its activities transferred to two German plants, proceeded to closure.

CONCLUSION

The closure of Akzo-Enka's Breda facility demonstrated over its ten-year history several of the most important issues facing multinationals. In the end, management's 1972 view of the problems and the solutions were borne out in fact. Over the intervening years, meanwhile, the company's experience constituted a sort of laboratory, in which competing views of job security as well as employee and government participation in decision making were tested.

Job Security

Management's first approach to the problems was based on an analysis of the long term. Despite the fact that neither management nor the unions could have foreseen, as early as 1972, the impact of two "oil crises" and the prolonged recessionary climate of the 1970s and early 1980s, management appears to have correctly forecasted the gradual erosion of its fibers' market and, more significantly, the irreversibility of the overcapacity problem. The union's analysis of the problems appeared to have yielded a sequence of short-term solutions, the laudable but failed aim of which was to preserve as many jobs as possible.

[54] *Ibid.*
[55] Interview between Dr. Herbert R. Northrup and Dr. Hans Günther Zempelin, Enka's chairman, in Wiesbaden, Germany, April 28, 1982.
[56] *Ibid.*

MNEs and the OECD Guidelines

These long- versus short-term perspectives reflect competing definitions of job security. As Northrup and Rowan have observed: "Job security is the key worker issue in Europe, and to the European worker, security means work in the plant where he is now employed."[57] Translated into policy, this latter view meant cutbacks at all facilities rather than the complete closure of some. The preservation of loss-making capacity, one approach to job security, was in part financed by the drain on the company's profits, thus preventing the other approach to job security, job-creating, new investment.

The solution of gradual cutbacks imposed costs that became apparent in the ultimate failure of that approach to maintain jobs or to prevent plant closure. From a level of 101,000 employees worldwide in 1972, employment at Akzo-Enka fell to 78,000 by the end of 1981, with the majority of jobs shed in the company's fiber operations.

Whether the company could have created as many jobs as those lost over these years through profitable new investment is unanswerable. As early as 1972, however, management observed that the subsidization of unprofitable capacity could jeopardize employment in the entire company. The mechanism would be the drain on profits. At the end of 1972, after plans to close the Breda facility had been shelved, Akzo's annual report noted that "the financial consequences will be 'more unfavorable' because it did not close the plants." Finally, following a loss-making year at Enka in 1981: "Dr. Hans Gunther Zempelin, Enka's chief executive, said the group would have operated profitably in 1981 if it had been able to push through restructuring measures more quickly."[58] The view of job security that links profits with jobs appears, therefore, to have been subordinated to a series of short-term approaches that proved inadequate solutions to the company's problems.

It is interesting to view the events at Akzo-Enka during these years from the standpoint of the perception, discussed elsewhere in this study, that multinationals create employment instability by investing and disinvesting at will. It would be recalled that an independent Committee of Experts, in analyzing the company's economic problems, did not hold the company at fault for the creation of the overcapacity situation. Ironically, moreover, it is probably true that only a company of considerable resources, such as Akzo, could have afforded the exploration of alternative economic deci-

---

[57] *Multinational Collective Bargaining Attempts*, p. 197.
[58] "Enka hopes to eliminate losses this year after modest upturn," *Financial Times*, January 28, 1982, p. 23.

sions over a ten-year period, even if this exploration ultimately resulted in the termination of jobs.

Information and Consultation

Management's accommodation of alternatives to its own decisions would appear to demonstrate attentiveness to concerns other than profit maximization and, particularly, to the will of employees and their representatives. Yet, a recent document by the European Trade Union Confederation (ETUC) charged Akzo with actions "whereby the rights of the workers and legal provisions were simply ignored."[59] The charge appears a curious one, given the extraordinary measures to which the company went in seeking to provide information that included not only the local but also the "big picture" to the unions and works councils, and in consultations with these bodies. Following their publication in 1976, management endorsed the OECD guidelines, and the fact that no claim of wrongdoing by the company under the guidelines has been alleged appears in itself to demonstrate management's exemplary conduct over these years.

It is equally apparent, however, that union interest in information, consultation, and worker participation has evolved considerably since 1972, as, indeed, have European laws on these matters. The ICEF's initial involvement in the Akzo matter seemed linked to establishing the principle and precedent of multinational collective bargaining. In 1975, meanwhile, the ICEF-affiliated unions involved in the Akzo-Enka situation sought "to obtain from the company agreements to consult regarding investment strategy and policy as the quid pro quo for agreement on restructuring."[60] The event demonstrated an expansion of both the locus and the scope of industrial relations from the unions' point of view.

Legislation in the Netherlands and in other EC member states during these years appeared to keep pace with union and employee representatives' interest in expanded participation in decision making. A directive stipulating disclosure and consultation duties of management in cases of collective dismissal was formulated and passed in the middle of the decade. Dutch law pertaining to the rights of works councils was considerably strengthened during the same period:

---

[59] "Survey and documentation on disputes in European subsidiaries of multinational groups of companies," (Brussels: European Trade Union Confederation, 1982), p. 27.

[60] *Multinational Collective Bargaining Attempts,* p. 200.

The opinion of the works council, which was already required in respect of important decisions such as a major change in the organisation of the undertaking, total or partial closure or relocation, considerable reduction or expansion of activity, merger or association, is henceforth also required for major investments or loans, collective recruitment and the setting up of new undertakings.[61]

At the present time, lastly, both the Fifth and the Vredeling directives have become the subjects of active discussion at the European Community level.[62]

It is difficult to fault Akzo-Enka's record in information to and consultation with employee representatives over the past ten years. The record tends to show that the company's decision-making authority was not at all unilateral, but sought compromise in the attempt to bridge economic concerns with social ones. The inherent compromise in the company's decisions was not, however, characterized by the smooth accommodation of all the competing demands facing the company. The social demand for worker participation would appear to have been given as much if not more weight than economic imperatives. From Akzo's experience at least, it remains unclear how the accommodation of all the claimants to corporate decision making will aid the latter in responding to changing economic conditions.

---

[61] *Workers' Participation in Decisions within Undertakings* (Geneva: International Labour Office, 1981), p. 217.

[62] See Chapter VI, pp. 94–97.

Index

ACAS. *See* Advisory, Conciliation and
Arbitration Service
Advisory, Conciliation and Arbitration
Service (ACAS), 40, 41–42, 43–44, 45,
46
affirmative action, 166. *See also* antidiscrimination legislation
in the EC, 166–67
and employment of the disadvantaged,
169–71
and Paragraph 7, 161
in the United States, 164
Age Discrimination in Employment Act,
168
airline groupings. *See also* KSSU;
ATLAS
history of, 228
status of as multinational enterprises,
228–33
Akzo-Enka
closure of Breda facility, 140
Amalgamated Union of Engineering
Workers (AUEW), 39, 45, 123
antidiscrimination legislation. *See also*
affirmative action
and age discrimination, 168–69
in the EC, 165–67
and employment of the disadvantaged,
169–71
and Paragraph 7, 161–73
types of, 162–68
in the United States, 164–65
Association of Scientific, Technical and
Managerial Staffs (ASTMS), 46
ASTMS. *See* Association of Scientific,
Technical and Managerial Staffs
ATLAS airline grouping
history of, 228
ITF attempts to negotiate with, 227–34
OECD activity regarding, 228–34
AUEW. *See* Amalgamated Union of
Engineering Workers
Australia
antidiscrimination legislation in, 162
Apprenticeship Training Commission,
123
collective agreements in, 37, 56
collective dismissals in, 132

compulsory arbitration, 37, 76
legality of strikes, 180
manpower training by MNEs, 125, 127
works councils, 51, 54, 73, 124

Badger (Belgium) NV Company, 7, 8, 139,
152–54
Baker, M., 24
Belgium
age discrimination in, 168
collective agreements, 37
disclosure of information, 78
employment of disadvantaged, 170
employment stability, 22, 29
foreign investment, 24
General Telephone & Electronics, 157
impact of MNEs, 19, 24–25
job security, 138
plant closure in, 19, 138, 140
principle of limited responsibility, 140
Royal Decree of 1973, 73, 91
training programs, 122, 123
transnational bargaining initiatives by
the government, 200
union recognition difficulties, 24
wages and working conditions, 31, 109
works councils, 73, 81, 91, 124
Bellace, Janice, 167
Bendix Corporation
alleged violation of Paragraph 3, 102
sale of Dutch subsidiary, 102–05
BIAC. *See* Business and Industry
Advisory Committee
Black & Decker, 39, 41, 46
Spennymoor Plant, 39–41
Blake, David, 28
Blanpain, Roger, 22, 23, 24, 25, 114, 139
Bloom and Northrup, 164, 167, 168, 171
BOCI-Viggo
CIIME activity relating to, 205–17
impact of investment plans, 210–14
investment plans, 205–14
major issues involved in investment
decisions, 213–14
relevance of Swedish Codetermination
at Work Act to investment plans,
208–10

281

Racial Policies of American Industry Series

Order from: Kraus Reprint Co., Route 100, Millwood, New York 10546

Order from University Microfilms, Inc.
Attn: Books Editorial Department
300 North Zeeb Road
Ann Arbor, Michigan 48106

*Order this book from the Industrial Research Unit, The Wharton School, University of Pennsylvania, Philadelphia, Pennsylvania 19104